TODAY'S
ISMS

Tenth Edition

TODAY'S ISMS

Socialism
Capitalism
Fascism
Communism

Alan O. Ebenstein
Antioch University of Santa Barbara

William Ebenstein
late of University of California at Santa Barbara

Edwin Fogelman
University of Minnesota

PRENTICE HALL, *Englewood Cliffs, New Jersey* 07632

Library of Congress Cataloging-in-Publication Data

Ebenstein, Alan O.
    Today's isms: socialism, capitalism, fascism, communism / Alan O. Ebenstein,
    William Ebenstein, Edwin Fogelman.--10th ed.
        p. cm.
    Rev. ed of: Today's isms / William Ebenstein. 9th ed. 1985.
    Includes bibliographical references and index.
    ISBN 0-13-138595-X
    1. Comparative government. 2. Comparative economics. 3. Communism.
    4. Fascism. 5. Socialism. 6. Capitalism.
    I. Fogelman, Edwin. II. Ebenstein, William. Today's isms.
    III. Title.
    JF51. E218 1993   93-948
    335--dc20   CIP

Editorial/production supervision, interior design,
    and electronic page makeup: Shelly Kupperman
Acquisitions editor: Charlyce Jones Owen
Copy editor: James Tully
Cover designer: Design Solutions
Prepress buyer: Kelly Behr
Manufacturing buyer: Mary Ann Gloriande
Editorial assistant: Nicole Signoretti

BUSCA

© 1994, 1985 by Prentice-Hall, Inc.
A Paramount Communications Company
Englewood Cliffs, New Jersey 07632

Printed in the United States of America
10 9 8 7 6 5 4 3 2

ISBN   0-13-138595-X

Prentice-Hall International (UK) Limited, *London*
Prentice-Hall of Australia Pty. Limited, *Sydney*
Prentice-Hall Canada Inc., *Toronto*
Prentice-Hall Hispanoamericana, S.A., *Mexico*
Prentice-Hall of India Private Limited, *New Delhi*
Prentice-Hall of Japan, Inc., *Tokyo*
Simon & Schuster Asia Pte. Ltd., *Singapore*
Editora Prentice-Hall do Brasil, Ltda., *Rio de Janeiro*

To the memory of my parents and Joy

Contents

2 *Capitalism* 39

3 *Fascism* 79

4 *Communism* 110

Preface

This edition of *Today's Isms* marks two milestones for the work. It is the tenth edition of the book, and its publication occurs forty years after the first edition in 1954. *Today's Isms* is unique in its longevity, perspective, and continuing relevance.

This edition is the most fundamental revision of the book ever. All chapters have been completely reviewed and rewritten as necessary. In addition to the removal of much dated material, major additions include sections on monetary policy, capitalism and democracy, and cultural conservatism in the chapter on capitalism; on the future of fascism in the fascism chapter; and on the demise of the Soviet Union, the Deng era in China, and the future of communism in the chapter on communism.

The order of chapters has been altered for the tenth edition. Socialism and capitalism are first, followed by fascism and communism. The reason for this shift is that socialism and capitalism are the systems with which students are most familiar; and in temporal order, it was first fascism and then communism that posed the major challenge to democratic socialism and capitalism during the twentieth century.

In the original preface to *Today's Isms* William Ebenstein stated: "The major conflict of our age is the struggle between aggressive totalitarianism and the free way of life. Not long ago the chief threat to liberty was fascism; today it is communism." For the most part, this conflict is over. *Today's*

Isms seeks to blend the theory, history, and practice of the major ideologies that have shaped the modern age.

I remember my father in his later years commenting that *Today's Isms* was in need of fundamental revision. I hope that this tenth edition sets the stage for more years of use.

Several acknowledgments are in order. First and most important of all, I would like to thank Ed Fogelman for the opportunity to write this edition and for his work on the previous two editions. Second, two reviewers David E. Blank and John M. Nickerson—provided particularly helpful suggestions. Finally, I would like to thank Gordon Baker, my brother Rob, Susan Mills, and Sandy McDonald for their assistance and encouragement.

Alan O. Ebenstein

TODAY'S ISMS

1

Socialism

Socialist ideas and principles—by whatever name they may go (and in the United States, they surely do not go by the name "socialism")—have been the animating force behind most of the growth in government throughout the world during this century. This growth in government has been in proportionate and absolute *size*. Federal government spending in the United States, for example, increased from 2.5 percent of gross national product in 1929 to 27 percent in 1992, and spending by governments at all levels in the United States has increased over a thousandfold this century, from under $2 billion to over $2 trillion. Government has also expanded in *scope*. That is, government regulates, controls and influences more areas of social life today than it has in the past. From local zoning controls, to food and drug requirements, to safety regulations, to pollution standards—government affects individuals in many ways other than what it taxes from and spends on them. The fuel behind this expansion in government, again, is an ideological perspective that is best termed *socialist*.

It should be strongly noted before commencing this discussion of socialism that there are at least two broad meanings of it. The first relates to collective ownership of the forces of production in a society, either through worker cooperatives or state-run businesses. This form of socialism is on the decline everywhere, and was never practiced much in many places, including the United States. The second meaning of socialism is a

communitarian outlook of the proper way that society should be organized, as reflected in public assistance and works programs and projects
of all sorts, and significant sovereign collective involvement in the lives
of the people. This latter form is the type of socialism that has expanded
so greatly.

SOCIALIST HISTORY AND THEORY

Historical Background

It is not easy to determine when socialism first appeared. To some,
the ideal commonwealth in Plato's *Republic* is socialist, inasmuch as its
ruling class has no personal property and shares all things. Others have
held that the Bible, particularly the Old Testament, constitutes the first
socialist code, covering the protection of workers, women, and the weak.
The early Christians rejected the concept of "mine and thine" and practiced communal ownership in their everyday lives; and in the Middle
Ages numerous sects and movements, mostly religious, attacked wealth
and commerce as wicked and incompatible with the Christian life. Such
sects frequently withdrew into isolation, living an austere existence and
sharing poverty in brotherly love as a protest against the greed prevalent
in the world around them.

During the Renaissance and the Reformation, there was a revival of
protest against inequality based on wealth. The new arguments increasingly combined the older faith with newer rationalism, as evidenced in
Thomas More's *Utopia* (1516), which idealized an egalitarian and communal social order. In the Puritan revolution in seventeenth-century England, there arose—side-by--side with the main movement of middle-class
origin—a more radical group, called "Diggers" or "True Leveler," who
sought to attain communal ownership of land not in use. This protest was
short-lived, but its attack on private landed property was not forgotten.

To the extent that socialism contains within itself an element of
protest against social inequality, it is as old as Western civilization itself.
Both Greek and Judeo-Christian thought categorically rejected the concept
of wealth as the basis for the good life. Another feature characteristic of
socialism, the protest against money as the chief tie among human beings,
is also not confined to the socialist tradition: Many nonsocialists have
voiced their disapproval of the "cash nexus." But if one looks to history
for something more specific and concrete than a vague protest against
social injustice, one finds that socialism as an effective, organized political
movement is a product of the Industrial Revolution. Despite all illustrations from earlier times, socialism as a major political force originated only
after modern industrial capitalism. Moreover, as it was Britain in which

capitalism and thus socialism first developed, it will receive the most attention here.

Socialism and capitalism derive their philosophical basis in large parts from the same source—the theory of property. This theory was put forward most ably by the English political philosopher John Locke (1632–1704), who held in his *Second Treatise of Civil Government* (1690):

> Every man has a property in his own person; this nobody has any right to but himself. The labor of his body and the work of his hands we may say are properly his. Whatsoever, then, he removes out of the state that nature hath provided and left it in, he hath mixed his labour with, and joined to it something that is his own, and thereby makes it his property.

That is, all people have property in themselves that is indisputably their own. Therefore, each person has a right to the fruits of his or her labors; these fruits thereby also become property.

The revolutionary import of Locke's theory has had several permutations, depending on the historical era in which it has been used. Originally, during early capitalism, the theory was used to bolster the place of the individual in contrast to that of the landed gentry. Because each person had the right to what he or she produced, individuals' productive efforts belonged to themselves rather than to the king, a noble, the church, or any other person or entity. Locke's ideas thus were used to justify reducing the size and scope of government.

In their second historical utilization, however, these same ideas were used to argue for an increased government role and against private *accumulations* of property. Because each person had an equal right to what he or she produced, it was not fair nor was it just for some to possess a great deal while others had very little. Every man or woman who worked had the right to his or her share of the collective production, and thus Locke's theory was used to advocate for ownership of enterprises by workers either directly or through the state.

Classical, nineteenth century socialism inherited from classical capitalism the basic goal of preserving the unity of work and ownership. In the seventeenth and eighteenth centuries, the early phase of modern capitalism, that unity was a reality. In the England of John Locke or the America of Thomas Jefferson, the average farm, store, or workshop was generally small enough to be owned and operated by one person or family. Work and ownership coincided. The chief threat to this unity came from the state, which sought to prescribe, to regulate—in short, to play the role of omniscient busybody in economic matters. The individual entrepreneur, who knew how to run his or her business without any unsolicited advice from self-confident state officials, resented this attitude, and constituted the major support group for capitalism and democracy.

As the nineteenth century progressed, however, the individual (or single-family) form of ownership and work was gradually replaced by an economic system in which large-scale enterprise swallowed up the original capitalist-owner-manager. As the size of industrial enterprise grew larger and larger, work became more and more collective, while ownership remained private.

In seeking to restore the classical harmony between work and property, the early socialist reformer faced two options:

1. The division of large-scale enterprises into small units, so that work and ownership could coincide again in one person or family
2. Collective ownership

The former method was and remains feasible in agriculture, where large landed estates can be physically broken up and divided among landless farm workers, as was done in France during the eighteenth century and has been done in various parts of the developing world during the twentieth century. The division of large-scale agricultural holdings has not always increased productivity, however, because individual proprietors may not be as knowledgeable or as efficient as competitive large-scale enterprise.

In industry, the solution of dividing the enterprise into units is physically out of the question. An automobile or aircraft factory cannot be divided into 10,000 portions, each owned and operated by one worker. The technological nature of modern industrial enterprise is such that there is no alternative to collective work and operation. Thus, in facing the problem of reuniting work and ownership in industry, collective ownership seemed to socialists the logical answer, just as the classical capitalist deduced the right to individual ownership from the fact of individual work. In both systems—classical capitalism and classical socialism—there is an underlying assumption that the right to property ultimately rests on work, effort, and industry, rather than on formal law, custom, or birth.

The filial link between socialism and capitalism can be illustrated by the first modern socialist, who was a wealthy and successful capitalist. Robert Owen (1771–1858), generally regarded as the founder of British socialism, first used the term *socialism*. A self-made capitalist, he had amassed a fortune by the age of forty. He was a man of sound, practical judgment, and he easily passed a test of experience often enunciated by conservatives as important to ask a reformer when he or she comes along with a plan: "Have you ever met a payroll?" Owen had. In *A New View of Society* (1813), he described himself as a "manufacturer for pecuniary profit."

His views were the result not of study in the British Museum (like Karl Marx) but of experience in his own industrial enterprises. Owen dedicated his book to the Prince Regent of the British Empire; he was no refugee from his own society, as were Marx and Lenin later, but a respectable, wealthy man. He considered drink an incentive to crime and a main source of misery, and his list of virtues and vices would have appealed to Benjamin Franklin.

Far from looking on capitalist Britain as a dungeon of inhumanity, he described the British constitution as being "among the best devised and most enlightened that have hitherto been established." Refusing to believe that evil can be transformed into good in a day, he advocated "progressive repeal and modification" of unjust laws and conditions. Strongly rejecting the allure of revolutionary change, he felt that "the British constitution, in its present outline, is admirably adapted to effect these changes, without the evils which always accompany a coerced or ill-prepared change." Realizing that love and fellowship cannot be conceived in hatred and born in strife, Owen appealed to "every rational man, every true friend of humanity," and he hoped for cordial cooperation and unity of action among the government, Parliament, the church, and the people.

Owen's rationalism also emerges from the fact that *A New View of Society* discusses one subject more than any other: *education*. Owen believed that the evils of his society were due to circumstances rather than to people's depravity, and he was convinced that, just as crime and degradation were the result of specific social and economic conditions, education in a new environment could produce human beings endowed with rationality and the habits of order, regularity, temperance, and industry.

In his own time, when children of six and seven years of age were employed in factories for twelve hours a day and more, Owen made the suggestion, bold and radical for the capitalist conscience of 1813, that a regular workday of thirteen hours, from six in the morning to seven in the evening, should not be imposed upon children under age twelve; after that age "their education might be finished, and their bodies would be more competent to undergo the fatigue and exertions required of them." Human nature, Owen said, is "universally plastic," and as education is the key to allowing people to become more rational and cooperative, "the best governed state will be that which shall possess the best national system of education."

Owen looked to society rather than to the state for important change, in the true nineteenth century liberal-capitalist tradition. A century before John Maynard Keynes and William Henry Beveridge, he emphasized the importance of full employment for the maintenance of a civilized society, yet he opposed the dole on the ground that the "industrious, temperate, and comparatively virtuous" should not be compelled to support the "ignorant, idle, and comparatively vicious." Owen clearly saw the human aspects of unemployment; yet he did not want the state to dispense employment but rather to provide an educational system good enough to equip every person with the skills with which to find employment in the open market.

A believer in the individualist principle of self-help, Owen started the cooperative movement and supported the incipient trade union organizations springing up throughout England and Scotland. For Owen, "cooperativism" was more than selling milk to consumers; he believed that producers' cooperatives rather than consumers' cooperatives would establish a new social order. He sank much of his fortune into producers' cooperatives in England and spent several years and the better part of his wealth in a cooperative venture in the United States. Although his best-known social experiment, the settlement of New Harmony in Indiana, did not succeed, his ideas had significant influence.

Elements of Socialist Thought and Policy

Socialism, like many other movements and ideas, has no bible or single manifesto because socialists do not have one set of beliefs or doctrines. Moreover, socialism has developed in a variety of countries in accordance with different national traditions, and has thus taken on different meanings for this reason. Further, as a democratic movement, it has never had a central authority to lay down a party line.

Despite the absence of universally valid statements of socialist doctrine, the outlines of its thought and policy can be culled from various writers and from the policies of socialist parties. What emerges, however, is not a consistent set of ideas and policies. The major strength—and weakness—of socialism is that it has had no clear-cut body of doctrine and has been nourished from many sources. This rich background gives socialism much strength, but also inconsistency.

The complex, and frequently self-contradictory, elements of socialist thought and policy, reflecting the complexity of the societies in which they exist, are well-exemplified by the British socialist movement. While not all of these elements are as prominent now in the British Labour party as they once were, their historical importance serves to enlighten roots of current socialist thought. The elements that stand out in the British socialist tradition are:

1. Religion
2. Ethical and aesthetic idealism
3. Fabian empiricism
4. Liberalism

Religion   Clement Attlee, who would later become Britain's prime minister, wrote:

> the first place in the influences that built up the Socialist movement must be given to religion. England in the nineteenth century was still a nation of Bible readers. To put the Bible into the hands of an Englishman is to do a very dangerous thing. He will find there material which may send him out as a

preacher of some religious, social, or economic doctrine. The large number of religious sects in this country, and the various tenets that many of them hold, illustrates this. (*The Labour Party in Perspective*, 1937)

The Christian Socialist movement, headed by two clergymen, Frederick Maurice and Charles Kingsley, reached its peak in the middle of the nineteenth century and was an important source for the later development of working-class and socialist organizations. The Christian Socialists had as their guiding principle the concept that socialism must be Christianized, and Christianity socialized.

George Lansbury, Attlee's predecessor as the leader of the Labour party, wrote:

Socialism, which means love, cooperation, and brotherhood in every department of human affairs, is only the outward expression of a Christian's faith. I am firmly convinced that whether they know it or not, all who approve and accept competition and struggle against each other as the means whereby we gain our daily bread, do indeed betray and make of no effect the "will of God." (*My England*, 1934)

During World War II, the archbishop of Canterbury, William Temple, came very close to socialism in his *Christianity and the Social Order*. Temple held that every economic system is, for good or ill, an immense educative influence and consequently the church must be concerned with it. The church is therefore bound to ask "whether that influence is one tending to develop Christian character, and if the answer is partly or wholly negative the church must do its utmost to secure a change in the economic system so that it may find in that system an ally and not an enemy."

This practical concern of Christianity was particularly strong in England throughout the entire second half of the nineteenth century. A sense of moral seriousness and dedicated disinterestedness characterized this period, and religion, while conceding that grace and faith were essential to salvation, nevertheless emphasized conduct and salvation by works. Many socialist leaders of the older generation (like Attlee) were steeped in an atmosphere in which religion was taken seriously.

Another religious influence of profound importance in Britain was the tradition of religious dissent, of *nonconformity*. In other European states Protestantism had resulted in freedom of the church in relation to Rome, but not necessarily in freedom *within* the church in matters of doctrine and church government. To the nonconformist in Britain, on the other hand, Protestantism meant freedom of individual conscience and the freedom to organize voluntarily in associations of like-minded believers. This principle of voluntary association was later translated from religion into politics, where it became the life principle of the democratic society.

It was in the village chapels of the eighteenth and nineteenth centuries that many local leaders of working-class organizations learned to think for themselves, as well as to conduct public meetings and administer finances. Wherever nonconformity was strong, labor unions and cooperatives were strong; in fact, trade unions have been aptly called the descendants of earlier nonconformist congregations. Nonconformity supplied more than a particular religious outlook: It was also the source, in the labor movement, of the idealism, the moral dedication, and the seriousness that historically has characterized the movement and its leaders.

The complexity of the religious roots of modern British socialism becomes apparent in the fact that nonreligious, rational humanism has also played a vital role in the evolution of socialist thought and action. Robert Owen was a rationalist; among more modern socialist leaders in Britain, Sidney and Beatrice Webb, Harold J. Laski, G.D.H. Cole, and Hugh Gaitskell, to mention but a few, have not been much inspired by formal religious beliefs. It remains of some interest, however, that the political leaders of the labor movement—men like George Lansbury, Clement Attlee, and Sir Stafford Cripps—were more often profoundly religious, while the principal intellectual figures, the people who formulate ideas rather than policies, have tended to represent the *rationalist* roots of socialism. Harold Wilson, a professional economist, came from a background of strong religious nonconformity, and religion meant a good deal to him. Although reluctant to express his religious feelings in public, he often preached in nonconformist churches. His type of socialism has been called by a fellow Labourite "Methodism, not Marxism."

In the United States, too, religion played an important part in the cooperative and communal settlements established in the eighteenth and nineteenth centuries. In the twentieth century explicit socialism in the United States was symbolized by Norman Thomas, who was a minister of religion before he took up the cause of socialism as his life's mission.

In contrast, religion has played a smaller part in continental European and Latin American socialism. In England religious dissent was the bridge between religious and political unorthodoxy; in the virtual absence of religious nonconformity outside of the English-speaking world, however, dissent from the established social and political order has usually included dissent from the established church or from religion itself.

Before World War I, Russian radical and socialist movements were notably free of any religious influence or inspiration. In his monumental study *The Spirit of Russia* (1913), Thomas Garrigue Masaryk, a renowned philosopher and later the first president of Czechoslovakia, observed that "Christian socialism is practically unknown in Russia." Masaryk's analysis in 1913 was later confirmed by the victorious rise of Leninist communism. In France and Germany there were small groups of religious socialists, but on the whole, socialists tended to be anticlerical or at least indifferent toward religion, since most churches in continental Europe openly supported the political and economic status quo. During World War II the struggle of many priests and ministers against Nazi-fascist oppression brought about a closer understanding between churches and most socialist parties. Since then, churches have become less committed to one particular set of social and economic theories, and socialists have abandoned much of their earlier anticlericalism.

Ethical and aesthetic idealism   Ethical and aesthetic idealism is another source of British socialism, although its impact cannot be measured in votes and membership cards. Expressed by writers like John Ruskin and William Morris during the nineteenth century, ethical idealism was not a political or economic program but a revolt against the squalor, drabness, and poverty of life under industrial capitalism. An art critic who turned to social issues, Ruskin deplored the capitalist system and the material and social results it produced. He sought an older and more traditional way of life, one in which natural and other forms of beauty would come before the economic bottom line.

Environmentalism continues to be an important issue to socialist parties around the world today. While not an exclusive preserve of the Left, environmentalism in part appeals more to socialist-oriented political parties because they do not emphasize material goods as much as do capitalist parties, which are more philosophically inclined to see humanity's control of nature as the cure of social ills than to see that very control as a large part of the problem.

While Karl Marx approached industrial capitalism in terms of cosmic laws—the development of world history according to inevitable social laws, philosophical materialism, and the law of the falling profit rate, to name but a few—William Morris kept his gaze closer to the ground. He saw around him ugly household goods and furnishings, and men and women who lacked joy and beauty in their daily lives. Once, when asked in a public meeting what he thought of Marx, Morris said: "I am asked if I believe in Marx's theory of value. To speak quite frankly I do not know what Marx's theory of value is, and I'm damned if I want to know." What Morris cared about was human beings, not this or that "system." He felt intensely that the arts must be brought back into everyday life and that people's creative impulses should be given expression in their daily activities and work.

The influence of Ruskin and Morris was more negative than positive. They showed what was wrong—physically and morally—with a civilization that was built on strife and squalor, but they did not formulate any specific program to improve the conditions to which they objected. Nevertheless, this aesthetic and ethical revolt was important in preparing the intellectual environment in which socialism could later find a sympathetic response.

Ruskin and Morris were read mainly by the more educated class, which absorbed from them—as well as from Charles Dickens, Thomas Carlyle, and other writers—a groping understanding of what industrial civilization does to a person, not only as a worker but as a human being. The aesthetic and ethical rebels of Victorian England undermined the self-confidence that prevailed and fostered self-criticism; out of that doubt and self-criticism more positive socialist ideas could later be developed step-by-step.

Particularly in town and country planning, the British Labour party has reflected directly and explicitly the message of Ruskin and Morris. The whole concept of community planning—more than tearing down slums and building neat little row houses of uniform size and style—owes much to the outlook of the early pioneers of socialist thought, for whom problems of industry merged with more general problems of creating a community in which each member would have access to the means of civilized enjoyment. Now the issue of a healthy environment combined with sound economic production is worldwide.

Fabian empiricism   Fabian empiricism is perhaps the most characteristically British aspect of the British labor movement. The Fabian Society, founded in 1884, was named after a Roman general, Quintus Fabius Maximus Cunctator—the "delayer." The early motto of the society was: "For the right moment you must wait, as Fabius did; but when the right moment comes you must strike hard, or your waiting will have been vain and fruitless."

The founders and early members of the Fabian society included George Bernard Shaw, Sidney and Beatrice Webb, H.G. Wells, and Graham Wallas. It was noteworthy that none of them came from the poorer classes and that there was a sizable proportion of writers in the group.

In Sidney Webb's historical survey of the basis of socialism, included in the *Fabian Essays* (1889), we find what is still the basic philosophy of Fabianism and, more generally, of British socialism. Webb looked upon socialism (eleven years before the foundation of the British Labour party) as an inevitable outcome of the full fruition of democracy, but he insisted that his "inevitability of gradualness" was sharply different from the Marxian inevitability of revolutionary, catastrophic change.

Webb emphasized that social organization can come only bit by bit and that important "organic changes" can take place only under four conditions: First, such changes must be democratic, acceptable to a popular majority, and "prepared for in the minds of all"; second, they must be gradual, causing no dislocation; third, they must not be regarded as immoral by the people; and fourth, they must be constitutional and peaceful.

Marxians in Europe and elsewhere aimed their propaganda at the proletariat. The middle and upper classes were to be liquidated, not converted to socialism. Because the propaganda was thus aimed exclusively at the proletariat, it tended to be highly emotional and sloganized, taking into consideration not only the educational level of the workers but also the fact that they were expected to be half converted before they were ever exposed to Marxist agitation.

The Fabian Society started from the opposite assumption: There could be no progress toward a just social order in Britain unless the middle and upper classes could be shown the reasonableness and equity of the basic claims of socialist thought and policy. Since government in England was by persuasion and consent, and since the governing classes of Britain were largely recruited from the middle and upper classes, there could be no change of policy without the consent of those classes. It was fortunate for the Fabians that they spoke the same language—literally and metaphorically—as did the governing classes and knew how to permeate the latter in ways that would have been closed to formal propaganda from those outside the same class.

The Fabian technique of permeation was based on the premise that one does not change a reasonable person through a single brilliant argument, lecture, or emotional appeal. It was Fabian policy to work on the minds and feelings of their listeners in a slow, gradual process rather than in one sudden act of conversion, and as often on social, informal occasions rather than on formal, official ones.

An emotional appeal to a high-level British civil servant, telling that individual that, according to the Marxian dialectic, the capitalist system is doomed and that such doom will be followed by the classless proletarian society, was likely to have less of a long-term effect than a casual reference at lunch to a new government report, written by a fellow bureaucrat, on the incidence of disease and crime in slum areas. Similarly, serious discussion of a recent book by a reputable and scholarly economist on changes in the distribution of income among various social and economic groups was likely to have more effect on a conservative political leader than the shorter appeals of "Down with Capitalism" and "Long Live Proletarian Solidarity."

Fabian leaders did not seek an immediate revolution in part because they thought such a revolution would be fruitless. As one socialist precursor, John Stuart Mill, wrote in his unfinished chapters on *Socialism*: "Sudden effects in history are generally superficial. Causes which go deep down into the roots of future events produce the most serious parts of their effect only slowly." One has only to consider the ultimately transitory effect of many "revolutions" this century to realize that gradualism may be more influential in the long run than a sudden burst of change.

Permeation of capitalist society by the Fabians also had another side. The Fabians did not consider it their job to pass resolutions, make appeals to kings and parliaments, or address themselves to the masses of the people. They were interested in convincing a small group of individuals who possessed two qualifications: First, they had to be people of continuous influence in public life, so that the long process of permeation, if successful, would pay off; second, such individuals would have to be reasonable, by which the Fabians meant not partisan extremists. Since such people could be found in all political parties, the Fabians cultivated conservatives as well as liberals.

This sort of Fabianism assumes a Fabianism in reverse, or else it would not stand a chance of success. For example, Fabians and other socialists in England read *The Times* not because they agree with its editorial viewpoint (generally conservative) but because it is "a good paper." In many other countries socialists have considered the local version of *The Times* a source of bourgeois contamination from which they should steer clear.

The difference between the Fabian and Marxist-communist approaches can best be seen by contrasting the writings of the two groups. Marx was little interested in the minutiae of life; his magnum opus, *Das Kapital*, is an attempt to give meaning to history as a whole, and much of his thought was devoted to fundamentals of economics and philosophy. Lenin wrote volumes on such subjects as *Materialism and Empirio-Criticism.* In contrast, more than 95 percent of all Fabian publications have been pamphlets rather than heavy tomes, and pamphlets lend themselves more to small subjects like *Municipal Milk and Public Health* (Fabian Tract no. 122) than to the future of Western civilization. The Fabian Society is rarely to be found in high intellectual altitudes, sniffing the thin air surrounding the metaphysical peaks; it is more often found " nosing about in the drains," seeking to remedy some immediate and specific condition.

Early in the history of the Fabian Society, Fabian Tract no. 70 (written by George Bernard Shaw) made it plain that Fabianism was no rival to existing philosophies trying to explain the whole cosmos and that it had "no distinctive opinion on the Marriage Question, Religion, Art, abstract Economics, historic Evolution, Currency, or any other subject than its own special business of practical Democracy and Socialism." This sense of practicality and concreteness is indicated by typical titles of Fabian tracts and other pamphlets: *Liquor Licensing at Home and Abroad; Life in the Laundry; Public Control of Electrical Power and Transit; The Case of School Nurseries; The Endowment of Motherhood;* and *The Reform of the House of Lords.*

Two Fabian pamphlets, *Metropolitan Borough Councils: Their Constitution, Powers and Duties* and *Borough Councils: Their Constitution, Powers, and Duties* were written by Clement Attlee in the spring of 1920, when Lenin was busy, not with the reform of borough councils, but with the destruction of states and empires.

The Fabian approach can perhaps best be shown in a simple illustration: If a slum clearance project is debated in terms of fundamental issues—such as socialism versus capitalism—agreement between advocates of the project and their opponents is unlikely. If, however, the pertinent facts can be brought out clearly—the cost (in dollars and cents) of a slum area in terms of disease, crime protection, and fire hazards, and as compared with the cost of building new houses with public assistance—the original gap has been considerably narrowed, and agreement will be likelier than it was when the arguments centered on issues of apparently irreconcilable ultimate values.

The successes of Fabianism have probably stemmed chiefly from this concern with reducing questions of principle to questions of fact. Fabians gambled on the notion that facts do matter and that the impact of facts ultimately determines how people think and act.

In his autobiography, *Power and Influence* (1953), Lord Beveridge had an interesting sidelight on the Fabian faith in facts. One of the greatest contributions of Sidney and Beatrice Webb was the creation of the London School of Economics and Political Science, which was founded to provide an adequate opportunity for the study of economics and allied subjects. The Webbs themselves chose the first four directors of the London School. Of the four, Beveridge tells us, the first two became Conservative members of Parliament, the third had socialist sympathies, and the fourth (Beveridge himself) was a Liberal. Beveridge says the Webbs "believed that the impartial study of society would further the Socialism which was their practical aim, but they were prepared to take the risk of being wrong in that belief."

The Fabian technique of trying to reduce apparently irreconcilable differences of principle to negotiable disagreements over facts is no invention or novelty but is implicit in the very nature of democratic society. There is peace in a free society to the extent that people are willing to keep to themselves conflicting fundamentals in religion, morals, and philosophy. Separation of state and church in the United States was brought about and has been maintained not because Americans are indifferent to religion but because the framers of the Constitution thought it wise to keep this fundamental issue out of politics and to concentrate on issues in which people of all religions can cooperate without injury to their religious belief.

Fabianism has frequently been described as reform without resentment, social reconstruction without class war, political empiricism without dogma or fanaticism. Despite its small size (its membership has never exceeded a few thousand, and is about 4,000 today), the Fabian Society has had an enormous impact. In the 1945 election, which led to the first Labour government based on a substantial parliamentary majority, 229 of the 394 Labour members of Parliament were Fabians, and more than half of the government, including Attlee himself (prime minister from 1945 to 1951), was Fabian. Hugh Gaitskell, who succeeded Attlee as leader of the Labour party, was also a long-standing Fabian, as is Gaitskell's successor, Harold Wilson (prime minister from 1964–1970 and 1974–1976). Wilson's successor, James Callaghan (prime minister from 1976–1979) also is a Fabian, as is

Neil Kinnock (Labour party leader from 1983 to 1992) and the current Labour leader, John Smith.

Liberalism   The term "liberal" has undergone significant changes in meaning from the nineteenth to twentieth centuries. In the nineteenth century, a liberal was generally one who favored a reduced role for government, because government (or tradition or culture) was perceived as the root of many problems. In the twentieth century, however, liberal has come to mean one who favors more government—government being perceived as being able to solve social ills.

Historically, the British Liberal party was, with the Conservatives, one of the two major political parties in Britain, and its eclipse in this century and replacement by the Labour party has seen many of its policies and attitudes incorporated into Labour policy. The Liberal party stood for free trade, free markets, free speech, and free nations (that is, the Liberals were generally anti-imperialist).

While the Labour party in the past favored larger government and nationalization of industries, these views were tempered by the Liberal legacy. While bureaucratic, the Labour party did not become statist. The individual has never been seen by the Labour party as finding his or her existence through the state; rather, the state exists to serve the people.

The decline of the Liberal party (liberal in a nineteenth century sense) during the early part of the twentieth century was not a result of its failure, but came about because success made it less necessary and no longer as relevant. Both the Conservative and Labour parties became committed to the Liberal principles of individual freedom of worship, thought, speech, and association.

Free trade has been in large part acceded to by both Conservatives and Labour. In the 1960s and early 1970s, the issue of free trade reappeared in the controversy over British entry into the European Economic Community, the EEC or Common Market. In 1973 a Conservative government led Britain into the Common Market; in 1974 a national referendum called by a newly formed Labour government confirmed the action by a vote of two to one. Since Britain's entry into the EEC, both the Labour and Conservative governments have supported participation in the EEC.

In the question of empire, too, the Liberal approach of the nineteenth century is no longer relevant, since virtually all of the empire is gone. The process of setting former colonies free after World War II occurred under both Labour and Conservative governments.

With many specific issues gone, many Liberals joined the Labour party, or vote Labour. Liberalism has generally been to the left of the Conservatives, and in a country with a two-party system, like Britain, if one wishes to stand to the left of Conservatism, the Labour party has had the only platform to stand on with a realistic electoral chance of implementation.

In the early 1980s, various renegade Labourites attempted to merge with the remainder of the Liberal party to form a new center alliance that would avoid the excessive bureaucracy of the Labour approach, while being more humane than what was perceived as the harshness of Margaret Thatcher's government. This approach ultimately failed, but once again the result was to draw both major parties closer to the center, with greater respect and appreciation for the individual in social life.

The Liberal party contributed (and still contributes as the Democratic Liberal party) much that is lasting in British politics. Because of the Liberal influence, socialist leaders have been more moderate and less doctrinaire than they might otherwise have been, and they have a deeper respect for individual liberty. Moreover, the Conservative party has incorporated free market economics as well as a healthy respect for individual rights into its platform. Liberalism turned the Labour party into a national party rather than one based on class, and it bequeathed to the Labour party the message that there can be reform without bitterness and class hatred.

In recent years, the Labour party has promoted more individual rights than the Conservative party in such lifestyle areas as homosexuality and abortion. Generally, socialist-oriented parties have been more inclined to allow freedom in personal activities, just as capitalist-oriented parties have been inclined to allow more freedom in commercial activities.

Socialism and Democracy

The link between democracy and socialism is the most important single element in socialist thought and policy. The history of socialism quickly shows that successful socialist movements have grown up only in nations with strong democratic traditions.

The reason for this parallelism is simple. Where democratic, constitutional government is generally accepted, socialists can concentrate on extensive economic and social reforms: to create more opportunity for the underprivileged classes; to end inequality based on birth rather than service; to open the horizons of education to all people; to eliminate discriminatory practices based on sex, religion, race, or social class; to regulate and reorganize the economy for the benefit of the entire community; to maintain full employment; to provide adequate social security for the sick, unemployed, and aged; to replan the layout of towns and cities; to tear down slums and build new houses; to provide medical facilities for everybody, regardless of income; and finally, to rebuild society on the foundation of cooperation.

All these goals of democratic socialism have one thing in common: *to make democracy more real by broadening the application of democratic principles from the political to the nonpolitical areas of society.*

Freedom of worship and freedom of political association, historically the first liberties to be won, are still the essential foundations of democracy. Where these foundations exist, therefore, socialists feel able to concentrate on what they consider the finer points of democracy.

In contrast, socialist parties have fought an uphill and generally losing struggle in nations in which democracy is not a living organism but an aspiration, a hope, an idea yet to be realized. For example, the Social Democratic party in Germany always worked under a heavy handicap. In the Second Reich (1870–1918), political autocracy was a reality, and parliamentary institutions were a cover for the virtual dictatorship of Bismarck and then of Emperor William II. In the 1870s Bismarck outlawed the Social Democrats as "enemies of the state," and the party leaders who escaped imprisonment fled to England, other free nations in Europe, or to America.

During the Weimar Republic (1919–1933), the German Social Democratic party was paralyzed again by the insecurity of democratic institutions; the main issue of the Weimar Republic was not a social reform in which the socialists could take a special interest but something much bigger: the issue of democratic government itself. Whereas in nations with long-established democratic habits socialists could argue over issues within democracy—taking the existence of democracy for granted—German socialists constantly had to fight over the issue of democracy itself. As fascism grew in the Weimar Republic, the German socialists became more concerned with the defense of republican and democratic institutions than with problems of economic reform.

In Russia before 1917 the situation was even simpler. The Czarist regime made no pretense of democracy or self-government; social and economic reform by peaceful means was thus virtually impossible, and the door for revolutionary communism was open.

Democratic socialists are keenly aware that without the opportunities provided by democratic, constitutional government, they could not get to first base. Once in control of the government, socialists often still maintain the psychology of the opposition, because they know that the possession of political power does not automatically solve the problems of social and economic organization. In other words, before socialists take over the government, they are in opposition to the government *and* to the wealthier interests; after they gain control of the government, this oppositionist psychology, directed as it is against the economic status quo, may persist.

Moreover, even in the purely governmental realm, socialists tend to preserve a certain degree of caution after they get into office, because they realize that though they can gain control of the legislature in an election, the other sources of political power—the civil service and the judiciary—may be hostile to them, as well as other vested interests in society.

Another factor essential to this discussion is all too frequently neglected. Examining the remarkably high state of civil liberties in nations with strong socialist movements, one tends to overlook the high respect for civil liberties demonstrated by opponents of socialism. If the conservative and propertied classes had shown less respect for the letter and spirit of constitutional government, the chances for socialist growth would have been slim. From the viewpoint of dollars and cents, the conservatives' genuine acquiescence in socialism and socialist practices means that they have valued democracy more than their pocketbooks and have been willing to be heavily taxed even for programs they considered undesirable or unreasonable.

Thus, both groups have taken a gamble: The socialists trust their opponents not to destroy the processes of democratic government in order to protect their financial interests; and the propertied classes trust the socialists not to abuse electoral victories, and to act reasonably and moderately when in office.

Socialism Compared with Communism

Socialism and communism have stood for two irreconcilable ways of thought and life, as incompatible as constitutional democracy and revolutionary totalitarianism. Although recent advocates of Eurocommunism attempted to play down the profound antagonism between communism and socialism, their claims were never tested in practice on a national scale, nor are they now ever likely to be, given the demise of communism around the world.

Because of the communist goal of revolution, it is understandable that socialist parties generally looked at communists as troublemakers who had to be kept out of unions or other organized working-class activity. It is also understandable why the communists worked with such energy for the control of organized labor. They knew that no amount of propaganda would convert the middle and wealthier classes to communism.

Socialists learned from elementary electoral statistics that parliamentary majorities cannot be obtained by appealing to one class only; a considerable proportion of the working class in England (about 40 percent) does not vote Labour, and if the Labour party is to obtain a majority, it must appeal to other groups. While communists think in terms of *class* and class antagonisms, socialists think in terms of *parliamentary majorities.*

The socialist rejection of Marxist thought also applies to the term *proletariat.* As former Prime Minister Harold Wilson put it: "The idea of a proletariat is nonsense. I am more interested in people as individuals than in the mass. I am interested in the family, because most happiness is family happiness. I am interested in Saturdays and Sundays and Bank Holidays." To say the least, these are not classical communist sentiments. Socialists have always been far more moderate than communists in Western European democratic nations.

In the crucial issue of public ownership, the gap that separates socialists from communists is unbridgeable. Communists visualize the transition from capitalist enterprise to public ownership as sudden and complete. There is no payment for expropriated property, because communists consider that capitalist ownership of property is no better than theft. In contrast, socialists do not believe that transition from capitalism to public ownership of the means of production can be either sudden or complete. Public ownership of the means of production is to be built up gradually, by installments; if one phase works, then the next will be tackled. Moreover, if one phase fails—as has been the case with many nationalized businesses—then this aspect of the socialist agenda will be dropped from electoral platforms. Responsible socialists feel that they must prove pragmatically, through actual accomplishments, the usefulness and practicality of their programs.

Concerning compensation, socialists share the general democratic conviction that no citizen may be deprived of property without due process and compensation. Important as public ownership of basic industries may be to their plans, socialists consider public ownership not an end but a means to an end, and a means that does not justify the violation of property rights.

There is another vital difference with regard to public ownership. Communists seek to transfer all means of production, distribution, and exchange to the state, preferring publicly owned property to private enterprise. By contrast, socialists consider and ponder whether a specific industry or service should be transferred to public ownership or control. Socialists have decided to nationalize because an industry is a monopoly, because it is financially ailing, or because it is of such vital importance to the national economy that it seems undesirable to leave its operation in private hands.

Philosophically and politically, the difference between communists and socialists is deeply rooted. Lenin's theory of the professional revolution (see Chapter 4) is based on the assumption that the Communist party has the job of leading the proletariat, and that within the minority of the party the professional revolutionaries are to formulate policies and assume leadership. Thus, a minority within a minority is the ruling elite. This elite concept is rejected by socialists, who believe in democracy and majority rule for party and nation.

Socialists believe in peaceful persuasion to promote their program. Communists feel that all means of communication, education, and propaganda are biased in favor of the capitalist status quo and that freedom of the press amounts to little if one lacks necessary funds to start a newspaper. According to orthodox Marxism-Leninism, socialist electoral victories are impossible. According to Lenin, workers under capitalism cannot be converted to socialist thinking until there has been a change in the economic structure of society. Only then, Lenin argued, will the workers be able to think along anticapitalist lines, because (as Marx said) the conditions of one's life determine one's thinking.

To the communist, every capitalist system, whether democratic or authoritarian, is a bourgeois dictatorship; specifically, democratic institutions in a capitalist system are considered a facade that does not make the capitalist system less dictatorial. Once capitalism—even democratic capitalism—is identified with dictatorship, the communist insistence on violence as the sole means of change is a logical conclusion.

Socialists, on the other hand, draw a fundamental distinction between two types of capitalist system, political dictatorship and liberal democracy. In a capitalist democracy, socialists believe in playing according to the rules of the game—provided, of course, all do the same.

Socialists reject the communist thesis that the choice in a democracy is between complete capitalism and complete collectivism. Democratic parties do not concern themselves with bringing about the millennium at a certain date but seek to tackle issues incrementally that are comparatively manageable and to avoid definitive solutions that are irrevocable. This is both a strength and weakness of democracy.

Socialists envisage the transition from a predominantly capitalist economy to a predominantly socialist economy not as a result of a sudden revolutionary coup but as the result of gradual measures, none of which by itself irrevocably alters the nature of the whole society. While communists think in terms of three absolutes—capitalism, revolution, communist dictatorship—socialists think in terms of three relative concepts: a predominantly capitalist economy as the starting point, a period of gradual change, and finally a predominantly socialized society.

Finally, in a deeply philosophical sense, communism stands for the complete sharing of all things, while classical socialism seeks only collective ownership of the means of production. Socialism has always been more individualistic, practical, and democratic as well as less revolutionary than communism.

SOCIALISM IN PRACTICE

Social-Economic Changes and Reforms

The victory of the Allied Powers in World War I provided a strong stimulus to socialist parties around the world. The war had been fought in defense of democracy against the authoritarian militarism of Germany and its allies, and during the war promises were made to the peoples of the major democratic belligerents, particularly Britain and France, that military victory would be followed by the establishment of a new social order based on greater opportunity and equality. This same pattern was repeated after World War II when the sheer evilness of the Axis powers and the

Allies'alliance with the communist Soviet Union moved the democratic world in a leftist direction.

In England the Labour party reflected in its growth and development the protest against the old social order. Founded in 1900, the party polled only two seats in the parliamentary elections of that year. By 1910, forty Labourites sat in the House of Commons, and the party ceased to be a negligible factor. In 1929 Labour became for the first time in its history the largest single political party in Britain, obtaining in the general election 288 out of 615 seats in Parliament. The coming of the world depression in 1929 weakened Britain economically, and the minority Labour government, being unable to follow socialist policies to cure the depression and unwilling to adopt conservative remedies, resigned in the summer of 1931. Thereafter, as long as the shadow of Nazi-fascist aggression hung over Britain, there was little chance for embarking on a major program of social and economic reform.

Between 1935 and the end of the World War II in Europe, there was no general election. In the first postwar general elections, held on July 5, 1945, the Labour party obtained 394 out of 640 seats, with the result that for the first time in British history, a Labour government was formed with a clear majority in the House of Commons.

Between 1900 and 1918 the Labour party was not officially committed to socialism, although it included many individual socialists. In 1918, when the party adopted socialism in its program, its commitment to the nationalization of industry was just about complete. But the party changed its outlook drastically and urged nationalization only where it had been proven pragmatically that public ownership would do more for the welfare of the nation than private ownership. In the election of 1945 the Labour party did not enter the campaign with a program of "socialism" in the abstract but promised to nationalize only specifically listed industries and services if elected to office.

In each case it explained why it believed nationalization was necessary. For gas and light, water, telephone and telegraph, and other utilities, the criterion of nationalization was the existence of a natural monopoly. Further, regardless of party, there was general agreement in Britain that the coal industry was so sick and inefficient that it could not be put on its feet except through nationalization. The iron and steel industries were declared to be so vital to the nation that their management could not safely be subject to the decisions of private owners. The nationalization of all inland transportation by rail, road, and air was proposed on the basis that wasteful competition could best be avoided by a coordinated scheme of transportation owned and managed by the public authorities. The Bank of England was proposed for nationalization on the ground that its purpose was obviously public. Finally, the election program of 1945 also promised to set up a National Health Service so that the best possible health and medical facilities might be available to every citizen without regard to ability to pay.

After the electoral triumph of 1945, the Labour party methodically carried out its program. With one exception, there was little argument over nationalization. Regarding the exception, iron and steel, the Conservatives argued that the industry was highly efficient and that the needs of the national welfare could be accommodated without nationalization.

The attitude of the British toward nationalization was generally one of indifference. The exception was, and remains, the National Health Service, because of its direct effect on the everyday life of the individual citizen. Although no one was compelled to join the National Health Service, 97 percent of the population and 96 percent of the doctors are in it. At first the administrative and technical difficulties in setting up the necessary machinery caused considerable delay and confusion. As the program developed, however, adverse criticism largely died down. Now the National Health Service is an established part of British life. The medical profession, while not enthusiastic about it, has nevertheless publicly accepted it as essentially sound. Public opinion polls have found that a large majority of those questioned are on the whole satisfied with the National Health Service. The British no longer discuss the basic issue of a national health insurance program but rather the ways of improving its practical operation. The United States remains the only Western industrial democracy without a national health insurance program of some sort. Whether or not to implement a health insurance program is a key question facing the Clinton administration.

The Labour government elected in 1945 also set up a comprehensive cradle-to-grave scheme of social security. The system provides protection against sickness, unemployment, and old age, supplemented by maternity grants, widows' pensions, and family allowances. Social security, as set up by the Labour government, was no invention of the Labour party but rather the culmination of several decades of social legislation enacted by Conservative and Liberal governments. A fully integrated system of social security was first proposed during World War II in the *Beveridge Report* (1942); in the middle of the war, both the Conservative and Labour parties pledged themselves, if elected to office after the war, to introduce a comprehensive system of social security.

A further policy of the Labour government in the years 1945 to 1951 aimed at greater social equality. The setting up of the basic institutions of the welfare state in itself contributed to greater social equality by bringing within the reach of large sections of the population many facilities and services that hitherto had not been available to them. Educational opportunities on the secondary and university levels, for example, were made available to children of lower-income families. In addition, several new colleges and universities were founded in an attempt to combine British educational features with the American goal of providing higher education for the many rather than for the select few.

In 1965 the Labour government tackled one of the keys to social equality—the secondary school. In Britain, as in most other countries, there are two main types of secondary school: an academic type, for a small minority, which leads to college; and a vocational type, for the mass of the people, that ends at age sixteen. The main disadvantage is that the system segregates members of different social classes at an early age. For these reasons, the Labour government started to adapt the British system of secondary education to the American pattern, in which most high schools combine academic with vocational education.

Taxation, however, was the greatest leveler. In 1910 a person with an income of £100,000 retained, after payment of taxes, about £94,000. By the 1970s, this had dropped to £20,000, before reforms introduced by Margaret Thatcher reduced the top marginal income tax rate to 40 percent Estate (or inheritance) taxes took about 50 percent of larger fortunes in 1938 but rose to 80 percent by the 1970s, before, again, being reduced by the Thatcher government.

As a result of high income and estate taxes, there has been a significant shift in the distribution of British wealth. In 1911 the top 1 percent of the British population held 69 percent of the nation's wealth; currently, the share of that 1 percent is about one-quarter. Similarly, the share of the top 10 percent has dropped from 92 percent in 1911 to about one-half of the national wealth today.

While the share of high incomes in terms of the national income has declined in Britain there has also been an increase of the middle-income groups, particularly skilled workers. The trend toward more social equality can be seen in the fact that the proportion of the national income paid in wages and salaries increased from 60 percent in 1938 to the current figure of well over 70 percent, while the income from dividends and interest declined considerably during the same period. All these policies have by no means brought about equality, but they have significantly reduced extremes of inequality.

Dropping much of the traditional socialist belief in nationalization, the Labour party came closer to the Conservative party, which in turn during the 1960s and 1970s dropped active opposition to the basic principles of the welfare state. Inasmuch as both political parties seem to be united on kindred principles of social policy, and because so much of the British economy depended upon factors external to it (such as its ability to compete with other countries in foreign markets), there was little room left for such differences in principles as characterized the classic nineteenth-century struggles between the Whigs and the Tories.

In the 1960s and early 1970s, British politics thus gave the impression of ideological peace and near-uniformity. This picture changed dramatically in 1979 with the advent of Mrs. Thatcher and her avowedly anti-welfare state policies. Not only were income and estate taxes dropped, but a number of nationalized state industries were privatized—including British Steel, British Gas, British Airways, and British Telecom. In addition, the Thatcher government curbed the power of trade unions.

It is significant that the area in which the Thatcher government experienced the least success was in actually reducing the size of the welfare state itself. While voters may decry big government in general, they rarely favor specific spending cuts. Individual programs, moreover, have sizable particular constituencies, whereas benefits that would accrue from the elimination of such programs are diffuse. As it is often more difficult in politics to overcome an assertive, organized minority than to promote a policy that has a small benefit to each member of the population-at-large, it was not to be unexpected that success in curbing the welfare state would prove difficult.

Mrs. Thatcher's three electoral victories (in 1979, 1983, and 1987), followed by her Conservative party successor John Major's slim win in 1992, have had a significant effect on the Labour party. Labour has been in search of a new program and set of principles that can inspire the country, for the impulses of early socialism—unionism, nationalization and social security—have largely been spent. Key components of the welfare state have been accepted by all political parties, and all parties—including Labour—recognize the need for economic efficiency.

On the Continent, the Scandinavian countries have had the most substantial record of social reforms, both in the interwar years and after World War II. Since the early 1930s the Scandinavian countries generally have been governed by socialist administrations based on parliamentary majorities. The Scandinavian socialist movements have emphasized economic development and social security rather than nationalization. Full employment, too, is a major goal in Scandinavian (as in British) socialism.

Economic necessity has to some extent caused a retrenchment in the Swedish welfare state, however. In September 1992, in order to cut its budget deficit, the Swedish government reduced housing subsidies on construction and mortgages, increased the age at which individuals qualify for pensions, trimmed health benefits, and required that health insurance will eventually be paid for by workers and their employers rather than by the state.

One of the important lessons of the social and economic reforms in Scandinavia over the past sixty years is the emphasis on socialization rather than on nationalization. One of the most serious political weaknesses of the British Labour party's program of economic change was the tendency to substitute state ownership and management for private ownership, thus increasing the tendency toward governmental centralization and inefficiency. In contrast, however, Scandinavian reform programs have experimented with other types of social ownership in lieu of private ownership.

The most significant contribution of Scandinavia to the socialist movement is the use of cooperatives rather than the state as the agent of social and economic reform. While in Britain, as in most other countries, the cooperative movement has been largely confined to retail and wholesale trading in selected groups of consumer articles, Scandinavian countries have set up cooperatives for slum clearance, health insurance, and industrial production, among other areas.

Socialism in Developing Nations

The distinction between socialism and communism has been of particular importance in developing nations. Poor countries desire to attain rapid economic growth. Without economic progress, developing nations feel there can be no genuine political independence or international leadership. Domestically, moreover, rapid economic growth is the only means to achieve better living standards, health, and education.

The history of the last two centuries has shown two methods of rapid economic development. The first is that of capitalism, in which the free market is the main instrument in producing rapid economic growth. While it is true that government has greatly aided this process (tariffs for infant industries; land grants for railways and educational institutions; legislatures, executives, and courts favoring the employer rather than the employee), it is also true that private initiative and capital have been primarily responsible for the economic progress of capitalist nations. Without any government-sponsored five- or ten-year plans, private individuals have decided how available resources—labor, capital, land, raw materials—are to be used, and individual consumers have decided how much of their income to consume and save.

Economic growth in capitalist nations has been for the most part greatly favored by factors that are largely absent in developing nations today: a stable government, a fairly efficient civil service, relatively high levels of education, adequate means of transportation and communication (highways, canals), and—perhaps most important of all—a considerable level of technological and entrepreneurial skill and initiative. Some nations—such as Great Britain, the Scandinavian countries, and the United States—had developed democratic political institutions before rapid economic expansion took place. As Alexis de Tocqueville noted in *Democracy in America* (1815), "democracy is favorable to the growth of manufacturing, and it increases without limit the numbers of the manufacturing classes."

The second historical method of rapid economic growth was communism In this method the state owns the means of production and sets an overall goal—as in Soviet Five-Year Plans—of what is to be produced and how the available resources of labor, land, and capital are to be employed. The freedom of the consumer, worker, and producer is replaced by the orders of the state. Because the communist state possesses totalitarian power, it can generally ensure that the plan is translated into reality. This may take a few decades, and millions of people may pay with their lives, but eventually a modern industrial economy can develop at a rapid pace. It is important to note that communism has proven ineffective as a means of economic development after the early phase of industrialism, and without great coercion. The economies of the Soviet Union and Eastern Europe broke down; China introduced market reforms into its economy.

In facing the issue of economic modernization, developing nations have generally wished not to imitate either the Western capitalist process of development or the communist path of complete state planning and ownership based on political repression. Almost all developing nations have liked to think that their economic and social problems can be solved through methods that are different from both capitalism and communism. A label attached to this "third way" has been often socialism.

Socialism means many things in the context of underdeveloped countries. First, it represents the ideal of social justice. In developing countries the differences between the rich and the poor are proportionately greater than in the wealthier countries. Socialism, then, stands for the commitment to raise the poor masses to a higher level and to narrow the gap between the small upper class of the privileged and the vast mass of the impoverished. Socialism means more welfare services for the poor, more schools for the uneducated, and more human dignity for the traditionally underprivileged.

Where tribal organization of society is still alive, socialism is but a new term for traditional tribal loyalty and solidarity given universal application. Thus, African socialism was defined by a leading Tanzanian political leader:

> The foundation and the objective of African Socialism is the Extended Family The true African Socialist does not look on one class of men as his brethren and another as his natural enemies. He does not form an alliance with the "brethren" for the extermination of the "non-brethren." He rather regards all men as his brethren—as members of his ever extending Family. (Julius K. Nyerere, "*Ujamaa*": *The Basis of African Socialism*, 1962)

When attacked for betraying socialism by encouraging private foreign investments in India's fertilizer industry, essential to its increased production of food, Prime Minister Indira Gandhi affirmed her government's commitment to both socialism and democracy. She then gave her definition of socialism: "What we all want is a better life, with more food, employment, and opportunity in conditions of economic justice, equality, and with individual freedom."

Second, the term *socialism* in developing countries often stands for nonalignment in international conflicts. The view among developing nations often has been that the fundamental division in the world is not political but economic. Developing nations, in the words of Julius Nyerere, "should be very careful not to allow themselves to be used as the 'tools' of any of the rich countries of the world," regardless of those countries' political orientation.

The third meaning of socialism in developing countries is an emphasis on planning. Because developing countries look on economic growth with a sense of urgency, they feel that the functioning of the free market may not ensure the kind of rapid economic expansion and growth that is called for. Some basic elements of a modern economy—highways, means of transportation, hospitals, housing, schools—cannot, in the very nature of things, attract private enterprise, since they are the framework within which private enterprise and profits can be generated but which in themselves usually do not create such profits.

Further, there is the kind of basic enterprise, such as the manufacture of steel, for which there is either not enough private capital available or which cannot hope to compete with established foreign enterprises. Only the state can build the foundations of a modern economy (highways and the like), and only the state can assume the risks of profitless enterprise over a number of years, if such enterprise is necessary for the economy as a whole.

The need for planning, to which many developing countries are committed, does not imply overall or even large-scale nationalization of the means of production. In the economic field socialism in developing nations means an economic structure in which some industries are completely private (such as farming, handicrafts, and small business), others have both a private and a public sector (as in heavy industry), and, finally, still others are dominated by the public sector (for example, transportation and public utilities). While this is the general meaning of socialism in the economic sphere among developing nations, the practical application varies in different countries. In general, it can be said that nationalization has gone furthest where political democracy is weak or nonexistent. Where constitutional government is a reality, private enterprise is more encouraged.

The meaning of socialism in developing nations differs from that in the wealthier countries, because the historical situation is different. In the West socialism has meant not how to industrialize an undeveloped country but how to distribute the fruits of a wealthy society in a more equitable way. As a result, the concept of the welfare state has virtually absorbed the idea of socialism.

By contrast, socialism in developing countries is confronted with the task not so much of distributing the fruits of an industrial economy, which hardly exists, but of building an industrial economy so as to raise the economic and educational level of the masses of the people. Further, while socialism in Western countries has generally developed within a framework of established constitutional government, socialism in developing countries frequently evolves with a burdensome tradition of authoritarian rule by foreign imperialists or native power holders. It is therefore to be expected that socialism in some developing countries will show a greater tolerance for authoritarian practices than has generally been true of Western socialism. When developing nations fail in their attempted synthesis of constitutional government and economic planning (including partial government ownership of industry), they consider constitutional government expendable but still pursue economic development through planning and public ownership of industry.

THE IMPASSE OF SOCIALISM

Problems of Nationalization

Socialist theory and practice have undergone drastic changes on the issue of nationalization over the last seventy years. When the British Labour party adopted a socialist platform in 1918, it demanded "the common ownership of the means of production, distribution, and exchange." At that time this formula expressed the prevailing socialist orthodoxy.

Today, not a single socialist party in the world, nor a single socialist leader of repute and responsibility, still adheres to the old formula of nationalizing *all* the means of production, distribution, and exchange. In 1951 the Socialist International, speaking for more than thirty socialist parties throughout the world, adopted a program that specifically rejected the older doctrine of total nationalization and conceded that socialist planning is compatible with private ownership in agriculture, handicrafts, retail trade, and small and medium-sized industries.

In 1959 the German Social Democratic party, the largest democratic socialist party on the European continent, adopted a new program in which freedom, justice, and respect for the individual were declared to be its highest values. As for nationalization, the program specifically stated that "efficient small and medium-sized enterprises are to be strengthened to enable them to prevail in competition with large-scale enterprises." Only where competition is impossible for natural or technical reasons does public ownership become a necessity. The following two general principles were included in the program: "Private ownership of the means of production is no longer identical with the control of power";

and "Every concentration of economic power, even in the hands of the state, harbors dangers."

In 1964 the Social Democratic party adopted a series of new resolutions spelling out its domestic and foreign policies in detail. This time the word *nationalization* did not even appear, so dead an issue had it become. The economic policy was summarized as follows: "Only a combination of the market economy and monetary and fiscal overall control and welfare policy can be the solution suited for our time." In its "Government Program" of 1969, the Social Democratic party spelled out its economic and social programs in detail, but again there was no mention or discussion of nationalization. The usual welfare and labor-union policies were advocated: secure employment, technological progress, regional planning, and tax reforms in favor of low-income groups.

The leader of American socialism over four decades, Norman Thomas, wrote in *Democratic Socialism: A New Appraisal* (1953) that "the state under the most democratic theory and practice will become too huge, too cumbersome, if it seeks to control directly all economic activity." Ten years later, in *Socialism Re-Examined* (1963), Thomas stated again: "American socialists nowadays generally accept, as they should, a mixed economy, controlled by the overall concept that production should be for the good of all. For the state, under any system, to try to own and operate anything would deprive us of some of the important values of private initiative and responsibility." Thomas spoke of the dangers of statism inherent in total nationalization, and like many other socialists, he stressed that the alternative to capitalism is socialization, not nationalization.

More recently, Michael Harrington, Thomas's heir as head of American democratic socialism, wrote in *Socialism: Past and Future* (1989):

> The equation of socialism and the state nationalization of industry was one phase of the movement's understanding of itself....But to say that is not to give up the vision of social ownership; it is to prepare a fresh way for taking it seriously.

Individual freedom is inextricably linked to the diffusion of power. This truism has always been admitted by socialists to apply to political government. They have now come around to the idea that in the economic realm, too, there can be no individual freedom unless there is dispersal of economic power.

The concept of socialization implies the diffusion of publicly owned property. Property is owned and managed not by the state but by producer or consumer cooperatives, labor unions, churches, educational institutions, hospitals, and other organizations, and these organizations derive their powers from voluntary association rather than from the sovereign authority of the state.

This approach has been successfully tried in Scandinavia, where most public housing has been built not by the state but by corporations that combine individual ownership and management with financial assistance from housing cooperatives and municipal agencies. In Scandinavia, too, as mentioned earlier, cooperatives are not confined—as they are in many countries—to the retail business but are common in the fields of manufacturing and wholesaling.

None of these solutions is final, and mistakes are constantly made, but these forms of socialization do seem to their advocates to avoid the worst evils of nationalization—monopoly and the resulting concentration of economic and political power. In a capitalist democracy the economic power of private monopolies can at least be opposed by the political power of the state. *When the monopolist is the state itself, who will protect the citizen against the state?*

Today, then, no socialist party advocates that all industries be nation-alized: Nationalization is recommended only for some industries. There seems to be universal acceptance among socialists of the idea that natural monopolies in the public utilities field should be publicly owned or managed. The concept of the "sick industry" and the criterion of the "key industry" have also been accepted as standards upon which nationalization may be based.

On the other hand, in industries that demand high adaptability to changing conditions—for example, industries that produce largely for export or industries that operate with a considerable element of risk—the case against nationalization or socialization is strong. Competition is necessary for rapid industrial and technological expansion. The automobile industry a generation ago and the computer industry today are the products not of preexisting giant enterprises but of relatively small corporations that were willing to put capital into new and risky products.

It remains to be seen whether the same spirit of adventure, risk, and experimentation can be shown by publicly owned enterprises. After all, it is one thing to gamble one's own money; it is quite another thing to use the public treasury for such ventures, or to persuade the taxpayer to do so. Moreover, it has been argued that under public ownership, declining industries (such as coal and railroads) are being artificially propped up by the government when, for economic reasons, they should be allowed to decline.

The traditional concern of socialists has always been with distribution rather than production. The most creative contribution of socialism has therefore been its revision of the internal social structure of nations in the direction of equality. It has not been shown that publicly owned enterprise is any more efficient in production than private enterprise or that it has materially increased the people's standard of living; in fact, quite the opposite is true. C.A.R. Crosland, a leading British economist and member of the Wilson cabinet, made important concessions in this regard. First, he admitted that the performance of nationalized industries in Britain had not been better than that of private enterprise, and that nationalized industries have been plagued by "bureaucratic centralization." Speaking of living standards, he also argued that further nationalization "cannot be said to be necessary to full employment and prosperity."

From the very beginning, public enterprise has found that three specific difficulties hamper its overall performance. First is the *managerial problem* of administering vast public enterprises with flexibility and initiative and at a low cost. The excessive tendency toward centralization and playing it safe is a serious matter. Moreover, it is not certain that the managerial situation will improve as nationalization continues. In the first phase of public ownership, the public corporation can draw upon managerial talent that has been trained in the tough environment of private competition, but if nationalization goes on, management of public enterprises will have to draw its top personnel from among its own ranks. It will then be seen whether persons trained and bred in the secure, sheltered atmosphere of bureaucratic monopoly will possess as great a capacity to operate large undertakings as is shown by graduates of the hard school of private, competitive business.

If the American experience can serve as a guide to managerial performance, the outlook for nationalized enterprise is uncertain. In American corporate business, industries that are near the bottom of the executive pay scale (and presumably attract less able executives) include regulated industries like public utilities. These industries are either monopolies or enjoy relatively little competition, since their existence generally depends on a governmentally granted franchise. There is relatively little product innovation in such industries, operations are often highly routinized, and seniority is a determining factor in promotions. By contrast, industries near the top of the executive pay scale (automotive, chemical, metals manufacturing, electronics, computers) are characterized by product innovation under the pressure of substantial competition. Promotion is less influenced by seniority, outside executive talent is more frequently brought in, and consequently there is a greater turnover of executive personnel.

In nationalized industries producing standardized goods or services (such as public utilities), the management problem may not be as serious. But in competitive industries, where flexibility and innovation are essential, nationalized industries will find it more difficult to attract top-quality executives for two reasons. First, as an industry becomes nationalized, it automatically becomes monopolistic and routinized and allows for less creativity and executive initiative than are demanded under conditions of private, competitive enterprise. Second, nationalized industries—like regulated industries in a nonsocialist economy—pay lower executive salaries, and able executives prefer more challenging positions that offer better pay to more routinized work at lower pay.

The problem of management in nationalized industries is closely connected with a second major problem. In private business the *system of profits and losses* operates in a crude but effective way to keep efficiency at a relatively high level, and the threat of bankruptcy is always real. In a public enterprise this system no longer operates to the same extent; if there are losses, no one goes bankrupt, and the losses of one division can be passed on to the whole enterprise. Even if the entire enterprise or industry is in the red, management can either increase prices or receive cheap credits or subsidies from the government because it has a monopoly.

Third, there is the *political difficulty*. How are public corporations to be related to the elected representatives of the people? If the public corporation is too closely supervised by Parliament or Congress, its management may become demoralized and lose efficiency. If parliamentary control is relaxed, on the other hand, up goes the cry that there is not much difference between the old and the new systems (since if management can do more or less as it pleases, what has nationalization changed?). More than four decades of nationalization in Britain has shown that whatever political control over nationalized industries is exercised is done so by the executive branch, not by the legislators.

Because of all these difficulties and complexities, many socialists have reconciled themselves to the virtually complete elimination of nationalization from the socialist program, emphasizing instead the concepts of equality and welfare. In his Fabian tract *Socialism and Nationalisation* (1956), Hugh Gaitskell, then leader of the British Labour party, concluded that "the most vital question is how far greater social and economic equality can be achieved without more nationalisation and public ownership." After Labour's electoral defeat in 1959, Gaitskell publicly advocated that the Labour party eliminate from its constitution clause IV, which called for common ownership of the means of production, distribution, and exchange, and which was finally eliminated by Neil Kinnock.

Denis Healey, a prominent spokesperson for the right wing in the Labour party and cabinet minister in the Wilson and Callaghan governments, went even further than Gaitskell. American writers like A.A. Berle had said that in the American capitalist enterprise, the real power is in the hands of professional managers rather than in those of the shareholders who legally own it. This viewpoint is now increasingly recognized by socialists as being equally applicable to publicly owned enterprises. According to Healey:

> Industrial power in every large, developed economy now rests with a managerial class which is responsible to no one. The form of ownership is irrelevant. State control over nationalized industries is as difficult as share-holder control over private firms.

For a high-ranking socialist to hold that the form of ownership is irrelevant marked a basic change of outlook.

More important than what socialist leaders and thinkers have said is the voters' clear and repeated expression of opposition to further nationalization. In the 1950s through the 1980s, numerous polls were taken on this question, some by independent polling organizations and others by Labour organizations. In every instance, from 65 to 80 percent of the voters opposed further nationalization; most significantly, even among Labour party supporters the number of those who favored further nationalization was generally only one-third to one-half of those who opposed it.

In recent elections the Labour party has de-emphasized public ownership and has concentrated on the topic of economic growth as Britain's number-one problem. Neil Kinnock campaigned in his second and last unsuccessful election for prime minister in April, 1992 on the slogan, "It's time for a change," referring to thirteen years of Conservative rule. Virtually not a word was spoken of nationalization; instead Kinnock's focus was on "the mixed economy and higher standards of social justice."

The economic challenge dominated the Labour government of Prime Minister James Callaghan, the last Labour government, which served from 1976 to 1979. Instead of pursuing distinctively social objectives, Callaghan was preoccupied with such problems as controlling inflation, reducing the balance of payments deficit, and maintaining industrial peace. By 1977 the bonanza of large-scale oil discoveries in the North Sea off the Scottish coast relieved British dependence on expensive imported fuel, but other economic problems were only exacerbated. Most important from the standpoint of a socialist government, the trade unions showed increasing reluctance to moderate their demands for higher wages and to support policies designed to stimulate investment, improve productivity, and expand exports. Paradoxically, the main obstacles to Labour's program for strengthening the economy came not from embattled capitalists but from embittered workers.

Serious internal divisions helped defeat the Labour party in the general elections of 1979 and to precipitate a formal split in the party. The defection of right-wing Labourites to form a new Social Democratic party, as well as ineffective leadership within the Labour party itself, not only cost the party successive elections, including the general elections of 1983, 1987, and 1992, but reflected a deeper ideological malaise. While Prime Minister Margaret Thatcher confidently espoused the policies of neoconservatism, opposition Labour leaders could chart no new direction to capture the popular imagination. Defeat at the polls attested to a depletion of ideas.

The Future of Socialism

Today, socialists everywhere find themselves bewildered and uncertain of the future. For more than half a century, the socialist movement was devoted to propaganda and organization outside the framework of governmental responsibility. Now that much of the socialist program has been realized, however, socialism faces a fate similar to that of organized political liberalism.

Just as political liberalism passed away largely because the causes it championed either died a natural death or were solved by conservatives and socialists along liberal lines, socialism too may gradually pass away, as far as its original program is concerned, even though political parties with the socialist label may continue.

In the field of international affairs, governmental responsibilities have modified the traditional socialist outlook. As long as socialist parties were in opposition and had to confine their political activities to propaganda and electioneering, they could steadfastly adhere to the classical socialist doctrine that capitalism was the root of all international tensions. From experience with both fascist and communist imperialism, socialists have learned that international affairs are much more complex, and that the forces of imperialism can be tied to any system of economic organization. Moreover, once socialist parties assume governmental responsibilities for foreign policy, they tend to follow established national interests on the one hand and economic realities on the other. At times, the requirements of national economic planning under socialist governments have given socialist foreign policies an element of isolationism, which is in sharp contrast to the traditional doctrinal commitment to internationalism.

The present difficulties in setting a socialist economic program are not likely to be resolved soon. One great objective of socialism, the welfare state—that is, the responsibility of the community for a minimum standard of social and economic security for every person—is no longer a monopoly of socialist parties. Other political parties in democratic nations also favor the welfare state. Some parties are more warmly for it than others, and some parties recommend more benefits than others, but as a general principle, the welfare state (in the minimum sense) is accepted by all parties and is no longer a matter of partisan controversy. Even American neoconservatives accept the principle of a "safety net" of government programs for those individuals who are genuinely destitute or incapable of self-help.

In Europe the concept of the welfare state no longer requires a separate political party. In fact, much of the welfare state in England was historically the work of the Conservative party, and the limits of the welfare state are increasingly set by the ability to pay for its benefits rather than by differences of ideology. Thus, the Labour government introduced charges for prescriptions and fees for eyeglasses and for dentures, breaching the principle of universal medicine without fees. It also overhauled the old-age pension system, so that contributions and benefits would be more closely correlated to earnings.

The principle of universality, under which the same benefits are given to everyone regardless of need or income, has been mainly defended by socialists on the ground that means tests are thereby avoided Yet the expe

rience of the welfare state has taught the Labour party that under this principle of universality, the needy do not receive enough benefits. Thus, the principle of "selectivity" has been debated in Britain. Under this principle, more
benefits are provided for those who need them than for those who do not. A
welfare system using the selectivity principle has some form of means test in
the provision of benefits. An analagous debate in the United States is the
extent to which social security benefits to the wealthy should be taxed.

The very fact that, after almost three generations of socialist activity,
the main principles of the welfare countries have been widely accepted in
democratic states has created a real dilemma for the future of socialism. If it
keeps on trying to convert the converted, it will lose the old fire and enthusiasm that made it a distinctive movement in the Western world. If its leaders are unable to formulate a new program, adapted to the needs of the
twenty-first century, the party may simply settle down to a fixed position
slightly to the left of the conservative parties, separated from the latter not
by a basically different economic or political philosophy but simply by its
own concentration on translating the conception of the welfare state into a
reality as thoroughly as possible.

The dilemma of socialist parties in the world today is well demonstrated by the ascension of Francois Mitterand's Socialist party to power in
France in 1981, following his election as president. Mitterand campaigned
for office on, and initially attempted to implement, a platform of moderate
socialist change in France: some nationalization of commerce, increased
social benefits, and a more egalitarian tax code. Three devaluations of the
franc soon followed as French capital fled the country. Mitterand then
abruptly reversed course, and France experienced more free- market policies during his tenure in office.

Democracy acts as a great check to dramatic change that is controversial. As it can be argued that a truly socialist program would take a long
time to effect, this indicates that the chances for socialist change are not
great in democratic nations except along incremental lines. Moreover, as
the example of France shows, private economic interests play a great role—
particularly in an international economy—in affecting public policy, thereby also lessening the chances of dramatic socialist change.

In recent surveys taken in various parts of the world, about two-
thirds of those polled rejected both capitalism—if capitalism means the
exploitation of the many by the wealthy few—and socialism—if socialism
means government ownership of the economy. Two-thirds of the intervie-
wees favored social welfare and private property.

Why "Socialism" Has Never Spread in the United States

The question is often asked why socialism, in the sense of collective
ownership of the means of production, has never been able to gain a

foothold in the United States. According to classical socialist writers, the United States as the world's leading capitalist country was bound to develop the "inner contradictions" out of which socialist mass movements would develop, yet nothing of the sort has happened. Is it because socialism is European? There are strong socialist parties in Canada, Australia, New Zealand, Chile, Japan, and other countries outside of Europe. Why the failure in the United States?

The Socialist party of the United States was founded in 1901. In the presidential elections of 1904 and 1908, it garnered about 400,000 votes. In the presidential election of 1912, it polled nearly 900,000 votes, or 6 percent of the total vote—the highest percentage it ever received in any election. It maintained its absolute strength of about 900,000 votes in the presidential elections of 1920 and 1932, receiving much less support in the intervening years of prosperity. The Great Depression of the 1930s filled the Socialist party with hope of further growth. In 1932 Franklin D. Roosevelt was elected president, and after four years of his vigorous New Deal policies, the Socialist party received only 187,000 votes. This downhill trend accelerated in subsequent elections, until the party decided to stop putting up presidential candidates.

Even in 1912, in its heyday, the Socialist party was strongest in the agricultural states of the west and not—as in Europe—in the industrial areas in the east. In these agricultural states—Arizona, California, Idaho, and a few other states of the west—the Socialist vote represented not the outcry of the "oppressed industrial proletariat" against capitalism but the protests of farmers against low prices for farm products, high interest rates, and corrupt politics.

Socialism bases its appeal on two main issues:

1. Social equality
2. The abolition of poverty

Social equality One of the driving forces of European socialism has been the protest against the inequality of social classes that Europe (and part of the extra-European world) has inherited from its feudal past. By contrast, the United States is a nation without a feudal past and has therefore developed without the legacy of such legally recognized inequality. Most Americans have considered themselves middle class; there is relatively less class consciousness in the United States than elsewhere. Social mobility is widespread, mainly because higher education is available to more people than it is anywhere else in the world. An American is a number of times more likely to get a college education than is a Briton. A black American's chance for a college education is higher than that of a white person in Britain, France, Germany, or Italy.

Racial inequality has been the persistent and pervasive form of inequality that has characterized American society from colonial days.

Unlike the inequality of classes, which affects the majority of people in other countries, racial inequality affects only 20 percent (12 percent blacks and 8 percent other nonwhites) in the United States, yet this comparative numerical advantage is deceptive due to the depth of racial tensions. Inequalities between classes are generally not as strongly felt and resented as racism is, particularly when historically based on slavery.

While the issue of capitalism versus socialism is relevant to the problem of social inequality, it has less bearing on racial inequality. Some capitalist societies are more racist than others, and the same has been true of socialist and communist states. Problems of racial harmony exist on all continents, whether the majority of the population is white, black, yellow, or brown, and in each case the degree of racial inequality is determined by many factors. In the United States the main thrust of the black response to racial inequality has not been in the direction of socialism. A few black leaders have been socialists. In recent years, however, the influence of socialist opinion has decreased in the radical black community in favor of more militant leaders who stress black racial solidarity and black power rather than the ideology of interracial and international socialism.

Abolition of poverty   Socialist groups in the United States have not been able to make the second promise of socialism—the abolition of poverty—a major popular issue. Early in this century Werner Sombart, the noted German economic historian, studied the American labor movement and predicted that socialism in the United States would founder on the abundance of "roast beef and apple pie." As the American historian Frederick Jackson Turner saw in the nineteenth century, the frontier provided the American poor with an escape from poverty and class war—a phenomenon that did not, and could not, exist in overcrowded Europe. When the frontier was closed around the turn of this century, economic opportunity in the expanding economy and the migration to the west replaced the agricultural frontier as the means of escaping poverty.

Poverty in the United States declined substantially during the decade of the 1960s, going from about 22 percent of the population in 1960 to about 13 percent in 1970. Since the 1970s, however, the poverty level has remained about the same, owing in part to the policies of the Reagan administration, which imposed major cuts on antipoverty programs.

Most of the poverty reduction in the United States was of the elderly, a result of the expansion of Social Security and Medicare during the 1960s. Poverty among children today is higher than ever. About one child in five in the United States lives in poverty, and poverty afflicts about one child in four under the age of six. Moreover, there has been a significant increase in the number of homeless people.

Poverty in America is closely tied to race. In absolute terms, the number of poor whites is almost double that of poor nonwhites. However, the incidence of poverty is much higher among nonwhites that whites. About 10 percent of whites in the United States are defined by the government as poor, as compared to almost 30 percent of blacks and Hispanics.

Incomes of blacks in the United States—like the reduction of poverty—made significant headway during the 1960s and early 1970s. Since the mid-seventies, however, black income as compared to white income has remained relatively static; indeed, by some measures it has even gone down slightly. The median income of black families in the United States is about three-fifths of that for white families. Accordingly, the political issue in the United States regarding poverty has generally been one of race rather than of socialism versus capitalism.

Today there is a renewed concern about poverty in the United States, signalled in part by the advent of the Clinton administration. The election of Bill Clinton as President in 1992 marks the first Democratic administration in twelve years. It remains to be seen exactly which path the new administration will take. While it can be expected that there will be somewhat more domestic spending than otherwise (as well as less military spending) and that the tax code will be made more equitable, with higher taxes on the more affluent, the basic economic structure of the United States will undoubtedly remain intact.

FOR FURTHER READING

HARRINGTON, MICHAEL, *Socialism*. New York: Saturday Review Press, 1972.

———, *Socialism: Past and Future*. New York: Penguin Books, 1989.

HAYEK, FRIEDRICH A., *The Road to Serfdom*. Chicago: University of Chicago Press, 1960.

HEILBRONER, ROBERT L., *Between Capitalism and Socialism*. New York: Random House, Inc., 1970.

HOWE, IRVING, ed., *Essential Works of Socialism*. New York: Bantam Books, Inc., 1971.

LANE, DAVID, *The Socialist Industrial State*. Boulder,Colo.: Westview Press, 1976.

LANGE, OSKAR, and FRED M. TAYLOR, *On the Economic Theory of Socialism*. New York: McGraw-Hill Book Company, 1964.

LASCH, CHRISTOPHER, *The Agony of the American Left*. New York: Vintage Books, 1969.

LICHTHEIM, GEORGE, *A Short History of Socialism*. New York: Praeger Publishers, Inc., 1970.

MYRDAL, GUNNAR, *The Challenge of World Poverty*. New York: Pantheon Books, Inc., 1970.

PELINKA, ANTON, *Social Democratic Parties in Europe*. New York: Praeger Publishers, Inc., 1983.

SCHUMPETER, JOSEPH A., *Capitalism, Socialism, and Democracy*. New York: Harper & Row, Publishers, Inc., 1962.

SIGMUND, PAUL E., ed., *The Ideologies of the Developing Nations.* New York: Praeger Publishers, Inc., 1972.

THOMAS, NORMAN, *Socialism Re-Examined.* New York: W.W. Norton & Co., Inc., 1963.

WILSON, HAROLD, *The Labour Government 1964–1970.* Boston: Little, Brown & Company, 1971.

2

Capitalism

Capitalism developed historically as part of the movement of individualism. In religion, that movement produced the Reformation; in learning, the growth of the physical sciences; in human relations, the social sciences; in politics, democratic government; and in economics, the capitalist system. The concept of a capitalist civilization, therefore, is a legitimate one; it suggests that capitalism is more than a particular type of economy—that it is a whole social system.

Capitalism developed in eighteenth-century Britain and was transplanted later to northwestern Europe and North America. From there, it has spread to much of the rest of the world. For the most part, Western industrial nations and much of the developing world operate the aspects of their societies that relate to the production of wealth along capitalist lines. Government may tax, spend, and regulate a great deal; nonetheless, most commercial activity has a strong private component.

CAPITALIST THEORY

Elements of Capitalism

A few basic traits have characterized capitalism from the beginning. These include the following:

1. Private ownership
2. Market economy
3. Competition
4. Profit
5. Stable prices

Private ownership   In the capitalist system ownership of the means of production (land, factories, machinery, natural resources) is held, for the most part, by individuals or corporations,   not by the state. This does not exclude public ownership of natural monopolies or basic public services (for example, public utilities or the post office), but such cases are considered the exception rather than the rule.

Capitalism's promotion of private ownership is based on two considerations. First, ownership of productive property means power over the lives of other people; it is better, from the capitalist viewpoint, that such power is diffused among many property owners rather than concentrated in one owner, the state. Were the state to control all productive property, the outlook for political as well as economic liberty would be uncertain. Second, the basic capitalist assumption is that economic progress is best attained when people are free to advance their own interests and have the personal incentive to do so. As the leading theoretician of capitalism, Adam Smith (1723–1790), expressed it in *The Wealth of Nations* over two centuries ago: "It is not from the benevolence of the butcher, the brewer, or the baker, that we expect our dinner, but from their regard to their own interest."

Market economy   Another principle of the capitalist system is that of the market economy. In the pre-capitalist era, the economy was generally local and self-sufficient; each family produced just about what it needed, supplementing its simple needs with some barter or exchange operations in a primitive local market. Division of labor was barely known, and each family had to do many jobs that are now spread among hundreds of various crafts and specialties. Also, the type of occupation a person held and the price one could charge for goods and services were largely predetermined by custom and usage.

In contrast, the market economy of the capitalist system is based on specialization of labor. Each person supplies only a fraction of his or her needs through individual skills and labors. The products or services are designed not for the producer's own household, but for the market. As to prices, supply and demand determine these.

Under fascism and communism, the government tries to plan the whole economy, but in so doing it encounters limitations on the span of its control. No planning group can anticipate all the possible contingencies in an intricate economic system that encompasses millions of people and requires economic decisions that run into the tens of millions daily, and the failure of command economies to provide adequately for the people living under them is what in large part has led to their abandonment. In the capitalist market economy, each decision-maker watches over a vastly smaller area; therefore, the span of attention and control is much more limited and manageable.

The comparatively unregulated operation of supply and demand is a most fundamental principle of the free market economy. Neither communism nor fascism believes in this; in fascism, ownership of the means of production is formally in the hands of private individuals, but this is unimportant, because fascism does away with the free or open market economy and substitutes the direction of the state. The state tells individuals where to work, what jobs to choose, what to produce, what prices to charge, and how to invest savings and profits. Under communism, both private ownership of the means of production and the market economy are abolished. Thus, the communist economy is also a command economy in which economic decisions are made by the state. In contrast, the market economy is one in which corporations or individuals may make their own economic decisions in the light of their own interest, experience, and capability.

The vital political implications of the market economy have been recognized by socialist economists. For example, British Fabian W. Arthur Lewis argued that the real issue is not between planning and no planning, but between planning by direction and planning by inducement. In the former, the government (as under fascism or communism) tries to get the right things done by direct control and regulation of output, wages, and prices. A government agent watches every step in the plan, and those workers or managers who fail to fulfill their quota may be punished as saboteurs, although neglect or incapacity rather than willful disregard may have been the cause of their failure.

In a democracy, the government stimulates certain economic activities indirectly by means of the budget, taxation, interest rates, and other policies of planning by inducement, thus avoiding the two main defects of planning by direction: bureaucratic centralization and economic inefficiency. In other words, government merely creates the climate within which private individuals and entities may then operate optimally. Far from rejecting the free market as the normal mechanism of economic adjustment, Lewis held that the aim should be to preserve free markets wherever possible. It is of no little interest that in accepting the principle of the market economy, Lewis was driven to the conclusion that the nationalization of all industry is undesirable because of the usual reasons against monopoly: inefficiency, lack of initiative, and concentration of power.

The function of the free market as a mechanism of political liberty is increasingly being recognized as it becomes apparent that political and economic liberty tend to go hand in hand. Thus, the distinction between a command economy and a market economy reflects in the economic field the more basic political distinction between coercive and democratic forms of government.

The symbiotic relationship between market economies and democratic political systems can be seen in comparative studies between democratic and nondemocratic forms of government, and even within nondemocratic forms of government. Political democracy and the free market go hand-in-hand; command economics are almost always politically coercive. Moreover, fascist Italy had more of a market economy than did Nazi Germany and was politically less despotic and, among communist states, Hungary—which was politically more liberal than most other communist countries—also moved further in the direction of a market economy than other communist economies.

An important feature of a market economy is consumer sovereignty: The consumer not only chooses among the goods offered for sale, but ultimately determines through such choices what and how much will be produced. Friedrich Hayek (1899–1992), one of the greatest capitalist writers of the twentieth century, maintained that consumer choice is the heart of the argument for a capitalist economy. In a free market, the government does not determine how many automobiles or television sets are produced; rather, these determinations are cumulative—geared to the individual choices of millions of consumers as opposed to the dictates of an all-powerful state. The state, Hayek argued, simply does not have the capacity to make economic decisions as effectively or efficiently as the free market does.

It should be noted again, however, that even in a market economy, the government will have a great bearing on economic activity through its taxation, spending, monetary, and regulatory policies. This influence, though, is fundamentally different from a government determining, as in a fascist or communist command economy, all aspects of economic production and distribution.

Competition   Another essential element of the market economy is competition. In the pre-capitalist economy, custom and usage dictated what goods and services were worth, and there were many people who could not compete at all because they were excluded from some occupations or trades. In the modern economy the alternative to competition is either private monopoly or the legal monopoly of the state. In both cases arbitrary determination of the prices of goods and services by a de facto authority (as in the case of private monopoly) or by a legal authority (as in that of the state) takes the place of the free interplay of buyers and sellers.

The principle of competition has been extended by capitalists in modern economies from merely competition within nations, to competition between nations. *Free trade* is always a controversial political issue because its benefits are general, while its costs are specific. Consumers benefit from being able to purchase imported cars, but American automobile workers lose their jobs. The capitalist view is that competition between nations prods economies as a whole to be as effective as possible, just as it leads businesses within an economy to be productive.

For example, in industry, research has become one of the keenest areas of competition. Research today means cheaper and better products tomorrow. By accelerating the rate of change in the economy, research promotes competition at an early stage, long before the product or service reaches the market. Research is also an important factor in competition between whole economies. One of the disturbing features of the American economy during the 1970s and 1980s was a decline in the proportion of private and public investment in basic research upon which technological leadership ultimately depends. The growing strength of Japan and Germany in world trade, at the expense of the United States, is attributable in part to their high investment in research.

Just as continued American dominance in the world economy will depend on being competitive with foreign nations, success within an economy depends on being competitive. Competition is the vital mechanism in a capitalist economy for assuring that economic resources are being used at their highest and best uses. As the great nineteenth-century British thinker John Stuart Mill stated: "Wherever competition is not, monopoly is; and...monopoly, in all its forms, is the taxation of the industrious for the support of indolence, if not of plunder."

Profit The profit principle is another basic characteristic of the capitalist system. A tremendous difference exists between capitalism and pre-capitalist systems: A capitalist economy provides more opportunity for profit than any other economy because it guarantees three freedoms that are not commonly found in other systems—freedom of trade and occupation, freedom of property, and freedom of contract. In the Middle Ages, products were made by guilds and sold at prescribed prices. The profit system was thus doubly limited. Only a member of the guild could enter the process of production; furthermore, prices were established not by freedom of contract between buyer and seller, but by the authority of custom, church, or state.

When the capitalist system is described as a profit system, it is frequently forgotten that the other side of the transaction is equally important—capitalism is also a *loss* system. Although it is true that never have so many made so much profit as under capitalism, it is equally true that in no other system have so many lost so much. In American economic development, bankruptcies and failures were very common in the early stages of the mining, railroading, and automotive industries. In the computer industry, the Radio Corporation of America, a giant company, tried in vain to get a permanent place in the business. After making computers for two decades, RCA finally decided to close down computer production. In a typical year, about four out of ten corporations report net losses. Of ten business firms started in an average year, five shut down within two years, and eight within ten years—lack of success being the main reason.

Stable prices   A presupposition of capitalism from the start, which received increasing prominence in countries around the world during the 1970s and 1980s, is the desirability of stable prices in an economy. As long ago as David Hume (1711–1776), who wrote in his essay "Of Money" (1752), "the high price of commodities be a necessary consequence of the increase of gold and silver," the relationship among prices, the amount of goods and services, and the money supply in an economy has been known.

Prices are a product of the amount of money in an economy and the amount of goods and services. If the amount of money increases at a faster rate than the amount of goods and services, then inflation will result. It is important to point out that inflation is the *general* rise of prices in an economy. In any free market economy, there will always be *specific* changes in prices—that is, prices will increase (or decrease) as a result of changes in supply of and demand for particular commodities.

The problems of inflation are many, as Western industrial democracies relearned during the 1970s and 1980s. In the first place, the role of prices as signals is muffled. During periods of price stability, the rise or decline of a price indicates that more or less of that good should be produced. Inflation distorts this information-sending message of prices by altering all prices.

Second and more importantly, inflation has serious long-term negative repercussions for a nation's economy. Inflation rewards those who have borrowed because the real (as opposed to nominal) value of what they must repay declines. Conversely, inflation punishes savers because the real value of what they have saved declines. In short, inflation discourages thrift and encourages consumption. In so doing, savings decrease and economies lack the investment pool of capital that savings provide for future growth. Thus, in the long run, inflation leads to less economic growth.

The major American proponent of anti-inflationary policies is Milton Friedman, who, in 1976, received the Nobel Prize in economics. In a series of articles and books dating back to the 1940s, he has argued that inflation is a monetary phenomenon that inevitably has pernicious effects on an economy. Most recently, in *Money Mischief: Episodes in Monetary History* (1992), he has written: "A change in the monetary regime can set the world sailing on uncharted monetary seas for more than a decade of instability and turbulence."

Stable prices are important to the capitalist regime, not only because they are conducive to economic growth but because they reflect the principle of private property. When inflation robs the value of money, this is as much a loss to someone as if his or her money were stolen. Moreover, since monetary policy is determined by government, this loss via inflation is in some sense government-sanctioned. Stable prices, thus, are consistent with the general capitalist premise of as little government involvement in people's lives as possible.

Capitalism and Democracy

It is a matter of historical record that modern democracy has developed exclusively in states practicing free markets in the production and exchange of goods. This is not to say that this practice has been completely free, nor that all states that have practiced some form of free markets have been democratic (for many have and are not). It is to suggest, however, a link between capitalism and democracy.

Capitalism is a type of freedom in the realm of economic activity. Democracy is the attempt to include all people, or as many as possible, in a collective governance of the community in which the majority rules, either directly or indirectly. What, then, is the connection between capitalism and democracy?

There are many would dispute–even vigorously–the contention that capitalism is a type of freedom. These individuals would argue: How can someone be held to be economically free if he or she lacks the material goods that make life possible on a level above that of mere subsistence? How, in short, can someone be starving and yet considered to be possessed of some sort of freedom?

These are valid questions, and ones to which capitalism does not have all the answers. There is no doubt the possession of a certain modicum of material goods is necessary to a satisfactory, much less an enjoyable, life. This is not to deny the value of spiritual goods; it is simply to recognize the realities of life, and that before a person can accomplish almost anything, he or she must first be fed, clothed, sheltered, educated, and have some form of health care. Individuals who do not possess these material bestowals usually are not able to lead productive or happy lives, although the mere possession of material goods in no way guarantees a fruitful life.

If, then, productivity and happiness are in some way predicated on the possession of material goods, how can capitalism possibly be a desirable system? Capitalism allows, after all, a few to possess much while many people may have little. A primary criticism, in fact, of both the Reagan-Bush years in the United States and the Thatcher era in Great Britain is that the relative emphasis on capitalist modes of thought during these periods resulted in situations where the rich became richer while the poor became poorer.

There is no question that capitalism allows—as it makes possible—greater accumulations of wealth than any other system. Capitalism and capitalist practices have created phenomenal wealth on a worldwide scale. And it is because of capitalism's success that the world's economy is today as it is. There is also no question that the economic policies of capitalist nations have shaped both themselves and noncapitalist countries; and because essentially capitalist economic policies have characterized much of the production and exchange of goods in Western Europe, the United States, and Japan in the period since the end of World War II (if not also earlier), much of the world's economy has been organized along capitalist and capitalist-influenced lines.

Moreover, this depiction of capitalism's place in the world economy neglects the fundamental role of colonial powers during the first half of the twentieth century and during earlier centuries in determining the economic paths of countries that gained their independence following World War II.

Finally, in a more deeply practical significance, capitalism's importance and success—at least from a material perspective—is demonstrated by the fact that the very existence of perhaps most of the people in the world today has been made possible by technological advances that have mostly been derived from the laboratories, assembly lines, and other productive complexes of capitalist nations.

The first and most important link between capitalism and democracy appears to be that capitalist practices are the most economically productive of any other system. This has been demonstrated not only in capitalist countries but also in noncapitalist nations that have moved in the direction of freer markets of production and exchange, such as China.

As the example of China also shows, however, capitalist economic practices do not necessarily imply democratic political ones; rather, they simply appear to be a precondition for them. As experience has shown in virtually every land, including the United States, economic deprivation and political liberty are a hard mix. Where people are economically dissatisfied, neither are they likely to favor the current government, whatever its policies may be. Thus, economic hardship is a threat to governments of all types, including democratic ones.

All of this is not to say that capitalism does not have its faults as a mere purveyor of economic goods; it does, as discussed above. It is to say that thus far capitalist practices have proven to be the most effective and efficient for creating wealth; moreover, because the distribution of wealth is dependent on the supply of wealth to be distributed, a system whose emphasis is maximum production of wealth may in the long run also have the largest absolute shares of wealth, even if relative shares vary more than would otherwise be the case. And, because tolerable economic circumstances are a precondition for the political stability that makes any form of government—including democracy—possible in the long term, capitalism is tied to democracy to the extent that it creates the larger circumstances within which democracy can operate.

Capitalism appears to be the only economic system that, quite literally, can deliver the goods. Certainly no other system has experienced anywhere near its success over a sustained period of time in maximizing economic output.

Indeed, socialism, as a practical program as opposed to a theoretical ideal, has achieved its greatest success when it has left the basic structures of private capitalist economy untouched or little touched. Socialism in the form of nationalized government industries has rarely achieved anything other than failure; and to the extent that socialism has concentrated on making the capitalist ideal more realizable, it has had the greatest positive impact. The welfare state, when it has resulted in more people being more well nourished and educated, has also resulted in these individuals being more personally productive. Personally productive individuals, in turn, fuel the economic engine of a nation.

The deeper tie between capitalism and democracy extends not just to capitalism's economic productivity but also to the values it engenders and sustains. Capitalism, at least in theory, is built in large part on individual initiative. A combined political-economic order, emphasizing the individual, furthermore, is more likely to result in a democratic outcome than an order emphasizing the group. Where it is held that it is the group, not the individual, that possesses ultimate rights, then individual rights generally are not as respected as in societies that place the individual first. The individual right to vote is, of course, the keystone of democracy.

What is the collective value system that undergirds democratic nations? For the most part, it is one that recognizes and encourages private ownership of means and outcomes of production. While there are a few partial exceptions to this (for the most part in smaller, unrepresentative countries)—and while there is extensive public ownership in many nations that are democratic—private property is the fulcrum of these nations' political and economic systems.

Private property is essential to democracy because when individuals do not control the fruits of their labors, meaningful freedom—which is an inextricable element of democracy—cannot exist. No country is democratic in which the right to hold private property (to some meaningful extent) is not recognized.

The concept of private property is that there is a material sphere in which individuals may exercise dominance. This dominance need not be absolute; the existence of zoning regulations in communities throughout America, for example, does not nullify the existence of private property in the United States. Neither must the sphere embrace all aspects of society or the economy; that Sweden has substantial publicly owned or controlled enterprises does not take away from its recognition of private property in many other aspects of its society. The sphere must be real, however, within whatever parameters it operates.

The right of private property does not exist in societies where the state directly owns, manages, or controls most property; it does not exist where the ostensible private property that does exist is not meaningfully private—namely, where government may at any moment seize that property as its own, or where government is unable to maintain the social order necessary to guarantee private property. For these reasons, the *rule of law* follows the recognition of private property as a distinguishing feature in the public value system of developed democratic nations.

The rule of law has at least two aspects: The first is more formal and the second is more substantive. The first aspect of the rule of law is that law exists. Where anarchy or chaos reign, law does not. A society in the throes of revolution cannot be said to be under the rule of law, notwithstanding that the revolution may have advantageous results. The second and more substantive aspect of the rule of law is that all members of a society must be equally protected by the laws. There can be no distinctions based on race, religion, caste, nationality, or economic class. All actual systems of law, of course, fall short of the absolute equality under the law demanded by the rule of law. But it is the extent to which a society recognizes the circumstances of legal equality ideally—as well as the extent to which it realizes them practically—that determines whether a nation is living under the rule of law.

Where individuals are treated unequally before the law, it is difficult to say that democracy exists, for the rights and privileges of some people in a society (including voting rights) are necessarily different from those of others. Meaningful, although not perfect, legal equality is a paramount feature of a democracy and is made necessary in no insignificant part by a capitalist economic order.

Significant civil rights are another aspect of democracies, and these follow in part from capitalism's emphasis on the individual. These rights include freedom of speech, freedom of the press and electronic media, freedom of religion, freedom of movement, the ability to engage in the trade or profession one desires (which is related to private property), and fair adjudicative processes (which is closely related to the rule of law). Once again, these rights may not always be practiced ideally in a democracy. The key factor is the extent to which they are, and the extent to which they are recognized as goals, even though they are imperfectly achieved. Because capitalism values innovation and experiments in new ways of material lifestyle, it helps to create the climate within which civil rights can flourish.

The final cornerstone of democracies, then, is the right to vote. It is this right that gives democracy its name, which is derived from the Greek, *demos* ("people") and *kratein* ("rule"). In a democracy, at least ideally, the people rule. Meaningful choice must exist in the candidates and propositions put before the people; most of the people must be able to vote; and the vote of the people must be respected, both in the process of fair voting and that the citizens must be able to vote on the most important issues, either directly or indirectly. Most democratic systems in the world today practice indirect democracy and are called representative democracies; that is, for the most part, democracy consists of electing public officials who make the decisions of government at all levels.

Again, capitalism furthers voting through its emphasis on the individual. While capitalist social democracy may not be "the end of history," as one political theoretician, Francis Fukuyama, has recently argued, it does appear to be the direction in which much of the world is heading at this time.

TWENTIETH CENTURY CAPITALISM

Stresses and Strains in Modern Capitalism

The theory of capitalism most closely approximated reality during its classical period, roughly from the middle of the eighteenth century to the end of the nineteenth century. In the twentieth century, capitalism has had to face unexpected stresses and strains.

The separation of ownership from the management of a business firm was made legally possible by the invention of the *corporate* form of business: Each shareholder in a corporation is liable only to the extent of the shares he or she owns, no more and no less. In the pre-capitalist economy, a partnership involved the full personal responsibility of each partner for the operations of the business. Partnerships tended to be relatively small, and each partner had a sense of personal involvement, financial and moral, in the business. In a large modern corporation, where 50 million or 100 million shares are owned by a half million or more shareholders, this link between the individual shareholders and the corporation of which they are part-owner is tenuous. The corporation may be located thousands of miles away from most of the shareholders; in most corporations only a small fraction of shareholders, generally less than 1 percent, attend the annual meetings in which officers are elected and other important business is transacted.

Management draws up the list of officers to be elected, presides over the elections, explains why its proposed policy decisions should be adopted, decides the salaries of management, and finally submits all its proposals to a vote: The vote is normally between 95 and 99 percent in favor of management. This is a comfortable majority, as compared with average majorities of 52 to 55 percent in political elections. "Like a stockholders' meeting" is a common phrase used to describe any perfunctorily run gathering. According to a recent study of 500 large corporations, the probability of a serious struggle for control in a large corporation occurs, on the average, once every 300 years!

The essence of the situation is simple. In government, democracy has established the principle that those who wield power must be accountable to the public. The people are the principle, the government their agent. Political power in a democracy must not be held for the benefit of the rulers; it is a trust, the purpose of which is to protect the interests of the citizenry.

In the economic realm, a situation prevails that runs counter to the basic concept of democracy: Corporation managers wield far-reaching power over stockholders and employees, and they constantly make decisions that affect the public interest without any clearly defined responsibility to the public. In a democracy, political policies are determined by processes of consent that begin at the bottom and move up to the top, whereas in a corporate business, economic policies are made at the top and passed down to the bottom. The character of modern industrial organization is hierarchical, founded on discipline and obedience. The traditional pattern in industry has been considerably modified by union negotiations, legislation, and public opinion.

The more that capitalism succeeds, the more it destroys its original institutional and ideological character by collectivizing the framework of business. The first collectivists in the capitalist era were not its critics, but rather were successful capitalist entrepreneurs—people like Andrew Carnegie, John D. Rockefeller, and Henry Ford—who created vast industrial empires.

Like other empires, industrial empires tend to become bureaucratic and conformity minded, to follow routine and precedent and, above all, to transform personal initiative and enterprise into impersonal rules of administrative routine. While the original individual capitalists were bold, daring, and adventurous, the present bureaucratic administrators of modern industrial empires tend to put security above everything else. While risk-taking was one of the characteristic traits of original capitalists, corporate business leaders today prefer the riskless investments of "safe bets." The danger is that as a business becomes bigger, the free enterprise system may gradually become a "safe enterprise" system.

In many respects there is less difference between large-scale capitalist enterprise and large-scale socialized enterprise than between small-scale capitalist enterprise and large-scale capitalist enterprise. Such defenders of capitalism as Justice Louis Brandeis and President Woodrow Wilson were afraid that the "curse of bigness" might eventually destroy not only big private enterprise but private enterprise itself. Again, this problem of bigness is not peculiar to the economic institutions of democratic capitalism; in politics, too, there is the threat of "big government" destroying the very elements that give life and vitality to democracy.

Who owns American business? About 60 percent of all corporate stock is owned by individuals; the rest is held by investment companies, insurance companies, foundations, and institutions. On the positive side, there has been a substantial growth in the number of individuals owning stock; on the negative side is the fact that fewer than 0.1 percent of the citizens own 20 percent of all individually held stock.

To get some idea of the role of big business in the American economy, consider that the 500 largest industrial corporations account for 80 percent of total U.S. industrial sales, for 75 percent of all profits in industry, and for 75 percent of employment in all industrial corporations. In some major nonindustrial sectors of the economy—such as banking, life insurance, and public utilities—concentration of ownership and control is even greater than in industry.

Yet there are other sides to the picture. First, the small business firm has by no means disappeared from the American scene. Retail trade and services have provided the largest opportunities for small business. Often, expanding big business is accompanied by a simultaneous growth of many new small businesses. For example, as people buy cars, there are new opportunities for small manufacturers of parts, for gas stations, garages, motels, and restaurants, and for all of the other services and trades associated with automotive travel.

Second, there is no hereditary aristocracy in big business. Of the hundred largest industrial corporations in 1909, fewer than one-quarter are still among the hundred largest today. Moreover, the competition is not only among individual firms in this top group; changing conditions of the economy entail keen competition among whole industry groups. Steel, coal mining, and textiles were much more important in 1909 than they are today, whereas the petroleum, chemical, and electrical equipment industries have risen sharply in their relative importance in the top hundred corporations.

Defenders of big business maintain that a big country and a big market need big business. Individual security, too, has a better chance with big business than with small enterprises, they argue, because the former can do a better job in long-term planning of production, stability of employment, and the provision of services like pension and health benefits. In labor-management relations the greatest progress has been made in mass-production industries like steel and automobiles, in which big business predominates; by contrast, labor unions have made little progress in agriculture and retailing, in which the small and middle-sized unit prevails.

In research, too, big business carries most of the work and responsibility. Occasionally, important inventions are made in small laboratories, but then it still usually takes the resources and organization of larger corporations to translate the inventions into economic realities. More and more, however, industrial research is carried out by vast corporations, because research requires large financial resources and many years of effort.

Concerning the impact of big business on competition, it is argued that the two are not incompatible. Big business produces a new kind of competition—internal competition. Not only is there competition between General Motors and Ford, but within General Motors itself the Chevrolet competes with the Pontiac, the Oldsmobile with the Buick. Moreover, there is competition in passenger transportation among automobiles, buses, and airlines.

The problem of competition in the changing American economy was the subject of *The New Industrial State* (1971) by John Kenneth Galbraith. In classical economics, the author points out, competition was conceived in terms of many sellers, each with a small share of the market, and restraint of excessive private economic power was provided by competing firms on the same side of the market. Galbraith concedes that this classical model of competition has largely disappeared, since many markets have come to be dominated by a few firms.

Yet Galbraith does not conclude from the widespread disappearance of traditional competition that there is no longer any restraint of private economic power left. New restraints have, in fact, taken the place of overt competition, and these restraints—termed by Galbraith "countervailing power"—are the products of concentration and bigness.

These new factors of restraint have appeared not on the same side of the market, but on the opposite side; not among competitors, but among customers and suppliers. The concentration of industrial enterprises has not only led to a relatively small number of sellers, but has also brought about the predominant position of a few buyers. In the field of labor, too, strong unions have developed mainly when faced by strong corporations, as in the steel and automobile industries. In contrast, there has been no equally powerful trade union in the retail business or in agriculture, the closest approximations in the United States to purely competitive fields.

The weakness of the concept of countervailing power lies in the fact that although the power of the large seller may be checked by that of the large buyer, the resulting benefit need not be passed on to the consumer. Monopoly benefits may be amicably split between the large buyer and the large seller, or between the large corporation and the large union, at the expense of the consumer.

The Rise of the Service Economy

In the initial phases of industrial development, under capitalism or any other system, the industrial working class constantly increases at the expense of artisans, landless peasants, and other social groups whose members seek employment in the expanding factories and mills. In a later and more advanced phase of industrial development, however, the industrial working class begins to decline in proportion to the total population.

In the United States the volume of industrial production and the number of people employed in industry have increased tremendously since 1900, yet the proportion of the industrial working class in the total work force has consistently declined for two reasons.

First, within industry itself there has been an increasing shift of employment from production ("blue-collar") workers to nonproduction ("white-collar" and service) workers and automation. Over the past twenty years, employment in goods-producing industries has about remained constant while industrial production has increased by almost 75 percent. Technological progress, particularly automation, has reduced the number of blue-collar workers needed to produce a given quantity of goods, such as steel, coal, or automobiles.

The second and more important reason for the sharp increase in white-collar workers is the rapid growth of employment in enterprises that provide services rather than produce physical goods. Since 1950, the total number of employed persons has almost doubled from just under 60 million to almost 120 million. Virtually, this entire increase is due to the growing number of white-collar and service-producing jobs, which rose from 27 million to 85 million. This increase resulted from a marked expansion in the service-producing sector of the economy (government, schools, wholesale and retail trade, health services, insurance, finance, real estate, legal services, communications media, entertainment). Among the fastest and most important growth area in the service sector has been government, particularly at the state and local level. Since 1950 federal employment has gone from 1.9 million to 3.0 million, while employment at the state and local level has climbed from 4.1 million to 15.6 million.

As a result of the massive shift in the American economy from producing goods to providing services, there has been a corresponding shift in the profile of employment. In 1950 less than half the labor force held white-collar or service jobs. Today almost 70 percent are employed in such jobs. While in 1950 blue-collar workers outnumbered white-collar workers, the latter now outnumber the former by about two to one. The office has replaced the production line as the typical place of work in the United States, and service has replaced physical goods as the typical form of economic output.

The new type of postindustrial economy is called a *service economy*, to distinguish it from the industrial economy that preceded it. The year 1956 was a milestone in economic history: For the first time in American history, or in that of any nation, the number of people engaged in producing goods was smaller than the number of people performing services. In recent years, a similar change has occurred in other industrially developed nations, such as Canada, Sweden, and Britain. No communist economy ever became, or is close to becoming, a service economy, since communist economies were either industrial (Soviet Union, East Germany), were in an early stage of industrialization (Romania, Poland, Bulgaria), or are still predominantly agrarian (China).

Farm workers and service workers are neither white-collar nor blue-collar workers. These two groups are not as important numerically as are blue-collar and white-collar workers, but they do show the same overall trend from goods-producing to service-rendering employment as living standards rise. In 1953, service workers for the first time exceeded the number of farm workers in the United States, and their numbers are consistently rising in absolute and relative proportion. Farm workers, however, have gone down in both absolute and relative size. Since 1950, the number of farm workers has declined from 7.2 million (12 percent of the work force) to 3.2 million (less than 3 percent of the work force). During the same period the number of service workers has risen from 6.5 million to 28.7 million, or from 9 percent to 23 percent of the work force.

The growth of the number of white-collar workers has important political implications, since the salaried person—in capitalist as well as in communist economies—tends to identify with the middle and upper classes rather than with the working class, even if his or her income is below that of the worker. Marx assumed that the transformation of the independent middle class of artisans and shopkeepers into a dependent salaried class would necessarily change the outlook of the middle class from bourgeois to proletarian. Yet the new middle class of salaried workers in the United States has generally opted not to join the ranks of organized labor, except in the area of government service.

Within the ranks of salaried workers, various segments have grown at an uneven pace. Since 1950, the top category of professional and technical workers has grown by about 150 percent, that of clerical workers by 112 percent, and that of salesworkers by only 50 percent. Thus, the white-collar group has increasingly moved upward in education and income —and also changed its political outlook, since professional personnel are not only better educated and financially better off than are clerical or salesworkers, but they are also more moderate in political attitudes. This upgrading of the labor force has also occurred among blue-collar workers. Politically, these changes are significant, because as workers become more skilled, they generally look upon themselves as middle class, adopt middle-class lifestyles, and tend to be politically more conservative than unskilled workers.

Finally, the rise of the service economy has profoundly affected the stability of advanced capitalist economies. Marx held that a major cause of the disintegration of capitalism is the recurring cycle of boom and bust, resulting in periods of inflation and unemployment. Economic experience has shown that substantial periodic changes in demand and employment occur in the goods-producing sector rather than in the service-producing sector, since goods can be overproduced and then have to be stored, whereas services cannot be stored. Thus, there is generally a better balance between supply and demand in the production of services than in that of goods, which leads to greater stability of employment in service-producing enterprises (government, schools, hospitals, banks). Because many services are provided by governmental or private nonprofit agencies, there is traditionally greater security of employment in such bodies than in goods-producing enterprises, which are almost invariably run by private business.

Before World War II the capitalist economies used to be racked by periodic slumps and economic depressions. Ever since the Great Depression of the 1930s, there has been no comparable economic collapse in the capitalist economies. Such stability has been partly due to welfare-state policies resulting in the maintenance of high levels of effective demand by means of governmental action. Of at least equal importance have been the structural changes of advanced capitalist economies from industrial to postindustrial service economies.

The Mixed Economy

The controversy of capitalism versus socialism has been altered by the profound structural changes effected in the economies of the most advanced Western nations. The public attention received by a constant political tug-of-war over specific economic issues conceals some long-term forces that are at work.

A primary change, for example, is the increased government responsibility for social and economic welfare, which is not the result of moral conversion or of partisan struggles between rugged individualists and do-gooders, but rather is a result of the increasing output of goods and services. Some of the more democratic developing nations have set up elaborate systems of welfare-state policies, but in many cases these systems exist on paper only, since the nations are too poor to pay for the desired welfare. By contrast, where economic levels are high enough to permit welfare policies, as in most Western nations, there is a realistic foundation for such programs.

Another structural change in capitalism has been the relative growth of the not-for-profit sector. Traditional economic analysis and popular thinking still concentrate on the private, profit-seeking sector of the economy while neglecting the importance of government and private nonprofit institutions, which together constitute the not-for-profit sector of the economy. In fact, the not-for-profit sector of the U.S. economy is growing at a faster rate than the profit-seeking sector, and currently comprises almost 45 percent of the gross national product of the United States.

What are the reasons behind the growth of the not-for-profit sector of the economy? In the expansion of government, defense (on the federal level) and education, health, and welfare (on all levels of government) have been the main areas of growth. Private nonprofit institutions have also enlarged their activities, mainly in education and health. Finally, the growth of the not-for-profit sector is due to an inherent factor in advanced economies that has nothing to do with capitalism or socialism. As an industrial economy advances, more and more labor goes into the rendering of services rather than into the production of goods. Since the scope of the not-for-profit sector includes services such as education, community services, health services, and social welfare rather than goods, its role in the economy is likely to grow as the shift from goods to services persists.

So far there has been little tampering with the traditional pattern of leaving the production of goods to private enterprise working for profit, and this pattern is likely to continue. Even socialist governments in Scandinavia have concentrated their socialization programs on services (health, pensions, education) rather than on industrial production. As an economically advanced nation progressively increases its wealth, demand grows for public provision of services considered essential but that many people cannot afford to buy, such as old-age pensions, health insurance, education, urban renewal, or cheap transportation in metropolitan areas.

Increasing wealth also makes it possible for private nonprofit institutions to enlarge their activities. Pension funds of labor unions or endowments of private colleges and universities in the United States run into many billions of dollars, and these vast funds have to be produced first in the profit sector of the economy before they can be channeled into the not-for-profit sector.

The profit sector and the not-for-profit sector are not antagonists engaged in a deadly struggle for supremacy. In health and education there is an interesting mixture of private profit, private nonprofit, and government. Most physicians are self-employed and are part of the private profit sector of the economy. Most hospitals are private nonprofit institutions. The largest general health insurance program is that of Blue Cross–Blue Shield, private and nonprofit, although there are also private, profit-seeking insurance plans as well as government health insurance programs (such as Medicare and state programs). Further, government contributes to the building of medical facilities.

In education, too, there is cooperation among the private profit, private nonprofit, and government sectors of the economy. Harvard University's endowment is worth almost $5 billion. Most of this endowment comes from gifts by wealthy capitalists, by nonprofit foundations originally set up by wealthy capitalists, or by individuals who generally earn their living in the private sector. Of Harvard's total operating budget of over $1 billion per year, about one-half comes from government sources;

the rest comes from interest earned on endowment funds, from student fees, and from annual gifts. Harvard, a private nonprofit institution, thus receives its funds from all three sectors of the economy: government, private profit, and private nonprofit. Its graduates then return to all three sectors of the economy, the majority working for private business or as self-employed professionals.

The traditional socialist charge against the profit motive in capitalism was coupled with the hope that the removal of profit would abolish poverty. Economic reality has worked differently. To the extent that the profit motive has given way to nonprofit service—whether it be private or public—the cause has been not poverty, but rising wealth and rising expectations of the people.

Also, nonprofit enterprise is not synonymous with absolute equality or uniformity. There is still room for ambition and even for competition. Labor unions, foundations, and colleges are all nonprofit, but their top salaries often compare favorably with executive salaries in private business. Frequently, successful people in any one of the three sectors of the economy move on to the other two. Former government officials, civilian and military, are to be found in important positions in business corporations or nonprofit foundations, and a top executive of an automobile company may become secretary of defense or president of the World Bank. As the number of men and women who have had experience in private business, private nonprofit institutions, and government increases, the result is likely to be lessening of ideological rigidity.

In adapting to the economic changes brought on by the expansion of the not-for-profit sector and to the social changes triggered by the welfare state, capitalism has undergone profound transformation. This new and constantly evolving system is neither capitalist nor socialist—if capitalism means laissez-faire and socialism means public ownership of the means of production. It is generally called a "mixed economy," combining predominantly private initiative and property with public responsibility for social welfare.

The Welfare State

The main principles of the welfare state are relatively simple: First, every member of the community is entitled to a minimum standard of living; second, the welfare state is committed to putting full employment at the top of social goals to be supported by public policy.

Particularly in the United States, adherents of the welfare state have believed that full employment can be attained without recourse to large-scale nationalization. Taxation properly adjusted to periods of prosperity and depression; interest rates determined by governmental decision according to economic needs; fiscal policies designed to redistribute purchasing power in harmony with the best interest of the nation; investment incentives in times of contracting business; public works for direct unemployment relief; government credits to builders or buyers of homes—these are but a few of the measures the government can adopt to stabilize the economy without changing its foundations.

In the United States the Great Depression from 1929 to 1939 undermined faith in the orthodox philosophy of laissez-faire, according to which the disequilibrium of the market would eventually be restored to a new equilibrium without any interference from the outside. When the American economy reached the stage in which one out of every four employable people was out of work, in which the farmer could not sell products at reasonable prices, in which more and more business enterprises went bankrupt or were unable to pay wages to their employees or earn profits for their shareholders, the feeling emerged that something had to be done. The New Deal, starting with the first term of President Franklin D. Roosevelt in 1933, was not so much a set of premeditated philosophical principles to be superimposed upon the American people as it was a series of emergency measures in response to urgent practical problems.

The Agricultural Adjustment Act attempted to help the farmer by raising farm prices to a level that would enable farmers to buy industrial products for the same relative amount as in the years from 1909 to 1914. To make such "parity" possible, farmers were to reduce production, in return for which they would receive higher prices (as a result of decreased supply) from the consumer and subsidies from the government. Traditionally opposed to government interference—in theory at least—the farmers have been content with that part of the welfare state which directly protects their interests.

The National Labor Relations Act, commonly known as the Wagner Act, established full statutory regulation of labor-management relations for the first time in the United States. In the preceding half-century, the employer in the United States was free to recognize or not recognize labor unions and to bargain or not bargain with them. Employers frequently discharged employees for union activities, and if unions became too strong, employers would use various means to break them, including company unions, private police, labor spies, lockouts, and professional strike breakers.

The main purpose of the Wagner Act was to encourage collective bargaining between labor and management, thus substituting peaceful discussion for violence. Although the law did not, and could not, compel both sides to agree, and strikes and lockouts still remained legal, the experience of collective bargaining quickly resulted in a dramatic decline of violence in labor disputes.

Dissatisfaction of management with some provisions of the Wagner Act led to its replacement in 1947 by the Labor-Management Relations Act, more commonly known as the Taft-Hartley Act. Although spokespersons for labor voiced deep dissatisfaction with the Taft-Hartley Act, it left the basic principle of the Wagner Act—collective bargaining—substantially unchanged.

The Social Security Act of 1935 marked another milestone in the establishment of a welfare state in America. In modern industry the individual is frequently at the mercy of large impersonal forces over which he or she has no control. The efforts of the family, private charity, and the local community have frequently proved insufficient to protect the individual against the hazards of old age, disability, or unemployment. Passage of the Social Security Act marked the recognition that government —on the local, state, and federal levels—is partly responsible for assuring its citizens of some protection against want and insecurity. Apart from its humanitarian motivation, Social Security also has important economic effects, since such payments provide people with a minimum purchasing power, which contributes to the stability of the economy.

In a significant extension of Social Security in 1965, Congress amended the law to include health insurance for people over sixty-five, covering both hospitalization and doctors' bills. Under this insurance program, popularly known as Medicare, the federal government pays the major cost of treating illness. Although federal Medicare covers only those over sixty-five, the federal government makes grants to state health insurance programs for families with dependent children whose income and financial resources are insufficient for necessary medical services. Numerous states quickly made use of this federal provision and set up supplementary state programs, known as Medicaid. While federal Medicare has an age limit but no means test, state Medicaid programs have a means test but no age limit, since each state prescribes the income level below which it provides health insurance. The issue of expanding public health insurance beyond the elderly and the needy is one of the most vexing concerns confronting the American public.

In education, too, the year 1965 was a turning point in the expansion of the welfare state. Under the Elementary and Secondary Education Act, the federal government now makes direct grants, amounting to several billions of dollars annually, to individual school districts with children from low-income families. The Higher Education Act also expanded the federal government's role. In addition to grants and loans to educational institutions for construction, training, and research, the federal government provides financial help to millions of college students. These programs include work-study aid, grants for disadvantaged students, direct federal loans, and federally guaranteed private loans, where the government guarantees repayment of the loan and pays the interest while the student is in school.

The major groups that receive social welfare benefits from federal funds include retired workers, their dependents and survivors; veterans and their dependents; recipients of public assistance, including persons receiving AFDC (Aid to Families with Dependent Children); and retired federal employees and their survivors. The figures do not include millions of people helped by Medicaid, children receiving federally subsidized school lunches, people getting food stamps, and more than 2 million college students receiving federal grants, loans, or insured private loans.

The growing commitment of the U.S. government to social welfare can be seen in the changes in the federal budget during recent years. The federal budget for 1971 was the first in twenty years in which more money was allocated for human resources (education, health, income security, and veterans' benefits) than for defense. In the budget for 1991, expenditures for human resources were earmarked at 57 percent of total expenditures, as compared with 25 percent for defense. By contrast, in the federal budget for 1963—before any major involvement in Vietnam—29 percent of the budget was spent on human resources, and 47 percent on defense.

NEOCONSERVATISM: AGAINST THE WELFARE STATE

In the years after World War II, support for the welfare state seemed to become part of a political consensus shared by liberals and conservatives alike. As no less a figure than President Dwight Eisenhower stated: "I am conservative when it comes to economic problems but liberal when it comes to human problems." The emphasis was often different: Liberals hoped to expand government services still further—as President Lyndon Johnson proposed in his plans for the Great Society; conservatives tried to revamp existing programs—as President Richard Nixon did in the areas of education and welfare. But until the 1970s, direct attacks on the welfare state could be dismissed as an extremist view.

By the close of the decade, however, two important changes in political leadership signaled a new direction: In 1979, Margaret Thatcher was elected as Conservative Prime Minister of Great Britain; and in 1980 Ronald Reagan was elected as Republican President of the United States. In these new administrations, opposition to the welfare state emerged as a dominant theme. Major shifts in policy confirmed the growing appeal on both sides of the Atlantic of an ideology that challenged basic assumptions of welfare liberalism—the ideology of neoconservatism.

Five main themes have been emphasized by neoconservatives: deregulation of the economy; deconcentration of government; privatization of public functions; nationalist foreign policies; and cultural conservatism.

Deregulation of the Economy

From Adam Smith onward, capitalism has promised economic progress spurred by private entrepreneurs competing in a free market without interference from government. But economic progress, which produced unprecedented growth in the wealth of nations, was accompanied by other, less benevolent developments: a tendency toward monopoly, which thwarts the benefits of competition in a free market; cyclical swings from prosperity to recession or depression, which disrupt the upward trend; inequality of wealth, which leaves many people vulnerable to the hazards of unemployment, illness, destitute old age, and other misfortunes over which they have little control; and a disregard for the environment, which degrades the quality of life not only in the present but for future generations. These unwelcome conditions prompted demands from many different groups for remedial action by government. Starting in the late nineteenth century, government intervened actively in the economy—first to curb monopolies and then to counteract the business cycle, guarantee a minimum standard of well-being, and safeguard the environment.

In part, government intervenes in the economy through a stream of regulations that prescribe, enjoin, and monitor how business is carried on. Regulations deal with everything from the health and safety of workers to preserving endangered animal species. From the standpoint of intended beneficiaries, these regulations provide protection against the hazards of a capitalist economy; from the standpoint of business people who must comply with a growing variety of detailed directives, the regulations impose a costly burden on private enterprise. Private enterprise is mired in a tangle of well-meaning but restrictive bureaucratic requirements.

Neoconservatives reemphasize the central belief of a market economy —that growth and progress result only from the creative efforts of private entrepreneurs competing in risky ventures for large profits. The wealth of every nation, as Adam Smith taught two centuries ago, lies in the productivity of its workers; and increased productivity depends on the innovations introduced by forward-looking, risk-taking entrepreneurs. Without the continuing improvements in production initiated by venturesome entrepreneurs in their quest for further profits, the economy stagnates. The ongoing process of replacing older products and outmoded methods of production with novel products and more productive methods—a process of "creative destruction," as Joseph Schumpeter called it—is the key to economic progress. Whoever stifles this process of "creative destruction" kills the goose that lays the golden egg.

Yet impediments to innovation are a by-product of the welfare state— impediments not only in the form of bureaucratic regulations but also in the guise of rising taxes to pay for the expanding public services and personnel. Although the welfare state aims to relieve the plight of the poor and unemployed, neoconservatives insist that such policies are self-defeating: They stifle the very forces that produce new jobs and general prosperity. Burdened by restrictions that hinder efforts to expand production, and by taxes that limit incentives for taking risks, capitalists turn away from creative innovation to more profitable but less productive investments—tax shelters, corporate mergers, precious metals, and other lucrative but nonproductive ventures.

Besides the practical question of what effects government restrictions and taxation have on economic progress, the call to deregulate the economy raises a basic issue of values. Government intervention in the economy is justified in the welfare state by a general concern for greater equality. To reduce disparities in wealth and opportunity is a positive goal. In an unregulated capitalist economy, successful entrepreneurs reap rich rewards while many other individuals earn only a modest income, and some face periodic unemployment and poverty. These market-based inequalities have been a major source of controversy in modern politics. Socialists condemn economic inequality as arising from the ill-gotten profits appropriated by owners and managers of capital through exploiting the workers by denying them fair wages. Liberals, too, challenge the extremes of wealth in a market economy, not because economic inequality is unjust in principle but because every citizen is entitled to freedom from want as a democratic right.

Neoconservatives, on the other hand, are more inclined to defend economic inequality as morally justified by the differential contributions particular individuals make to economic growth. Thus, neoconservatives believe that, because entrepreneurs drive the engine of economic progress that benefits everyone, they are entitled to exceptional rewards that the rest of society cannot claim.

Deconcentration of Government

Along with regulation of the economy and extension of public services, the welfare state brought a notable expansion and concentration of governmental power. Demands for government services have multiplied at every level, so that all units of government have increased their personnel and expenditures; but the most conspicuous expansion has occurred at the national level. Issues that once were predominantly in the domain of states and localities have fallen increasingly within the scope of national policy. Various national programs, many associated with Lyndon Johnson's Great Society, have dealt with medical care for the aged, training for the disadvantaged and handicapped, welfare for the poor, safety conditions for workers, protection for consumers, cleaning up the environment, preventing crime, loans for students, rebuilding urban neighborhoods, subsidies for higher education, and equal treatment for women and minorities.

Concentration of power occurs as the problems of contemporary society are considered as being national in scope, requiring national—if not international—solutions. Recession and unemployment, inequality of opportunity, and damage to the environment are not confined to single states or regions. Their effects are felt throughout the country, and remedies have been sought through national policies. In addition, the national government has the most resources to finance so broad a range of expensive programs. The more services and benefits that particular groups demand from government, the less able are local units to pay the costs. In fact, most states have responded only fitfully to the distinctive problems of an urban industrial society. State legislatures are reluctant to adopt costly measures to relieve the blight of inner cities, to provide inexpensive public transportation, to pay increasing claims for welfare, or to respond to other characteristic urban complaints. In part, national power has expanded into areas in which states and localities have been either unable or unwilling to act on their own.

To neoconservatives, the concentration of governmental power is undesirable on several grounds. Neoconservatives believe that policies initiated by national agencies are less adapted to people's actual needs and circumstances than are policies made locally. As the process of decision-making becomes more centralized, the resulting policies are less flexible in meeting the special conditions to which they apply. For example, a national minimum wage neglects differences in the cost of living between urban and rural areas, or between cold and warm climates, which affect how much income people need in one place or another. Other attempts to impose uniform regulations in such areas as welfare benefits, housing codes, aid to schools, health care, and protecting the environment are open to the same objection. Variations in local conditions are ignored by government officials far removed from the communities in which their policies actually take effect. The result is policies that may either be ineffective in solving existing problems or inefficient, squandering valuable resources.

Concentration of governmental power also means that layers of bureaucracy are added in the implementation of policies, which in turn raises the cost of public services and enhances the authority of appointed administrators who are not responsible to the people they are expected to serve. Career officials in a national bureaucracy have no direct incentive to consider the interests of local constituencies or even to consult the people who are affected by their decisions. Insulated from popular political pressures and charged with implementing policies that have been enacted without reference to special local conditions, national bureaucrats exercise their power as agents of a remote central authority.

To combat concentration of power, neoconservatives advocate abolishing some national programs entirely and decentralizing the administration of others. They recommend further that when states are unable to meet the cost of needed programs, the national government should grant them uncommitted funds to spend as the states themselves see fit; that is, block grants as opposed to categorical programs. In this way, control and responsibility for welfare and other programs are shifted from central to local authorities. The aim is to limit the activities of the national government while devolving as many public functions as possible to the states and localities.

Whether or not to regulate the economy thus involves not only practical judgments about how to ensure prosperity but moral beliefs about the value of equality. Neoconservatives approve as legitimate those inequalities of wealth and opportunity that liberals reject as unacceptable in a democratic society. Particularly during the first term of the Reagan administration, the focus was on the total supply of wealth in the economy rather than on its distribution.

Neoconservative recommendations for deregulating the economy, reducing social services, and cutting personal and corporate taxes proceed from a recognition that economic conditions in the 1990s are very different from those of the 1930s, when major policies of the welfare state were introduced. Six decades ago, the world was in the grip of the Great Depression; economic crisis was spreading from one country to another, paving the way for revolutionary politics. Communists on the extreme left and fascists on the extreme right attacked democratic government as being ineffectual and worthless. Conventional economic doctrine held that "in the long run" capitalist economies would recover from the crisis and resume their march toward prosperity. But in the words of John Maynard Keynes, the preeminent economist of the time and a committed liberal in politics, "in the long run we will all be dead." He meant that if the economic crisis was not solved in the short term, liberal democracy would not survive until the long run. Keynes proclaimed "The End of Laissez-Faire," and formulated an economic theory that prescribed direct government intervention and spending to offset the decline in private investment and purchasing power and to stimulate economic recovery.

In the United States, Keynesian doctrines were reflected in President Roosevelt's New Deal, which marked a historic change in the relationship between the public and private sectors. Critics of the New Deal denounced FDR as a "traitor to his class"—a charge he deeply resented; advocates of the New Deal hailed FDR as the savior of American capitalism.

Whatever the achievements or failures of the New Deal, circumstances now are clearly different from the time when Roosevelt's program was introduced. Successive hikes in oil prices imposed by OPEC after 1973 helped trigger a worldwide process of creeping stagflation for almost a decade—economic stagnation combined with mounting inflation. To control this inflation, while at the same time providing needed new investment, became the overriding objective of government. Moreover, before the 1930s government served mainly as an umpire of the economy; today it is the leading participant. Not only does government participate in the economy through its fiscal and monetary policies and through its regulation, but it is also a major purchaser of goods and services—especially for the military. Huge government deficits have become a perennial fact of economic life. To meet its deficits, the government can borrow, raise taxes, or increase the supply of money—in any case either contributing to inflation or absorbing income that might otherwise be invested productively in new industry. Unlike the 1930s, when liberals turned hopefully to government for a solution to the economic ills of capitalism, in the 1990s government itself has become an important part of the problem.

Recognizing the marked economic changes that have occurred during the last sixty years, neoconservatives point out that policies intended for one set of conditions cannot be expected to work under altogether different conditions. They also emphasize that liberals have been unable to reformulate their traditional proposals for extending the welfare state to address the new realities. Keynesian remedies for a severe economic depression— including budgetary deficits and intentional inflation—are no solution for governments already massively in debt and legally committed to entitlement programs under which a growing number of individuals claim their right to escalating benefits from publicly financed health, welfare, and retirement programs. Whether deregulating the economy is an effective alternative to liberal policies, as neoconservatives insist, or a regrettable step back toward the bad old days, as their critics allege, remains to be seen.

In opposing concentration of governmental power, neoconservatives echo Thomas Jefferson's ideal of a republic based on local self-government. Historically, this ideal was associated with Jeffersonian liberalism in contrast to Alexander Hamilton's vision of a strong central government actively aiding the growth of national power, both economic and political. But times have changed. Present-day liberals regard Jefferson's belief in limited central government with maximum local self-rule as no longer adequate for the needs of a complex, interdependent society characterized by large-scale organizations that operate across continents. Reliance on the national government to remedy the deficiencies of capitalism is thus a leading theme in contemporary liberalism, whereas neoconservatives reaffirm the autonomy of states and localities.

Privatization of Public Functions

Extensions of the welfare state depend on the desire of liberals to expand the scope of public functions to encompass activities formerly left either to individuals personally or to voluntary joint efforts. Liberals justify collectivizing an activity or service on the grounds that without government involvement, the activity will be performed inadequately or neglected entirely. Saving for retirement, for example, may be left to each individual as a purely private responsibility; but many people are unable to save because their income is low, while others will choose to spend all they earn on current consumption instead of saving for the future. The result will be that for one reason or another, a sizable proportion of elderly persons will find themselves destitute. Such widespread poverty—which did in fact exist before the welfare state—prompted liberals to demand a compulsory system of Social Security financed by taxes on both employees and their employers, in order to assure a minimum retirement income for everyone. Saving for retirement was transformed from a voluntary activity subject to the uncertainties of personal circumstance and choice to a collectivized activity mandated by law as a universal requirement.

For similar reasons, liberals have advocated public welfare for the poor, not simply private charity; legal enforcement of pollution standards, not simply voluntary compliance; government grants for scientific research, not simply private investment; public subsidies for the arts, not simply private contributions; and affirmative action guidelines for women and minorities, not simply voluntary nondiscrimination. In these and other instances, liberals have urged collectivization of a voluntary activity to assure that results they value will actually be achieved.

Perhaps no issue is more fundamental in the neoconservative critique of welfare liberalism than their insistence on privatizing activities that have been collectivized under the welfare state. As a general principle, neoconservatives see harmful effects from extending the scope of public functions. One main harm is a loss among the beneficiaries of public services of a feeling of self-reliance and a sense of personal responsibility. Neoconservatives believe, for example, that public welfare programs intended to aid the poor actually perpetuate their poverty by removing incentives to self-help: Instead of accepting personal responsibility for their situation and acting to improve it, welfare recipients become dependent on government aid and lose the motivation to work for a better life on their own.

Charles Murray is perhaps the most well-known neoconservative to advance this position. In his 1984 work, *Losing Ground: American Social Policy 1950–1980*, he argues that far from helping people, welfare programs actually hurt them. Increases in AFDC payments and other programs such as food stamps reduce disincentives to socially improvident behavior, weaken the family, and create a cycle of poverty. In time, dependence on public services as a way of life, perpetuated across generations, produces a permanent underclass composed of individuals who subsist on government programs with neither the desire nor the capacity to assume responsibility for their own well-being as self-sufficient citizens.

Such a prospect is both socially and morally disturbing: Socially, a significant segment of the population remains permanently nonproductive, sustained by the efforts of others; morally, these people lose the qualities of self-reliance and independence that are the strengths of a democratic society.

In addition, taxpayers who share the increasing cost of public services find their income reduced through rising taxes, and so lose the freedom to spend their earnings as they themselves think best. Private contributions to maintain welfare and cultural activities based on personal judgments about which enterprises should be supported shrink in importance compared to government appropriations based on the political and bureaucratic influence of organized interests. Collectivization drives out voluntarism as the primary source of funding. The result is not only a loss of personal freedom in deciding how one's income should be spent but also a decline in habits of public generosity and a sense of community spirit. Only by returning collectivized activities to private voluntary action can these unfortunate effects be reversed.

In urging privatization of public functions, neoconservatives reaffirm the primacy of nongovernmental institutions in developing qualities of initiative, responsibility, public spirit, and other important virtues. Families, churches, schools, private enterprises, and cultural institutions should be protected from government intervention, because it is in these private environments that the personal qualities needed to sustain a free society are nurtured and transmitted.

According to neoconservatives, the liberal penchant for invoking government to do good is more harmful than beneficial. Do-good efforts are too often self-defeating or counterproductive—whether by reducing incentives for entrepreneurs to innovate in the economy, by discouraging the poor and unemployed from helping themselves through personal effort, by creating new slums through subsidizing massive housing projects that people find oppressive to live in, or by perpetuating crime through ineffective programs to rehabilitate habitual offenders. More good is accomplished by relying on the judgment and resourcefulness of private individuals than by government intervention to remedy all the apparent ills of a modern society, many of which are beyond the ability of public officials to comprehend, let alone correct.

Neoconservatives challenge government programs that are intended to correct the abuses of an unregulated market and provide opportunities for the disadvantaged. Against liberal demands to use the power of government to fulfill social obligations, neoconservatives reassert the values of individual self-help and private initiative as the enduring bases of personal well-being and social progress. In the ideology of neoconservatism, the welfare state finds a vigorous critique.

Nationalist Foreign Policies

Neoconservatives have opposed not only the domestic programs of the welfare state but also liberal foreign policies. Neoconservatives have generally been less likely to embrace internationalist prescriptions for world problems and have instead concentrated on what a nation can do for itself. While this has not ruled out internationalist approaches, it has resulted in an attitude in which the United States has been more likely to go it alone. Foremost among the neoconservative criticism of liberals in foreign policy was the former's distrust of the latter's optimistic expectations from détente.

The Cold War   Prior to détente, for more than twenty-five years after World War II, relations between the United States and the Soviet Union were dominated by the Cold War. The Cold War arose not simply from competing national interests but also from conflicting ideologies. The distinction between ideologies and interests is not always clear. Political leaders no less than ordinary citizens view the world through a complex intellectual screen in which ideological beliefs and practical interests are often so closely intertwined that it is difficult to determine where one begins and the other ends. Yet the distinction is important, if only because it is easier to compromise about interests than over ideologies. When conflicts are regarded as differences not mainly of interest but of principle, there is less chance of reaching an accommodation. The Cold War involved important differences of interest, but it was also viewed on both sides as a conflict of principle.

Mistrust between the Soviet Union and the Western Allies arose even during their collaboration in World War II—notably over Western motives in postponing a second front in Western Europe, which would have relieved German military pressure on the beleaguered Russians. This disagreement about military strategy was the first in a series of basic differences between the Soviet Union and the Western Allies that emerged during the war, surfaced ominously at wartime conferences, and erupted afterward into the Cold War.

Underlying this mutual suspicion were fundamental differences of interest and ideology that the wartime alliance could conceal but not resolve. During the war ideological issues were muted. Joseph Stalin's wartime speeches made no mention of communism but stressed instead the patriotic defense of Mother Russia. Nationalism aroused far more intense loyalties among the Russian people than did communism, and Stalin put nationalism first.

The aims of the Western democracies were formulated in the Atlantic Charter, signed by Prime Minister Winston Churchill and President Roosevelt in 1941. Besides statements renouncing territorial ambitions, denouncing the use of force, and proclaiming "freedom from fear and want," the charter contained two articles that expressed distinctively Western objectives. One was political—the right of all people to choose the form of government under which they will live; the other was economic—the right of equal access to world trade and raw materials. These articles embody the characteristic democratic conceptions of politics and economics. The contradiction between these principles and postwar Soviet objectives would soon become apparent.

A primary interest of the Soviet Union after World War II was to assure the military security of its western borders. Three times in a century and a quarter Russia had been invaded from the west, each time with an enormous toll of death and destruction. To prevent another such calamity became an overriding concern among Soviet leaders. This meant that Russia must control or maintain a sphere of influence in Eastern Europe. From the Russian standpoint, the only acceptable governments in Eastern Europe were communist regimes firmly tied to the Soviet Union.

This political interest in security was reinforced by an economic interest in rebuilding and expanding the devastated Soviet economy. One means for doing so was to exploit the economies of Eastern Europe by physically transferring industrial plants to Russia and by imposing on these nations terms of trade advantageous to the Soviet Union.

Two obstacles to these basic Soviet interests soon emerged. One was nationalism—the unwillingness of Poles, Czechs, Hungarians, and other nationalities to submit to Russian domination. The most successful national resistance occurred in Yugoslavia, where Marshal Josip Tito, though himself a staunch communist, asserted his independence from Russian control.

The other obstacle to Soviet control of Eastern Europe was the Anglo-American commitment, affirmed in the Atlantic Charter, to democratic self-government. The first showdown between Russian interests and Western principles came in Poland. Would the Soviets permit democratic elections in Poland, as President Truman insisted was required by the Yalta Agreement of 1945 (signed by Roosevelt, Churchill, and Stalin) and the subsequent Declaration of Liberated Europe? Whatever the terms of these official statements, Soviet troops were present on Polish soil, and Stalin was not about to surrender vital Russian interests in favor of "bourgeois" notions of democracy. In fact, the fate of Poland had been sealed in the wartime decisions that allowed Russian armies to liberate Eastern Europe while the Western forces halted their advance. Now the Russians made a token gesture toward broadening the pro-Soviet communist government they had already recognized unilaterally. President Truman denounced Soviet actions in Poland in strong terms; the chill in Soviet-American relations was well underway.

The freeze deepened through a series of Soviet and American actions and reactions, both at home and abroad, which began during the late 1940s and led to the bitter and dangerous Cold War confrontations of the 1950s and 1960s. From the day he came into office, following the death of Roosevelt, President Truman took a strong stand against communist expansion. He regarded the consolidation of Russian control in Eastern Europe as provocative, rather than defensive, and he was determined to resist any further extension of Soviet influence. If the security and prosperity of the

Soviet Union depended on control of the governments and economies of Eastern European satellites, the security and prosperity of the United States depended on the existence, especially in Western Europe, of regimes able to resist the threat of Russian encroachment and to function as active members of a free world economy. The imposition in Western Europe of communist regimes tied politically and economically to the Soviet Union would leave the United States isolated and vulnerable in a world of hostile powers.

A comprehensive response to the communist challenge came in 1947, in the far-reaching Truman Doctrine. The immediate occasion was the civil war in Greece, initiated by communist guerrillas trying to dismember that nation. Economic and military aid had been supplied to the Greek government by Great Britain, but by 1947 the British recognized that they were no longer able to keep up their former international commitments, including assistance to Greece and Turkey. President Truman, strongly supported by Dean Acheson, his future secretary of state, saw an opportunity to assert America's determination to resist communist expansion, by force if necessary. The United States intervened in Greece with arms, aid, advice, and personnel. A hard line of political and military containment—the heart of American policy in the Cold War—was being drawn around the Soviet Union and the communist world.

In 1947 another significant response to the communist challenge was unveiled by Secretary of State George Marshall. Under the Marshall Plan the United States pledged $17 billion to help the countries of Western Europe—including West Germany—rebuild their economies. The economic reconstruction of Europe was an essential requirement for maintaining a strong and prosperous free world. Underlying the Marshall Plan was the realization that communism could not be contained by military means alone; only in healthy societies with productive economies would resistance to communism be effective.

At its height the conduct of the Cold War was based from the American side on several major assumptions. First, it was assumed that there was no significant difference between the expansion of the Soviet Union and the success of national communist movements outside Russia. This meant that all communist regimes, regardless of their relations with Moscow, were considered equally antagonistic. In fact, important divisions had developed within the communist world. Although the adjacent countries in Eastern Europe remained satellites of the Soviet Union, this was hardly true of all communist regimes. Yugoslavia and China were anything but docile instruments of the Soviet Union; on the contrary, both were as jealous of their independence in foreign policy as they were zealous about implementing communism in domestic policy.

Other communist governments were able to assert greater or lesser degrees of independence—including Romania, Albania, and North Vietnam. These divisions might have been recognized years earlier as a basis for improving political and economic relations with at least some communist regimes. But as long as the communist world was viewed as a single monolithic whole, disregarding national variations, there was no room for flexible responses geared to specific countries and circumstances.

Second, the confrontation between the free world and the communist world was seen in global terms, as a conflict extending to every corner of the earth, in which a gain for one side was necessarily a loss for the other. This meant that the United States must be prepared to intervene in any situation on any continent, wherever there was danger of a communist success. The suggestions of people like Walter Lippmann and later George Kennan that disengagement might be possible in certain areas, or that some remote regions were simply of no strategic value, went unheeded. It also meant that countries which attempted to follow a policy of neutralism between the two blocs were sometimes regarded as hostile. There was little middle ground between the two sides: A country was either for us or against us.

Third, the conflict was viewed largely in military terms, as involving threats of aggression and territorial expansion. This led the United States to sponsor a series of collective security arrangements around the world, including military alliances with countries that potentially were unstable, like South Vietnam, or overtly authoritarian, like Franco's Spain. The fear was of a "domino effect" in which first one country and then another would fall to communism.

The most important military alliance was the North Atlantic Treaty Organization (NATO), in which the United States joined a collective security arrangement with the countries of Western Europe—initially Britain, France, Italy, Belgium, the Netherlands, and Luxembourg. The success of NATO as a military shield behind which Western Europe could resist Soviet threats while regaining its economic strength encouraged the United States to initiate similar alliances in Southeast Asia. But Southeast Asia is very different from Western Europe. European governments enjoyed mass support in societies that were willing and able to rebuild themselves after the devastation of war into viable and thriving communities. With American aid they were ready to assume their responsibilities as genuine partners in collective self-defense. Moreover, the members of NATO were democratic systems, committed to the same basic values as the United States.

American allies in other parts of the world were different from the European nations. Some were unstable, undemocratic, or both. The whirlwind from this policy was reaped in South Vietnam, ostensibly an equal partner of the United States in the Southeast Asia Treaty Organization but actually a client state with neither the political viability nor economic capacity to act effectively in resisting invasion and subversion.

Finally, the Cold War was assumed to be rooted ultimately in irreconcilable differences of principle and morality. At stake were basic beliefs and convictions; the Cold War was finally a struggle for people's minds. Anticommunism became not simply a policy but a creed, a moral crusade demanding ideological fervor and uncompromising dedication.

Détente   The Cold War dominated Soviet-American relations for more than a quarter century, from the late 1940s into the early 1970s. But in the 1970s a new theme emerged—détente. The main architects of détente on the American side were President Richard Nixon and his secretary of state, Henry Kissinger. There is some irony in the fact that as a congressman and senator, Nixon had been an ardent advocate of the Cold War; but as President he could move toward détente without provoking accusations that he was "soft" on communism.

The roots of détente lay in profound changes within the international system that led both the United States and the Soviet Union to recognize that, despite their ideological antagonism, there were areas of common interest in which joint action would be mutually advantageous. The notion of détente was a relaxation of tensions.

A central feature of the Cold War was the nuclear arms race between the United States and the Soviet Union, in which each country sought to neutralize and overcome any military advantage the other might have. An arms race is nothing new in international relations: In a world of competing independent states, military strength has always been and still remains an indispensable basis for achieving vital national objectives, including physical security. But in one critical respect the Soviet-American arms race was unique: The deployment by both sides of vast arsenals of nuclear weapons introduced for the first time in history the possibility of assured mutual destruction for both great powers.

The underlying motive for every previous arms race was to gain a relative military advantage over one's opponent; but the devastation from nuclear weapons raised the specter of absolute destruction for victor and vanquished alike. Beyond a certain point, the accumulation of additional weapons brought no relative advantage; once the threshold of assured mutual destruction was passed, there was no good reason to continue the enormous expense of developing and deploying new systems of nuclear weapons. Consequently, limitation of nuclear arms appeared as a basic common interest for both superpowers.

The promise of détente was obvious. The prospect of a nuclear war between the United States and the Soviet Union was mind-numbing: Life, as it is known now, would have come to an end. Nonetheless, such a war was, by no means, beyond possibility. Strategists in both countries long ago began "thinking about the unthinkable," planning how to carry on after a nuclear holocaust. No right-thinking person could have looked forward with anything but horror to such a catastrophe. Any developments that lessened its likelihood were welcomed. It is in this light that Soviet-American détente seemed most promising.

At the same time, the scope of détente went beyond Soviet-American dischord to a wider range of East-West relations. Initiatives for détente originally came from Western Europe, notably from West Germany during the chancellorship of Willy Brandt. These efforts, intended to achieve an "opening" to the East, had a marked effect on relations among the countries of Europe. Trade, travel, and information all flowed more easily between East and West. A more flexible attitude toward the satellite regimes was also reflected in American foreign policy. A momentous instance of détente was the recognition by the United States of the People's Republic of China in 1978 after decades of determined hostility. These changes comprised a significant departure from Cold War principles. Indeed, the easing of East-West tensions outside the sphere of Soviet-American relations was probably the main achievement of détente.

From détente to confrontation   Neoconservatives believed that optimistic American expectations from détente reflected a misguided assessment of Soviet objectives, and that the benefits from détente were one-sided, in favor of the Soviets. Pointing to Soviet or Cuban intervention in Eastern Europe, Africa, the Middle East, Latin America, and, most blatantly, Afghanistan, neoconservatives insisted that long-term Soviet ambitions had remained consistently expansionist. The promise of détente served mainly to beguile Western nations into softening their opposition to aggressive Soviet actions. While continuing to pursue expansionist goals, the Soviets used détente to weaken Western resolve in confronting communist threats to security. In their eagerness for international peace and stability, the West succumbed to wishful thinking about Soviet aims and intentions, which had never really changed since the days of the Cold War.

Distrust of détente led neoconservatives to recommend a number of policies: an arms buildup by both the United States and its allies to strengthen deterrence; use of military force to resist expansion of the Soviet Union or its surrogates, primarily Cuba; caution in negotiating arms-limitation agreements and other cooperative ventures with the Soviet Union; control of trade, technology, loans, and other exchanges as sanctions against the Soviet Union and other communist regimes; and support for anticommunist authoritarian regimes as bulwarks against communist expansion.

The buildup of American and allied military forces was a cornerstone of neoconservative foreign policy, even though the enormous cost of new weapons systems worsened the federal budget deficit and threatened to escalate the nuclear arms race. Any "window of vulnerability" through which the Soviets might be tempted to launch a military attack had to be securely shut.

The assured capacity to inflect nuclear devastation under all possible circumstances, including a first nuclear strike by the Soviets, was one means to deter aggression and thus to preserve peace. Another method was the attempt to develop a defensive capacity to prevent Soviet attack, the controversial strategic defense initiative ("star wars"). Neoconservatives argued that ensuring national survival took precedence over such concerns as reducing federal budget deficits and curbing the arms race.

The need to achieve an arms buildup guided some of the Reagan administration's major policy efforts. Despite warnings from his advisers that increased budgetary deficits might stifle economic growth, President Reagan persuaded Congress to adopt his proposals for higher military spending; despite widespread popular demonstrations in Europe against deploying American medium-range nuclear weapons, he ordered installation of Pershing and cruise missiles on European soil; despite strong resistance in Japan to a policy of rearmament, he convinced Japanese leaders to expand that country's armed forces; and he persisted in securing funding for the strategic defense initiative in the face of broad opposition. These actions all reflected the neoconservative belief that enhanced military power was the necessary foundation for an effective foreign policy.

Willingness to use military force in resisting communist expansion was demonstrated by the Reagan administration in 1983 in the invasion of the Caribbean island of Grenada. Supported by small neighboring countries fearful that Grenada was becoming a base for revolutionary activity against them, and ostensibly to rescue endangered American medical students on the island, the United States struck with decisive force to occupy Grenada and disarm the national militia.

Grenada's unpopular ruler, who had recently seized power in a bloody coup, was deposed; large stores of Soviet-made weapons were confiscated; and Cuban construction workers stationed on the island to build a modern airport were expelled. The action signaled President Reagan's resolve to use troops if necessary in meeting threats of communist takeovers. Additional pressure, short of invasion, was placed on Nicaragua in Central America during the Reagan and Bush administrations.

A major achievement of détente was SALT 1—the first strategic arms limitation treaty between the superpowers. SALT 1 was intended to be followed by further arms agreements; but a proposed SALT 2, agreed to by President Jimmy Carter as well as President Leonid Brezhnev, was blocked by conservatives in the U.S. Senate. After President Ronald Reagan's election, caution in entering cooperative arrangements with the Soviet Union, especially in arms control, became the prevailing attitude until the advent of Mikhail Gorbachev, when the United States and the Soviet Union reached an agreement eliminating medium-range and short-range ballistic missiles on terms that were almost entirely American. The Reagan-Gorbachev arms control agreement was followed by more agreements limiting conventional and nuclear weapons between President Bush and Gorbachev, and then between President Bush and Russian President Boris Yeltsin.

Beyond their caution toward Soviet-American cooperation, neoconservatives advocated restrictions on trade and other exchanges as a means of penalizing communist governments for actions the United States opposed. To express disapproval over the invasion of Afghanistan in 1979, for example, the Reagan administration denied to the Soviets sophisticated machinery for completing a mammoth gas pipeline between Russia and Western Europe.

The ban was soon lifted in the face of an intense reaction from European countries helping to build the pipeline as a vital facility for supplying needed energy. Similarly, following the suppression of Solidarity in Poland, an embargo was imposed on trade with that country to express American disapproval over the Polish government's actions. During détente trade and other exchanges were encouraged as a means of fostering closer ties between East and West, but in the confrontational approach favored by neoconservatives, such exchanges were viewed as a potential sanction to invoke in situations of conflict rather than as an opportunity to promote international cooperation.

A highly controversial aspect of neoconservative foreign policy, articulated most clearly by President Reagan's ambassador to the United Nations, Jeane Kirkpatrick, involved extending aid to authoritarian regimes to help them resist communist subversion. Especially in Latin America—where revolutionary movements abetted by Cuba operated openly in a number of countries and, in Nicaragua, had succeeded in winning control of the government—the United States supported regimes whose records of domestic repression had been repeatedly condemned by international human rights organizations.

Two main arguments were used to justify support for such regimes: First, aiding authoritarian regimes enabled the United States to exert pressure upon them to become less repressive; and, second, such regimes were in any case preferable to communist totalitarianism, which was not only hostile to American interests but was perceived to be far less likely to undergo internal reform. On both counts, providing military and economic aid to pro-American authoritarian regimes, however repressive they might have been, was considered better than watching them succumb to communist subversion. The policy of selective American support for, and pressure on, authoritarian regimes seemed to bear fruit, as many countries moved in the direction of democracy throughout the 1980s, particularly in Latin America.

The elements of neoconservative foreign policy reflected distrust of détente, a more confrontational approach to relations with the Soviet Union and a greater willingness to assert American national interests. While advocates of détente saw Soviet-American cooperation as the basis for avoiding the cataclysm of nuclear war, neoconservatives saw a forceful response to Soviet ambitions as the basis for American security and international stability. To what extent the dissolution of the Soviet Union and the collapse of communism were a result of neoconservative policies, Mikhail Gorbachev, or both, remains in dispute.

Cultural Conservatism

A final important strand of neoconservative thought, related to its general distrust of government, is its belief that a stable society must have at its core a system of moral and cultural values that result in responsible citizens capable of implementing democracy. Unless the citizenry is responsible, moral, and prudent, neither economic prosperity nor democracy is possible, neoconservatives argue.

The neoconservative movement has, thus, tended to support traditional institutions in society such as family, church, and neighborhood schools. The neoconservative view is that recent governmental policies have eroded these and other pillars on which society is constructed. In this outlook, the neoconservatives have adopted a broader vantage point than some of their liberal critics—that is, the neoconservatives view is that society is more than government; political policies, while vital, are not the whole of a society's way of life. Unless certain cultural traits are present in a population, free government is not possible.

Moreover, the neoconservative critique of the trend of governmental policies during recent decades is that such policies have been in opposition to the cultural prerequisites that have made the form of government that enacted these policies possible. To take first the neoconservative views on sexual matters, the role of the family, and the place of women in society: The prevailing culturally conservative attitude is that the 1960s through the 1980s were a time in which the condition of the family took a monumental step backwards. Out-of-wedlock births, divorce, and extramarital sex skyrocketed.

Furthermore, this decay of traditional family structure has had marked negative effects on the social order. Poverty in the United States is most prevalent among single-parent, female-headed households, and opportunities for children living in these circumstances are considerably less than they are for children living in traditional, two-parent families. Criminal behavior is much more likely to develop, as is drug use and a host of other social ills.

Neoconservatives blame a general attitude of permissiveness in society for the dissolution of the family. Too often, individuals value the present above the future and, in so doing, condemn their future. Individuals need to be gratification-delaying. As it is an apparently ineradicable tendency in human beings to "live for the moment," it is essential that institutions exist in society that reinforce individuals' capacities to defer present pleasures so that they might experience a more pleasant future.

Foremost of the historical entities that encouraged people to look toward the future was the church. The vision of heaven and the nightmare of hell acted as powerful inducements to individuals to behave morally. For this reason, neoconservatives decry the waning influence of religion in modern life, and also criticize governmental actions of whatever sort that act to weaken organized religion.

In the area of cultural permissiveness, neoconservatives have generally opposed the "anything goes" attitude that currently characterizes accepted definitions of free speech and freedom of expression. Neoconservatives are more likely to favor restrictions on obscenity and pornography, for example, and to hold that burning an American flag is not an acceptable form of freedom of expression.

The conservative critique of modern society in the area of culture is more than just an unspecific wailing over the loss of the "good old days." Rather, it is that government policies themselves are in large part responsible for this loss. The secular emphasis of modern government policies has eroded religious faith; government welfare policies diminish the family; high taxation requires both parents in a family to work, thereby leaving children unattended; affirmative action and similar programs destroy individual initiative.

In the areas of economics and foreign policy, neoconservatives have had a reasonable amount of success, if not in persuading others to implement their full policy, then at least in encouraging others to consider their point of view. This same level of success has yet to be experienced by neoconservatives in the area of cultural attitudes, as Patrick J. Buchanan's failed 1992 presidential campaign demonstrated. Indeed, culturally conservative rhetoric by individuals such as Buchanan, who at the 1992 Republican National Convention described the condition of American society as befitting a "religious war," seemed to move the public at large in a direction opposite of its intention.

Both Margaret Thatcher and Ronald Reagan were able to leave conservative leaders after them: John Major in Britain and George Bush in the United States. Neither Major nor Bush has been as ideologically motivated as were their predecessors, however, and the defeat of Bush in the 1992 presidential election by Bill Clinton ended twelve years of Republican presidential domination.

The problem with the neoconservative movement—which in large part has been to restore to Western nations values that characterized the economy, society, and politics in an earlier time—is that it simply may not fit the present and future. The welfare state has transformed social life and created sizable constituencies. An increasingly complex world— politically, economically, and environmentally—may not be able to implement the outlook of an earlier time. From both a practical and electoral perspective, the future of neoconservatism is uncertain.

FOR FURTHER READING

BELL, DANIEL, *The Cultural Contradictions of Capitalism*. New York: Basic Books, Inc., Publishers, 1976.

BELL, DANIEL, and IRVING KRISTOL, eds., *The Crisis in Economic Theory*. New York: Basic Books, Inc., Publishers, 1981.

BERLIN, ISAIAH, *Four Essays on Liberty*. New York: Oxford University Press, 1969.

COSER LEWIS A., and IRVING HOWE, eds., *The New Conservatives*, New York: Quadrangle, 1974.

FRIEDMAN, MILTON, *Capitalism and Freedom*. Chicago: University of Chicago Press, Phoenix Books, 1963.

————, *Free to Choose*. New York: Harcourt Brace Jovanovich, Inc. 1979.

GALBRAITH, JOHN KENNETH, *Economics and the Public Purpose*. Boston: Houghton Mifflin Company, 1973.

GILDER, GEORGE, *Wealth and Poverty*. New York: Bantam Books, Inc., 1981.

HEILBRONER, ROBERT L., *Business Civilization in Decline*. New York: W. W. Norton & Co., Inc., 1976.

HEILBRONER, ROBERT L., and LESTER THUROW, *Five Economic Challenges*. Englewood Cliffs, N.J.: Prentice-Hall, Inc., 1981.

HOWE, IRVING, ed., *Beyond the Welfare State*. New York: Schocken Books, Inc., 1982.

KRISTOL, IRVING, *Reflections of a Neoconservative*. New York: Basic Books, Inc., Publishers, 1983.

KRISTOL, IRVING, *Two Cheers for Capitalism*. New York: Basic Books, Inc. Publishers, 1978.

LINDBLOM, CHARLES E., *Politics and Markets*. New York: Basic Books, Inc., Publishers, 1977.

McCONNELL, GRANT, *Private Power and American Democracy*. New York: Vintage Books, 1970.

SCHOLOSTEIN, STEVEN, *The End of the American Century*. New York: Congdon & Weed, Inc., 1989.

STEINFELS, PETER, *The Neoconservatives*. New York: Simon & Schuster, 1979.

3

Fascism

Fascism was the first major twentieth-century revolutionary, totalitarian challenge to the democratic way of life. While it is true that Russia experienced its communist revolution in 1917, five years before Mussolini's March on Rome, until the Soviet Union emerged victorious from World War II its system was generally perceived to be inapplicable to other nations.

Stripped to its essentials, fascism was the totalitarian organization of government and society by a single-party dictatorship, intensely nationalist, racist, militarist, and imperialist. In Europe, Italy was the first to go fascist (1922); Germany followed in 1933; and then Spain through a civil war that began in 1936. In Asia, Japan became fascist in the 1930s, gradually evolving totalitarian institutions out of its own native heritage. In the Western Hemisphere a semiconstitutional government of a landed oligarchy was destroyed in Argentina in 1943 in a revolt of dissatisfied military officers, and a fascist dictatorship was subsequently built up under the leadership of Colonel (later General) Juan Perón, lasting until its overthrow in 1955.

BACKGROUND OF FASCISM

Social Conditions of Fascism

While communism has been historically linked with poor and underdeveloped nations (Russia in Europe, China in Asia), fascism typically grew in comparatively wealthier and technologically more advanced nations (Germany in Europe, Japan in Asia). In the Americas, fascism saw its most intense development in Argentina, the wealthiest of all the Latin American republics.

While communism has been very largely the product of predemocratic and preindustrial societies, fascism was *postdemocratic* and *postindustrial*: Fascists were unlikely to seize power in countries with no democratic experience at all. In such societies dictatorship might have been based on the military, the bureaucracy, or the personal prestige of the dictator, but it lacked the element of mass enthusiasm and *mass support* (though not necessarily majority support) characteristic of fascism. Moreover, although no fascist system arose in a country without some democratic experience (as in Germany or Japan), there was never fascist success in countries that experienced democracy over a long period.

Paradoxically, experience proved that, in general, the more violent and terroristic fascist movements were, the more popular support they tended to have. Thus, fascism in Germany was both the most brutal and the most popular political movement; in Italy, fascism was less brutal and less popular. Such fascist dictatorships based on mass support are not to be confused with traditional dictatorships such as have existed throughout much of the developing world in the post–World War II era.

In Latin America there have been numerous dictatorships, but they have not been fascist (with the exception of Argentina from 1943 to 1955), for usually they have rested on the personal force of one person, typically a general. Relying as they did on the goodwill of the army, Latin American dictators had no need for—and rarely enjoyed—the mass support that characterized fascism.

Another condition essential to the growth of fascism was some degree of industrial development. At least two principal points of contact existed between fascism and relatively advanced industrialization. First, fascist terror and propaganda required a good deal of technological organization and know-how. Second, as a system of *permanent mobilization for war*, fascism could not hope to succeed without industrial skills and resources.

It may be argued that the connection between fascism and modern industry went even deeper. Every industrial society brings about social and economic tensions. Such tensions can be dealt with in one of two ways: the democratic way or the coercive way. A democratic society recognizes the variety of economic interests and their inevitable conflict (such as between labor and management, agriculture and industry, skilled and unskilled workers) and seeks to reconcile such conflicts by the experimental method of peaceful, gradual adjustment. A fascist state either denied the existence of divergent social interests (abhorring the notion of variety, especially in the form of departures from state-imposed uniformity) or, if it halfheartedly conceded the existence of divergent social interests, it resolved such differences by force.

The difference between communism and fascism on this point may be briefly (and with some oversimplification) formulated in this way: Communism is the coercive way of *industrializing an underdeveloped society*; fascism was the coercive method of *resolving conflicts within an industrially more advanced society.*

In its social background fascism appealed to two groups particularly. First, it attracted a numerically small number of *industrialists* and *landowners* who were willing to finance fascist movements in the hope of getting rid of free labor unions. Industrialists have not, as a class, been any more fascist-minded than other social groups; in countries with strong democratic traditions, industrialists have demonstrated neither more nor less faith than other people in the democratic process. But where democracy was weak, as it was in Germany, Italy, and Japan, it took only a few wealthy industrialists and landowners to supply fascist movements with ample funds.

Where the pressure of public opinion was strongly democratic, individual industrialists who were inclined toward fascism found that supporting fascist groups was bad business. Where democratic traditions were weak, however, leaders of big business, like Thyssen and Krupp in Germany or the Mitsui trust in Japan, found it possible to side openly with the cause of fascism.

The second main source of fascist support—and numerically by far the most important—came from the lower middle classes, mostly in the salaried group. Many individuals in this class dreaded the prospect of joining (or rejoining) the paid-by-the-hour working class and looked to fascism for salvation of their status and prestige. Salaried employees in Germany, Italy, and elsewhere felt jealous of big business, into whose higher echelons they would have liked to rise, but fearful of labor, into whose proletarian world they would have hated to descend. Fascism very cleverly utilized these jealousies and fears of the lower middle classes by propagandizing simultaneously against big business and big labor. Although such propaganda was neither logically nor politically consistent, its very inconsistency both reflected and appealed to the confusion of the salaried class, uncertain as that class was as to where to turn politically.

Widespread negative emotions such as envy and fear, thus, were an important ingredient to allow a successful fascist movement, as was an enemy who could be blamed for social problems. In Germany, Jews were scapegoated as being behind both big business and big labor. Fascism and racism went hand-in-glove because racial hostility generally was stronger in psychologically more insecure lower-middle-class groups than in the better-educated and more affluent middle and upper classes.

Paradoxically, organized labor frequently contributed to the uncertainty and demoralization of salaried employees without meaning to do so. For psychological and other reasons, white-collar workers were typically unwilling to organize into unions during the fascist era. As a result, the incomes of blue-collar workers, particularly those organized in unions, tended to improve much faster than the incomes of salaried workers.

As the gap between the economic status of workers and that of salaried persons widened, the latter became resentful of losing what they considered their rightful place in society and turned to fascism, which promised to keep unions in their place. The leaders of organized labor pointed out that the weak economic position of salaried individuals was their own fault, and that such persons were in error in refusing to organize in order to bring pressure on their employers—an argument that, though valid logically, was not psychologically persuasive. In times of prosperity the divergence between labor and the salaried class may not have been too upsetting politically, but in times of crisis and economic depression the smallest class antagonisms could turn into political dynamite.

Another important social group that showed itself particularly vulnerable to fascist propaganda was the military. Even in a strong and well-established democracy, professional military personnel tend to overestimate the virtues of discipline and unity; where democracy is weak, this professional bias of the military becomes a political menace. Thus, in the early stages of Nazism in Germany, the military class of that nation either openly supported Adolf Hitler or maintained an attitude of benevolent neutrality. The top military leaders of Germany knew that a high proportion of Nazi bosses were criminals and unscrupulous psychopaths, yet they supported the Nazi movement as a step toward the militarization of the German people. In Italy, too, fascism in its early stages received considerable support from army circles, and in Japan fascism developed with the active and enthusiastic support of the army, which had every reason to be the main pillar of a regime committed to imperialist expansion. In Argentina, semiconstitutional government was overthrown in a revolt of the "younger officers" under Juan Perón.

Yet it should be pointed out that the military has often played a leading role in getting rid of fascist regimes, as well as other kinds of dictatorial government. Juan Perón learned this lesson in 1955, and the same thing has happened to many other dictators since the end of World War II, particularly during the 1980s. In countries without an established record of democracy, the military may be as likely to relinquish the reigns of government as to seize them. As a result of the independence often practiced by a nation's military, fascist leaders (like communists) engaged in periodic purges of the armed forces because they realized that the military was one of the few institutions left that retained genuine popular support.

Although fascism was not a direct or necessary result of economic depression in capitalist states, as Marxist-communist theory suggested, there was a connection between the two. In times of economic depression, fear and frustration undermined faith in the democratic process; and where faith in rational methods weakened, fascism was a potential gainer. Owners of small businesses blamed big business for their troubles; big business blamed the unreasonableness of labor unions; labor felt that the only way out was to soak the rich; farmers believed they were not getting enough for farm products and that the prices they paid for manufactured goods were too high; and, worst of all, there was a large mass of unemployed people.

It is often not sufficiently understood that the worst feature of unemployment is not economic suffering, but the feelings of being useless, unwanted, and outside of the productive ranks of society. It is among the spiritually homeless that fascism made serious inroads during a depression: By putting unemployed people into uniform, a fascist movement made them feel that they "belonged," and by telling them that they were members of a superior race or nation, such a movement restored some of their self-respect.

The sense of not belonging is, in a way, characteristic of life in modern industrial society in general. Industrialization and urbanization have debunked and frequently destroyed traditional values, usually without providing adequate substitute values in their place. The disorientation and confusion resulting from these effects of industrialization provided the social and psychological background of fascism and its attempt to restore the old, preindustrial way of life in a modern nation.

Thus, the Marxist interpretation of fascism in terms of class (identifying fascism with, in Stalin's words, "the most reactionary, most chauvinist, and most imperialist elements of finance capital"), is not borne out by the facts. Fascism cut across all social groups. Wealthy industrialists and landowners supported fascism for one reason, the lower middle classes for another, and blue-collar workers for yet a third. Finally, there were the many nationalists and chauvinists in every country who proved themselves vulnerable to promises of conquest and empire. In terms of explicit programs, fascist movements had to make the most contradictory promises to satisfy all their adherents; such contradictions were a main weakness of fascism. But in terms of implicit psychological background, fascism looked within all social groups for the great common denominators of frustration, resentment, and insecurity. These psychological attitudes could easily be turned into hatred and aggression, against both internal and external "enemies."

Because these social and psychological attitudes were not the monopoly of any one social class, fascism managed to appeal to large masses of people in some countries. When Adolf Hitler joined the Nazi party in 1919, he was member No. 7. Within fourteen years Nazism became the greatest mass movement in German history, numbering in its ranks representatives of all groups of German society, from hobos to members of the imperial family. By 1932 the Nazi vote had mounted to 14 million, and in March 1933, some 17 million Germans (almost half the total ballot) voted for Nazi candidates. Several more millions voted for nationalist and militarist parties that were Nazi in all but name. It is obvious that 17 million voters cannot consist exclusively of wealthy bankers and industrialists and that only a party with national, rather than class, appeal could have obtained so many votes. In no other country was fascism ever as widely popular as in Germany, but all fascist regimes possessed considerable public support.

Psychological Roots of Totalitarianism

The clue to understanding fascism in nations like Germany and Japan lies in broad social forces and tradition. In these countries the authoritarian tradition was predominant for centuries, while the philosophy of democracy was a frail newcomer. In both Germany and Japan, democracy was negatively associated with Western powers who had invaded these countries during the nineteenth century. As a result, the German or Japanese citizen with fascist tendencies was no outcast and might well have been considered perfectly well-adjusted to his or her society.

Much in the implicit habits and customs of German and Japanese culture tended toward the authoritarian way of life, and the road from authoritarianism to fascism was short. In democratic societies, on the other hand, the appeal of fascism can be more fruitfully judged from the angle of individual psychology. Traditional analysis of political dictatorship has centered on the motivations of dictatorial leaders, driven by lust for power and sadistic cravings for domination. The followers and subjects of a dictatorship are viewed exclusively as "victims" who just happen to fall into the misfortune of oppressive rule. Every insurance company knows that some people are more accident-prone than others, and every police officer knows that some individuals are more likely to commit crimes than others.

Similarly, it is not inaccurate to suggest that some nations are culturally more "dictatorship-prone" than others. Plato's psychological insight led him to suggest in the *Republic* that constitutions grow not "from stone to stone," but "from those characters of the men in the cities which preponderate and draw the rest of the city after them." The very existence of an authoritarian mass movement like fascism depends on the desire of many individuals to submit and obey.

Rational democrats may not understand why individuals would prefer to obey rather than to take the responsibility of making decisions for themselves; rational democrats take it for granted that citizens should make their own decisions rather than have their actions dictated by others. But this democratic attitude overlooks the comfort of having others make one's decisions for one. Children love the feeling of being sheltered and secure behind the benevolent power and authority of their parents. The mark of a mature adult is the willingness and capacity to stand on one's own feet, to take responsibility and to be independent of others. Yet relatively few people fully attain this sort of maturity; the process of growing up is painful, and many people fear a cold, competitive world where they must struggle for themselves without the care and omnipotence of parental love and security. In human beings there is a latent tendency toward dependence based on the parent-child relationship. The totalitarian system, whether communist or fascist, appeals to those who seek the parent-child relationship, those who grasp for security through dependence.

What are some of the traits that characterize an authoritarian personality, particularly the personality attracted to the fascist type of authoritarianism? Some characteristics are a tendency to conform compulsively to orthodox ideas and practices; emotional rigidity and limited imagination; excessive concern with problems of status and strength; strong loyalty to one's own group, coupled with vehement dislike of perceived outsiders; and stress on discipline and obedience rather than on freedom and spontaneity in human relations such as education, sex, family, religion, industry, and government. The group (or ethnocentric) element in the fascist personality was perhaps the single most important one, although no one element in itself conclusively defines a personality as authoritarian.

The key role of the family in the formation of basic attitudes is brought out by all clinical and theoretical studies; but the family is not, after all, an isolated and independent agent. Rather, it reflects the predominant goals and values of a society, and it constitutes to the child the cultural and psychological representative of society at large.

No nation is ever completely authoritarian or completely democratic, just as no single human being is. In each case it is a question of quantity and degree, though differences of quantity eventually become differences of quality. Although there has been no major fascist mass movement in the United States, it is a matter of record that some Americans looked upon German and Italian fascism in the 1930s as the "wave of the future" (as it was called in a book of that title) and that others sympathized with Spanish and later Perónist fascism.

Dependence and submission in a totalitarian society give a person the security for which he or she hungers but deny individual self-expression and self-assertion, the needs for which are as deeply embedded in human nature as is the desire for security. Thus denied, these drives turn into repressed hostility and aggression, for the expression of which fascism provided two channels; one for the ruling class, and one for the ruled. Within the apparatus of a dictatorial party and government, there is a typical pattern: kneeling before the superior above, pressing down on the subordinate below. Only the leader need not kneel before anyone. Below the top leader—"Big Brother," as George Orwell called this authoritarian figure in his novel *1984*, the classic fictional portrait of totalitarianism—each member of the party and government hierarchy must kowtow to someone higher up, although in return he or she may tread on those lower down.

Those people outside the ruling class, however, have no one to command; they have only to obey. How can they express their hostility and aggressiveness? Since the vast majority of people in a totalitarian state form the group of those who must take orders but not issue them, this is a serious problem for every dictatorship. Although dictators claim officially to be universally beloved, they know that there is much repressed hatred and hostility directed (or capable of being directed) toward them and their regime.

The solution of totalitarian dictatorships is to direct this latent hostility of the people against *real or imaginary enemies*. For the communist, the enemy might have been the bourgeoisie, Trotskyites, or Wall Street. Hitler chose Jews as the target of German aggression, and 6 million Jews perished in the Holocaust as a result. Later, new enemies took their place with the Jews: Britain, the United States, Churchill, Roosevelt, Bolshevism, the churches. When the end of the war was near, Hitler and his cohorts unleashed their vengeance on the German people themselves by refusing to negotiate a surrender; if they had to go down, the German people had to be destroyed with them. In Perónist Argentina, American imperialism and international finance were the chief targets of fascist hate propaganda.

To those who cannot be masters of their own fate, fascism promised mastery over others; and if fascism could not deliver the triumphs it promised, the hatred of the people turned against their leaders, as it did against Benito Mussolini, who was tried before a committee of Partisans in northern Italy in April 1945, executed, and then strung by the heels from a lamp post in Milan for public display. Having taught his people violence and hatred, Mussolini reaped what he had himself sown.

The psychological interpretation of totalitarianism—fascist or communist—is of particular value where the prevailing cultural pattern is not authoritarian; that is, where it takes some personal deviance to break with the democratic pattern of the environment. Thus, in societies like Britain or the United States, the psychological analysis of people who have embraced communism or fascism is of great value, because from such an analysis emerges a definite pattern of personality factors that are typical of many American fascists or communists. These people are often misfits.

It would be futile, however, to explain the strength of fascism in Germany or Japan, or of communism where it has been successful, by means of personal psychology alone. It can be argued that an American or an English citizen who embraces communism or fascism is not well-adjusted, comes from a broken home, or has had an unhappy childhood, for example—but the same can hardly be said of the 17 million Germans who voted for Hitler in 1933 or of the many millions of individuals who sincerely embraced communism throughout a score of countries. Where totalitarianism assumes the proportions of a mass movement, its main avenues must be the great social, economic, historical, and cultural forces and traditions of a nation.

FASCIST THEORY AND PRACTICE

Doctrine and Policy

Although fascism, like communism, is a movement that has existed in many places, it has no authoritative statement of principles such as communism does in the *Communist Manifesto*. Moreover, there is no fascist state in the world today. During the Nazi regime (1933–1945) Germany was the most powerful fascist state in existence, and world fascism was very largely directed, financed, and inspired by German intelligence and resources. After the defeat of the fascist Axis powers (Germany, Japan, and Italy) in World War II, however, there was no major fascist state; Spain and Argentina never possessed anything like the worldwide influence that Nazi Germany had until 1945, nor were they as fascistic.

The absence of a universally recognized, authoritative statement of fascist principles is not total. Hitler wrote *Mein Kampf (My Struggle)* (1925–1927), a guide to his tortured thought, and Mussolini's *Doctrine of Fascism* (1932), a more moderate statement of fascist principles, expresses the Italian brand of fascism. The latter served as a model for most other fascist movements in the world because it is broader in outlook—Nazism, a specifically German brand of fascism, proved less suitable for export, except by force. There is even less of a written statement of Japanese fascistic principles, evolving more gradually as did rather than emerging relatively full-grown as in Germany and Italy.

Although there is no fascist manifesto with undisputed authority, it is not too difficult to state the basic elements of the fascist outlook:

1. Distrust of reason
2. Denial of basic human equality
3. Code of behavior based on lies and violence
4. Government by an elite group
5. Totalitarianism
6. Racism and imperialism
7. Opposition to international law and order

Distrust of reason is perhaps the most significant trait of fascism. The rational tradition of the West stems from ancient Greece and is a basic component of the West's characteristic culture and outlook. Fascism rejected this tradition of Western civilization and was frankly antirationalist, distrusting reason in human affairs and stressing instead the irrational, the sentimental, and the uncontrollable elements in people. Germany emphasized "blood and soil" and the concept of *Volk* ("the People"); Japan sought to revive in altered forms the ancient practices of Shinto (Japan's indigenous religion) and Bushido (a feudalistic code for military men, emphasizing loyalty, bravery, and the valuing of honor above life) to bolster a militaristic state religion.

Psychologically, fascism was *fanatical* rather than reflective, *dogmatic* rather than open-minded; consequently, each fascist regime had its taboo subjects such as race, or empire, or the leader—the nature of which demanded that it be accepted on faith alone and never critically discussed. During the fascist regime in Italy (1922–1945), Mussolini's picture was shown in every classroom in the country over the caption "Mussolini is always right."

Communist states, too, have had the taboo issue of Marxism-Leninism, a set of final truths that could not be questioned. In addition, there were more passing taboo subjects as defined by the top party leaders in the former Soviet Union and other communist states, and as are still defined in China and elsewhere.

As a matter of basic principle, democracy recognizes no taboo issue: There is no subject that cannot be questioned or challenged, not even the validity of democracy itself. In practice, of course, democracies do not always live up to that ideal. Under conditions of stress and strain, an individual as well as a group may take refuge in the temporary shelter of a taboo and postpone facing reality, even if it is impossible to shut it out forever. Since totalitarian regimes operate in a permanent state of high tension and crisis, the taboo is part and parcel of their normal environment. Democracies succumb to the temptation of the taboo and its false security only in periods of exceptional strain. Along these lines, it is significant that the United States Supreme Court's decision upholding the Smith Act (under which advocacy of revolution was a criminal offense) took place in 1951, at the height of the Korean War. In the 1960s a more tolerant mood prevailed, and the Supreme Court progressively eliminated restrictions on the constitutionality of revolutionary propaganda and organizations.

The *denial of basic human equality* was a common denominator of fascist movements and states. While democratic societies do not always live up to the ideal of human equality, they at least accept some concept of equality as a long-term goal and presupposition of public policy. By contrast, fascist societies affirmed human inequality and defined it as an ideal.

The concept of human equality goes back to the three roots of Western civilization. The Jewish concept of one God led to the idea of one humankind, since all people, as children of God, are brothers and sisters. The Christian notion of the inalienability and indestructibility of the soul led to the ideal of the basic moral equality of all people. The Greek-Stoic concept of reason posited the oneness of humankind on the basis of reason as the most truly human bond that all people share.

Fascism rejected the Jewish-Christian-Greek concept of equality and opposed to it the concept of inequality, which can be spelled out most simply in the contrast of superiority and inferiority. In the fascist code, men were superior to women, soldiers to civilians, party members to nonparty members, one's own nation to others, the strong to the weak, and (perhaps most important in the fascist outlook) the victors in war to the vanquished. The chief criteria of equality in the Western tradition are a person's mind and soul, while the fascist affirmation of inequality was based ultimately on strength. In Germany, there was the Führer; in Italy, *Il Duce*; and in Japan, the god-king: ultimate symbols of inequality.

The fascist code of behavior stressed *violence and lies* in all human relations, within and between nations. In democratic governments, politics is the mechanism through which social conflicts of interest are adjusted peacefully. By contrast, the fascist view was that politics is characterized by the friend-enemy relation. Politics began and ended, in this fascist way of thinking, with the possibility of an enemy—and that enemy's total annihilation.

The democratic antithesis is the *opponent*, and in democratic nations the opponent of today is considered the potential government of tomorrow. (The party out of power in the British Parliament is officially called "Her Majesty's Loyal Opposition," and the leader of the Opposition receives a special salary to do that job well.) While occasionally, as at the 1992 Republican National Convention, outer elements of a political organization can brand its adversaries in harsh moral (as distinct from political) terms, this is the exception rather than the rule and should not be confused with the fascist conception of the "enemy."

The fascist knew only enemies, not opponents, and since enemies represent evil incarnate, total annihilation was the only solution. This doctrine applied to domestic as well as to foreign enemies; thus, the Nazis first set up concentration camps and gas chambers for German citizens and only later used them for non-Germans.

Concentration camps and slave labor camps, as under Hitler and Stalin, were not incidental phenomena in totalitarian systems but were and remain at their very core. It is by means of concentration and slave labor camps that totalitarian regimes have sought to destroy the moral person in men and women and to deprive them of the last residue of individuality. The technique of brainwashing deliberately seeks to warp a person's mind to the point where the person will publicly confess to crimes that he or she did not commit and perhaps could not have committed. After a period of brainwashing, victims no longer have a mind of their own; they merely play back, like a cassette tape, what is expected of them. The example of China, among other places, demonstrates that concentration and slave labor—or "reeducation"—camps sadly remain a practice of governments in the world today.

By institutionalizing organized mass murder and torture in concentration camps and slave labor camps, totalitarian regimes have demonstrated to the entire population what is in store for anyone in disfavor with those in power, and at the same time have provided the shock troops of the regime with a peacetime outlet for savagery and fanaticism. Immediate death was often considered too humane a penalty by such regimes; moreover, the slow death suffered in concentration or slave labor camps had greater demonstration value than the clean, old-fashioned method of the execution squad or the gallows.

Government by an elite group was a principle that fascists frankly opposed to what they called the "democratic fallacy," which is that people are capable of governing themselves. The concept that only a small minority of the population—qualified by birth, education, or social standing—is capable of understanding what is best for the entire community, and of putting it into practice, was not an invention of twentieth-century fascism. Plato, one of the first Western political philosophers, strongly believed that only one class, the "philosopher-kings," is fit to rule a society. The contrary belief, that the people as a whole are capable of self-rule (especially including women, minorities, and nonproperty-owners), is of relatively recent origin.

Although the fascist idea of government by a self-appointed elite was undemocratic, such a government did not always lack popular approval. Strange as it may seem to the democrat, throughout history people frequently have approved of autocratic governments. Approval alone, however, is not evidence of democracy. What makes a government democratic is that it is based on popular consent given regularly in free elections. In fascist regimes, even when the government enjoyed popular approval, it was carried on independently of popular consent—without free elections, a free press, or a freely functioning opposition.

The fascist leadership principle expressed the extreme form of the elite concept. It reflected the irrational emphasis of fascist politics; the leader was said to be infallible, endowed with mystical gifts and insights. In a conflict between popular opinion and the fascist leader, the will of the leader prevailed; the leader alone represented the public interest—the way all people would think if they knew what was best for the whole community, while the people expressed only individual whims and desires not necessarily in harmony with public good.

Totalitarianism in all human relations characterized fascism as a way of life rather than as a mere system of government. Many dictatorships, particularly in Latin America, applied the authoritarian principle only in government. As long as the people did not make any trouble politically and did not interfere with the rule of the dictator and his henchmen, they could often lead their own lives relatively freely. Education, religion, business, and agriculture have not been touched very much by simple political dictatorships. By contrast, fascism was totalitarian; it employed authority and violence in *all* kinds of social relations, whether political in nature or not.

With regard to women, fascism was antifeminist. Women, said the

Nazis, should stay in their place and their concern should be the famous three K's—*Kinder, Küche, Kirche* (children, kitchen, church). Since women were considered incapable of fighting in war, they were automatically second-class citizens according to the fascist view, and they were excluded from leadership positions in government and party. They may have had the right to vote, but since that right in fascist countries meant only the right to be enthusiastic about the leader and his party, it was not much of a practical asset.

Within the family the father was the leader, and his wife and children may have received a strong dose of domestic authoritarian government, which had more effect on their everyday lives than the operations of the political government in the nation's capital. In the extreme case of Nazi Germany, the contempt for women was finally demonstrated in the official ridicule of the institution of marriage as a false Judeo-Christian prejudice, and German women were encouraged to produce children for the fatherland outside of wedlock.

Fascist countries also preferred to employ male teachers in schools. From the fascist viewpoint, the purpose of schools was to teach discipline and obedience, specifically to prepare boys for military service and girls for domestic activities. In a program of such importance, fascist educators felt women teachers should play subordinate roles.

Thus, it can be seen that fascist totalitarianism, unlike traditional dictatorships, sought to control all phases of human life, political or not. In Germany, fascism began this control before birth by promoting certain population policies; and it reached beyond life into the grave by deciding who should live and who should die.

Fascism was also totalitarian in its means. It used any form of coercion, from verbal threats to mass murder, to obtain its goals. By contrast, the traditional authoritarian dictatorship was, and is, more restrained in its means and resorts to murder only on a limited scale. Thus, when Latin American leaders have been ousted, they often have been permitted to assemble their family and peacefully depart to a foreign country.

Racism and imperialism expressed the two basic fascist characteristics of inequality and violence as applied to the society of nations. Fascist doctrine held that within a nation, the elite is superior to the mass and may impose its will upon the latter by force. Similarly, among nations, the elite nation is superior to others and is entitled to rule them. German fascism went furthest in racist, imperialist policies. A straight line led from the theories of German-Nordic "race" superiority to the murder of millions of people. The German objective of world domination included the elimination of some nations through genocide and the enslavement of the rest. After Germany's expected defeat of Britain and the Soviet Union, the United States was next on the list.

Italian fascism was for a long time (from 1911 to 1938) remarkably free of exaggerated race theories; early Italian fascist propaganda concentrated on the idea of reviving the old Roman Empire. In 1938, however, Mussolini announced that the Italians were a pure and superior race, and he became more closely tied to Hitler's Germany. Japanese racist theories found practical expression in the concept of "co-prosperity", under which Japan would dominate Asia and the Pacific.

Racism and imperialism have not been an exclusive monopoly of fascism, however. During World War II the Soviet Union annexed Estonia, Latvia, and Lithuania. After the war it held onto portions of Germany, Czechoslovakia, Poland, Finland, and Romania. Russian domination of the multinational Soviet Union became increasingly stressed as time went on, differing only in degree from the Great Russian superiority concept held in czarist Russia. Indeed, Russian ethnocentrism contributed in no small part to the breakup of the Soviet Union. During the 1960s, and 1970s, China, too, used the propaganda argument of race and color in its struggle with the Soviet Union for supremacy in the communist world and for leading developing nations—mostly composed of nonwhites.

In democracies as well there is racism; tribalism is as old as the human race. In the United States, for example, racial discrimination has corroded the application of democratic ideals. The fundamental question in determining whether a particular government is seriously or truly racist, however, is the extent to which racism is imbued as an official policy of government and of what that racism consists. Fascist states were officially racist, and their racism could be very substantial indeed.

Opposition to international law and order, or war, is the logical outcome of fascist beliefs in inequality, violence, elitism, racism, and imperialism. While nonfascists (except nonresisting pacifists) accept war as a tragic fact of life, as something that should be abolished if it were possible, fascists raised war to the level of the ideal. As Mussolini put it, "war alone brings up to their highest tension all human energies and puts the stamp of nobility upon the people who have the courage to meet it."

Any type of international organization assumes some form of government by consent, which is directly contradictory to fascist *government by force*. Also, equality of states before the law of nations is a basic principle of international order. The fascist concept of the elite led to the leadership of one nation over the society of nations, as it did to the leadership of one person within a nation's government. Fascist states limited or declined from participation in international organizations in which they were expected to abide by majority decisions and in which policy-making was carried on by methods of discussion rather than by force.

The fascist regimes of Italy and Germany had no use for the League of Nations; Germany withdrew in 1933 and Italy in 1937. In the Organization of American States, Perónist Argentina did all it could to prevent effective cooperation among the American republics—a policy later copied by Fidel

Castro in Cuba. Fascist regimes opposed international law and order because they opposed national law and order. Politics was simply the expedient, and no means were out-of-bounds. What happened internationally was merely an extension of principles used to govern domestically.

Fascist Economics: The Corporate State

The corporate state applied fascist principles of organization and control to the economy. The fascist economy was subdivided into *state-controlled* associations of capital and labor, and each association had a monopoly in its trade or occupation. Thus, in fascism as in communism, the one-party state was the ultimate arbiter of capital and labor.

The philosophy of the corporate state rested on two assumptions: First, the individual should not be a politically articulate citizen, but only a worker, entrepreneur, farmer, doctor, lawyer, or whatever. General political problems were assumed to be too complicated for the masses, who were expected to understand only those issues that bore directly on their vocational or professional work. Second, members of the ruling elite were supposed to understand broad problems that affected the entire society; therefore, they alone were qualified to govern.

The democratic concept rejects the corporate approach to economic and political organization for several reasons. First, it is not always easy to separate economic from political aspects. Tariffs seem to be a purely economic issue, yet they directly affect political and diplomatic relations with other states. Immigration seems at initial glance to be an economic problem, yet involved in it are a host of political and diplomatic issues. Economic aid to other nations has profound military and political aspects as well as economic effects. Moreover, a free economy appears to be a prerequisite of a free political system, just as a command economy is appropriate only for a nondemocratic society.

Second, democratic theory holds that only the one who wears the shoe knows where it pinches; the mystic knowledge or insight of a ruling elite is no substitute for the experience of the ruled—or, as Aristotle put it, the guest is a better judge of the meal than is the cook. Fascists insisted that the cook not only ought to be the final judge of the product but should impose that judgment on the guests, by force if necessary.

Finally, democratic theory rejects the fascist assumption that members of one particular class are superior in judgment to the rest of the people and are therefore the nation's natural rulers. It also rejects the assumption of fascist doctrine that only an elite group has insight into the public good. From the democratic viewpoint, only the divine has a perfect understanding of Truth with a capital *T*, but everyone is capable, at least partially, of seeing truth with a small *t*.

What the one-party state, with secret police and concentration camps, was to the political side of fascism, corporatism was to its social and economic sides. Just as in the political sphere fascism replaced the pivotal concept of individual liberty with unlimited state authority, so in the economic sphere it replaced the free welfare economy—be it capitalist, socialist, or middle of the road—with state coercion. The objective of the corporate state was to guarantee the power of the state, not promote the welfare of the individual.

More specifically, the ultimate objective of corporate organization of the economy was the preparation of a *permanent war economy*, because aggressive imperialism was the ultimate aim of fascist foreign policy. It is true that virtually all nations have a military, but then national security is the first requirement of all states. What differentiated the fascist war economy from that of other countries in times of peace was that fascist states saw war as an end in itself, glorified war, and positively sought war to pursue expansionist ambitions.

The Italian fascist regime set up a corporate state that was to show the Italians and the world that fascism was not a mere reaction against democratic capitalism and socialism but a new creative principle of social and economic organization. The economy was divided into syndicates, or associations, of workers, employers, and professionals. Only one syndicate was recognized in each branch of business and industry, and although membership in a syndicate was not obligatory, the payment of dues was. Syndicate officials were either fascist politicians or persons demonstrating loyalty to the fascist regime. In effect, these associations of workers and employers were instruments of state policy, with no will or life of their own. Because each syndicate had a monopoly of organization in its field, state control was made that much easier.

To make this method of control more nearly complete, the fascist government established *corporations*, which were administrative agencies in a given industry designed to unite and control the syndicates of workers and employers in that industry. According to law, the syndicates were autonomous; in reality, however, they were run by the state. The corporation, supreme instrument of fascist economic organization, made no pretense of autonomy, being but an administrative agency of the state in no way different from the other tools of fascist government.

Despite the name, the fascist corporation was in no way similar to the business corporations of democratic countries. They had nothing in common. The Italian fascist corporation was a government unit, whereas the typical business corporation was and is a company of limited liability, owned by private citizens, and engaged in competitive enterprise.

It is a mistaken conception that fascist enterprise was in some sense "capitalism with a demonic face." Fascist industries were operated according to government edicts to accomplish government ends. There is all the difference in the world between enterprises run by the sovereign authority to accomplish its purposes and those operated by private, profit-seeking individuals and entities in a competitive market to satisfy the demands of independent consumers.

Though in the fascist economy some private owners of capital were allowed to retain nominal ownership and some of the fruits of their productive energies, this increasingly became less the case in Germany, Italy, and Japan as World War II progressed. All of these nations' resources—material and human—were thrown into the war effort. These countries' economies, in fact, far from representing some form of degenerate capitalism, came in time to resemble nothing so much as what the Soviet Union's economy presented in its decrepit stage.

As in politics, so in economics: Those countries that emphasize political freedom also practice economic freedom (of whatever shade), and those nations that have been politically unfree have also generally not practiced economic liberty. The reasonably closer approximation of fascist economies to communist economies stems in part from mutual roots of the two. Mussolini started out as a collectivist socialist, and Hitler had the insight to realize that the most likely converts to Nazism were communists, not democrats whether of the socialist or capitalist stripe.

Italy's much-advertised corporate state did not represent any new principle of social and economic organization; rather, it merely signified that economic relations, like all other aspects of society in the totalitarian system of fascism, could not be left to the free interplay of competition. In Mussolini's own words, the essential bases of the corporate state were a *single party, a totalitarian government,* and an atmosphere of *strong ideal tension.* The Fascist party provided the first two essentials of the corporate state; the strong ideal tension was induced by ceaseless propaganda of expansionist imperialism.

The first real test for the corporate state in Italy came with that country's entry into World War II in June 1940. Fascist Italy revealed itself wholly unequal to the task of fighting a major war, not only from the military and political viewpoint but also from the standpoint of economic efficiency. For twenty years the corporate state had sacrificed the welfare and happiness of a poor people to the dream of a powerful empire and the megalomania of a would-be conqueror of continents, yet when the first real test of battle came, Italian fascism failed on the economic front as conclusively as it did on the military front. In its ultimate economic non-productivity, too, fascism resembled communism. The economic legacy of the corporate state was not wealth and empire but the loss of world standing, followed by poverty and destitution.

In Germany under Hitler there was some initial economic growth, but this was tied in large part to war preparation. Whether Germany's fascist economy would have been productive in peacetime circumstances is a moot question; Hitler's program was based on war, and it brought Germany ultimately both military and economic destruction.

After the execution of Mussolini in the spring of 1945, the Italian people destroyed whatever vestiges were left of the corporate state and embarked on a new chapter of economic rehabilitation based on a mixture of economic freedom and political democracy. Much of the fascistic economic ruin of Italy and Germany was ultimately paid for by the American taxpayer, as the United States poured billions of dollars into these countries after World War II to help them recover from fascism and war, and to secure them from communism. After the war the economies of Germany and Italy (as well as Japan) were among the fastest-growing in the world, and they have provided standards of living undreamed of during the fascist era.

In the Western Hemisphere, Colonel Juan Perón, speaking for the fascist regime in Argentina just after its successful coup of June 1943, declared his admiration for the fundamental conceptions of the corporate state at the very moment when Italian fascism, the model and inspiration for Argentine fascism, had reduced Italy to ashes and ruins. To Argentina under Perón, as to other nations, the corporate state brought inflation and meatless days—in a country that had been the world's largest exporter of meat. Above all, corporatism in Argentina (called (*justicialismo*) meant the end of free labor unions and their replacement by government-sponsored puppet organizations. Employers, too, were put under the control of the government. Finally, the Perónist regime followed the corporate systems of other fascist states, and command economies everywhere, in dedicating the economy to the rushed development of heavy industry and the manufacture of armaments. Thus, *justicialismo*, which set out to defend justice against both capitalism and socialism, became the servant of a militaristic dictator and his political machine, until both were overthrown in 1955.

SPANISH FASCISM AND CONTEMPORARY FASCISM

It will be noted that fascism is referred to in the past tense here, reflecting the author's view that fascism properly understood possesses very little chance of even minimal reemergence on the world stage for the foreseeable future. As long ago as 1954, in the first edition of this book, its original author wrote: "Is fascism still a threat in the leading democratic nations? The tendency now is to say emphatically "No!"

Not all political scientists share the perspective of the present author. Before considering contemporary fascistic movements or potentialities, however, it is worthwhile to review the experience of Spain, both because of its intrinsic interest and because virtually it alone provides a case history of a fascist regime that endured for a number of decades. Thus, the Spanish experience with fascism rounds out presentation of the subject proper, and by offering the most recent example of a fascistic nation suggests what the real possibilities for fascism may be today.

Spanish Fascism

Following the collapse of the Axis powers in World War II, there remained three fascist countries: Spain, Portugal, and Argentina. Of these, *perónismo* was overthrown in Argentina in 1955, and the experiences in Portugal were not as significant as those in its larger Iberian neighbor, Spain.

Francisco Franco came to power in Spain in a civil war that lasted three years, took 600,000 lives, and became in the late 1930s an emotional cause comparable to the Vietnam War in the 1960s. The Spanish Civil War began in 1936 when Franco and several other nationalist generals rebelled against the government of the Spanish Republic. The generals were actively aided by two other anti-Republican forces: a varied group of monarchists, who wanted to overthrow the Republic in order to restore the Spanish monarchy; and the Falangists, a group of self-conscious fascists who hoped to create in Spain the kind of system that already existed in Italy and Germany. During the course of the war, General Franco emerged as the leader of the Nationalist (anti-Republican) forces and adopted the fascist ideology of the Falange as the rallying creed of his new regime.

The occasion for the revolt in Spain was the growing inability of the Republican government to maintain order in the face of mounting and often violent unrest among important segments of Spanish society. One source of conflict was regionalism: the demand of several provinces, notably Catalonia in the northeast and Basque provinces in the north-central sections of the country, for greater autonomy from the central government in Madrid. Republican efforts to grant greater autonomy to Catalonia heralded, from the standpoint of Spanish nationalists, the disintegration of central authority and so were bitterly opposed by them.

A second source of conflict was the issue of clericalism, another long-standing division in Spain. The Catholic Church had been a staunch supporter of the Spanish monarchy, and the attitude of organized Catholic groups toward the Republic was mixed. The most conservative clerics denounced the Republic, and some priests later took up arms in the Nationalist cause; more moderate Catholics initially supported the Republic and participated in the elected government. This support was undermined, however, by strongly anticlerical clauses in the constitution of the Republic directed against ordinary priests, who were being paid from the public treasury; against influential religious orders, especially the Jesuits; and against parochial schools, which dominated the educational system. The constitutional clauses reflected the intense anticlericalism of the Republican forces. Among the anarchists—the most extreme Republicans—anticlericalism was literally a burning issue, for they sacked and razed numerous churches and monasteries.

A third source of conflict was economic, involving basic unresolved issues in both the agricultural and industrial sectors. In the 1930s Spain was still predominantly an agricultural country; but it lay stagnant and underdeveloped in the hands of landowners who behaved like feudal barons rather than modern landlords. The laborers or tenants who worked this land lived in grim poverty and insecurity. To begin the long overdue process of reform, the Republican government passed an Agrarian Law that distributed unworked estates to individual peasants or peasant cooperatives. This hardly endeared the Republic to the landowners and their agents. At the same time, in the recently developed industrial areas of Spain, conflict was aroused by two special circumstances: the effects of a worldwide economic depression and the growing strength of the anarchist movement.

Unlike both socialists and communists, whose aim was to win political power by gaining control of the institutions of government—in one case democratically, in the other by revolution—the Spanish anarchists aimed at direct appropriation of farms and factories by the workers who labored there. The goal was not to seize the state but to dismantle the government and replace it with associations of workers who would own and control the resources, tools, and organizations of production and distribution. In addition, the anarchists used distinctive tactics in carrying on their revolutionary struggle: periodic political strikes leading to paralyzing general strikes, and sporadic acts of violent destruction.

The anarchists posed a continuing threat not only to business interests and landowners who were the immediate objects of their strikes and violence but also to the political leaders of the Republic. Whatever steps the government might take to deal with pressing economic and social issues were subject to disruption through the extreme actions of the anarchists. In fact, the government had little real chance to solve the country's deep-seated economic ills, for throughout its life the Republic felt the chilling effects of worldwide economic depression.

Bitterly divided over basic issues of separatism, clericalism, and socialism, the political groups of both Left and Right became increasingly polarized, as the authority of the Republic declined. By the election of 1936—the last legislative election of the Spanish Republic—the opposing forces had coalesced into two major blocs: the Popular Front that supported the Republic; and the National Front, made up of its enemies. Although the Popular Front emerged as the single strongest group in the electorate (the registered voters) and the Cortes (the Spanish parliament), the Republic's days were numbered. Arrayed against it were monarchists, the Catholic party, fascists of the Falange, and conservative elements in the army. Although divided among themselves on a number of important issues, these groups were able to coordinate their actions with growing effectiveness. On the other side, the Popular Front comprised an uneasy coalition of moderate liberals, democratic socialists (themselves divided into competing factions), communists, Trotskyites, and anarchists. They drew together in defense of the Republic but agreed on little else. Even in the throes of the ensuing civil war, communists and anarchists carried on their bloody fratricidal struggles, as much intent on murdering their opponents within the Republican ranks as in fighting the common enemy.

As dissatisfaction with the Republic continued to grow, militants on both sides began to arm and train for combat. Conspiracies flourished, coups were attempted, and assassinations became commonplace. The country was slipping into chaos. Then several generals, including Franco, a hero of wars in Morocco, intervened to restore order. This was hardly unusual in Spanish politics: The army had a long history of political intervention. Within the preceding century the army had imposed a liberal constitution, supported a succession of military coups, deposed one monarch and restored another, and established a military dictatorship. On July 17, 1936, the generals acted again, as they saw it, to secure the unity and greatness of the Spanish nation. The civil war that followed lasted three bloody and devastating years.

From the very beginning the civil war was not confined to Spain alone but involved the governments, soldiers, and ordinary citizens of the major world powers. The Spanish Civil War became one of the melancholy preludes that prepared the way for World War II. Both sides in the Spanish Civil War appealed for help to the outside world, and the responses foreshadowed the greater tragedy soon to follow. The Western democracies—France, Britain, and the United States—to whom the Republicans appealed for help, adopted a policy of nonintervention, including an embargo on all shipments of arms; the dictatorial governments of Italy, Germany, and Portugal, to whom the Nationalists appealed for help, paid lip service to nonintervention but eventually supplied arms, matériel, and several divisions of troops to aid the Nationalist cause; the Soviet Union encouraged the Republicans with strong words and sent limited aid to stave off disaster at least temporarily. In view of the vital assistance provided to the Nationalists by Italy and Germany, the democracies' policy of nonintervention and embargo in effect condemned the Republic to defeat, while the showdown with fascism was postponed only briefly. The Spanish Civil War provided Hitler with an ideal opportunity to try out the weapons and strategies that would be used on a much grander scale a few years later.

Following the final defeat of the Republic in 1939, Franco, self-proclaimed *El Caudillo*, or Leader, proceeded to consolidate his power and exacted bloody retribution from his enemies. His *New State*, or National Revolution, bore striking similarities to Mussolini's *Fascismo* and Hitler's *National Socialism*. Like his fellow dictators, Franco affirmed the totalitarian nature of his regime. He declared that "Spain will be organized from a broad totalitarian approach by means of all national institutions guaranteeing its totality, unity, and continuity."

In keeping with this conception, all political opposition was outlawed and suppressed, the economy was organized into corporatist structures subordinated to Franco's political objectives, and trade unions were replaced by a *Syndical Organization*, led by active Falangists, to which all workers were forced to belong. One way or another, Franco handled the basic issues that had bedeviled the Republic—separatism, clericalism, and socialism. Catalonia was occupied as a conquered territory and ruled under a policy of subjugation designed to destroy not only its political expressions of separatism but also its cultural roots. The Catholic Church regained its position of privilege and influence, and Franco won warm approval from the Catholic hierarchy in Rome as well as in Spain. Agricultural and industrial workers were forcibly integrated into syndicates in which they could raise no independent voice of protest, and their standard of living fell sharply. In every city and town heavily armed troops patrolled the central streets—the visible strong arm of an oppressive police state.

Yet from the outset there was a fundamental difference between Franco and his fellow dictators. While Mussolini and Hitler rose to power as leaders of revolutionary political parties dedicated to fascist ideology, Franco came to power as a victorious general whose primary base of support was the Spanish army, not the fascist Falange party. Franco made effective use of the Falange—both its ideology, which provided a doctrine for his National Revolution, and its militant members, who provided loyal managers for his New State. During the first decade of the regime, from 1939 to about 1950, its distinctive Falangist character was especially evident. But unlike his Italian and German counterparts, Franco was first and foremost a conservative general rather than a revolutionary fascist, and as political circumstances changed, he gradually restricted the role of the Falange while relying increasingly on the traditional bulwarks of Spanish conservatism—the army, the Church, the landowners, and, at the end, the monarchists.

A major political circumstance that directly affected the character of Franco's regime was the defeat of the Axis powers in World War II. Reminded of the debt he owed from the civil war, and urged to join the international fascist cause, Franco sent his Blue Division to fight beside Hitler's army in Russia. Yet he avoided a formal declaration of war against the Allies, which the more militant Falangists advocated and the Axis would have welcomed. No doubt Franco's military sense that Spain was simply too weak to fight another war overcame whatever ideological fervor he felt for the fascist cause. In any event, by 1942, with the Allied invasion of North Africa, it was clear to Franco that he had nothing to gain by joining the Axis side; the fascist dictators would face their Armageddon alone, without Spain. This policy of neutrality saved Franco's regime but confirmed Spain's unenviable position as a country isolated politically as well as economically backward.

It is one of history's unanswered questions what would have been Spain's course of development had the fascist states emerged triumphant from World War II. But it is a matter of historical record that while Franco relatively stressed more fascistic principles of economic organization during the 1940s, Spain experienced stagnation and recurring economic crisis. Whether measured by real income, volume of output, or rate of capital accumulation, the achievements of the regime were negative or meager. By 1950 per capita income had yet to regain its prewar level. Franco's fascist corporatism was not conducive to growth. Only after 1951, with the introduction of capitalist-style competitive markets, did significant advancement occur.

Conditions of life began to change in the 1950s. Caught up in the Cold War with the Soviet Union, the United States saw Spain as a likely place for military bases, and the prevailing political and economic neglect came to an end. The Pact of Madrid, formally ending Spanish isolation, was signed in 1953. Benefiting both from large-scale American loans and investments as well as Franco's newly capitalistic economic program, Spain started on the road toward economic development and political change.

Economic progress was rapid and marked; political change was slower and less certain. In the 1950s industrialization proceeded at a steady pace despite serious difficulties with the high inflation and balance-of-payments deficits. The experience confirmed the confidence of Spanish leaders in capitalist economic policies. During the 1960s and into the 1970s, Spain benefited from the general European prosperity; tourism became a major industry, contributing nearly $2.5 billion annually to the economy by the early 1970s, and thousands of Spanish workers streamed over the border to factories abroad, sending home millions of dollars more in remittances to their families. But the sustained growth during this period was due primarily to sound domestic policies: a Stabilization Plan, which dealt with inflation, and three subsequent Five-Year Development Plans. Inevitably, the economic progress had its effects on politics.

The economic growth of the 1950s bore political fruit in the 1960s, with an outbreak of strikes and mass protests. During the 1950s new signs of opposition appeared, rooted not so much in memories of the Republic but in immediate dissatisfactions. By the early 1960s conditions were ripe for major expressions of protest. In 1962 a wave of strikes spread across the country, which clearly revealed the strength and determination of restive workers; in 1965 more than 6,000 students held a mass meeting of protest in Madrid, a dramatic demonstration of increasing pressure for liberalization. Winds of change were also felt in the Catholic Church. A growing liberal faction, composed mainly of younger clergy, sided with the workers and dissidents and demanded the severing of official ties between the Church and the Spanish state. Some accommodation by the government was obviously required.

However visible these signs of opposition had become, there was never a real possibility of overthrowing the dictatorship. The regime itself was enjoying new-found strength. On the international scene Franco had been transformed from political pariah, whose downfall would have been generally welcomed, into valued ally in the Cold War, recipient of substantial American aid. At home, prosperity led to increased support for the regime among middle- and upper-class groups who were the main beneficiaries of the economic upturn. Even the recurring strikes, though troublesome to Franco's government, were not directed toward political reform but toward economic objectives such as higher wages and control of inflation. Among Franco's genuine opponents—former members of the Republican Popular Front—the old dissensions of a generation earlier broke out once again. Anarchists, socialists, and communists resumed their ideological polemics and jockeyed for leadership. Unity on the Left was once more lacking. In these circumstances Franco felt confident enough to permit political concessions: A few independent political groups were allowed to organize, some political prisoners were released from jail, censorship was partially relaxed, and police brutality was muted. During its last years, Franco's regime vacillated between liberalization and repression, but the general trend was in the direction of liberalization. Spain in a sense became a fascistic Yugoslavia; that is, as Yugoslavia under Tito was to communism, Spain became during Franco's later years to the ideology of fascism.

On November 20, 1975, Franco died, peacefully in his sleep. Juan Carlos, whom Franco had designated as his successor in 1969, became King of Spain. The accession of Juan Carlos marked the beginning of a new era. Franco enjoyed widespread popular support until the end—more than 400,000 people filed past his body to pay their last respects—and the response of Francoists to political change was by no means certain. In addition, fears of divisiveness on the Left remained.

In his inaugural speech King Juan Carlos touched upon the broad issues facing his new regime and gave general indications of his own intentions. He acknowledged the popular demand for "profound improvements," the legitimacy of regional claims and the importance of "social and economic rights." He noted that "a free and modern society requires the participation of all in the centers of decision, in the media, in the different levels of education, and in the control of the national wealth."

Within six months Juan Carlos felt ready to move decisively toward democratization. In July 1976 he appointed Adolfo Suarez prime minister. With the king's support, Suarez began to dismantle the Francoist political structure. Amnesties were granted to political prisoners; public meetings were legalized; political parties were allowed to organize; independent trade unions were permitted, as well as the right to strike; Franco's National Movement party was abolished; and a comprehensive Political Bill was enacted to reintroduce basic political rights in anticipation of a general election to be held within the year. Political competition, stifled for so long under Franco's repression, burst into life with remarkable vigor. New parties and coalitions of parties sprang up on all sides.

A month before the election, the Communist party was legalized, and its leader, Santiago Carrillo, an outspoken advocate of Eurocommunism, promptly acknowledged the legitimacy of the monarchy as well as his intention to work for political reconciliation within a democratic regime. Long-time political exiles returned to Spain, including the fabled Dolores Ibarruri, *La Pasionaria*, president of the Communist party since the days of the Republic. It was an emotional time of celebrating and hope, tinged with apprehension about what the future might hold for the fragile institutions of Spanish democracy.

On July 15, 1977, for the first time in forty years, the people of Spain went to the polls in a free election to choose their representatives for the Cortes. Of the eligible voters, 80 percent turned out to cast ballots. The results vindicated the moderate approach of King Juan Carlos and Prime Minister Suarez. Of the 350 seats in the lower house of the Cortes, 165 were won by the Union of the Democratic Center, headed by Suarez; the Socialist Workers Party was second, with 118 seats; the communists third, with 20 seats; and the Popular Alliance (hard-line Francoists) fourth, with 16 seats.

One of the most significant actions taken by Suarez's new government was to apply for membership in the European Community, and later membership in NATO. These moves solidified as they reflected Spain's transition from paleo-fascist holdover to mainstream Western industrial democracy. This transition was capped by the 1992 Olympic games held in Barcelona.

The most serious threat to the new regime came in February 1982, when a group of Right-wing officers, dismayed over the government's apparently irresolute response to continued terrorism on the part of some Basque separatists, attempted a coup to install a military dictatorship. The king's immediate denunciation of the attempt, and the obedience of the armed forces to the king's personal orders, led to the quick collapse of the coup and the arrest of its leaders. A direct challenge to constitutional democracy was convincingly thwarted, thanks in large part to the intervention of Juan Carlos himself.

Most emphatic confirmation of the growing legitimacy of Spanish democracy was the peaceful advent into office in 1983 of a socialist government headed by Felipe Gonzalez following legislative elections. A situation that once might have provoked armed confrontation between Left and Right was accepted as a normal change in democratic politics. The outcome was testimony to the new-found moderation and political responsibility of both the Right and the Left. Groups on the Right, including the military, acknowledged the legitimacy of a socialist premier selected through constitutional procedures, despite their deep opposition to a number of socialist policies; at the same time, the socialists—and even the communists—acknowledged the legitimate role of the armed forces as defenders of the state and refrained from provocative attacks against the military. Like the repudiation of a military coup from the Right, the orderly transfer of power to a government of the Left was evidence of the new stability of Spanish politics.

Fascism Today

With the transition of Spain and Portugal to democracies in the mid-1970s, the last remnants of self-proclaimed fascist states vanished from the globe. And, to consider even these countries truly fascist in the latter decades of Franco's and (in Portugal) Antonio Salazar's reigns would be inaccurate. By the 1960s if not sooner, these countries had essentially become military dictatorships; the trappings of fascism left within them were merely vestigial.

Military dictatorship may be bad, and fascism may be bad, but this does not mean that military dictatorships are fascist. The distinction between the two can be elucidated by exploring further the distinction between *authoritarian* and *totalitarian* forms of government. The latter sought (and in a few countries regrettably still seek) the complete control of all aspects of human social life. There is no part of human endeavor, under a totalitarian regime, that does not fall within the purview of the state, which is typically run by one individual. Stalinist Russia, Nazi Germany, and Maoist China are classic examples of totalitarianism. Pure fascism was totalitarian.

Authoritarianism, by way of contrast, is not as intrusive into each individual's life and leaves significant areas of social experience relatively untouched. Freedom of religion, a fair amount of latitude in economic affairs, a certain degree of leniency in the areas of artistic and even some political expression—all of these characterize the lot of nations living under authoritarian rule. In addition, authoritarian nations are more likely than totalitarian regimes to have some sort of collective governance by a few, even if one man or woman holds the predominant position.

This certainly is not to justify authoritarianism; nor even is it to downplay its significant deficiencies. Rather, it is to define in broadest terms some of differences between totalitarian and authoritarian regimes. There have been various forms of totalitarianism. Fascism was one of them.

Now, to be sure, the word "fascism" is much used today, even though there are no totalitarian-fascist nations extant. To the extent that "fascist" is intended to mean one with whom another disagrees politically, particularly one with a right-of-center view (just as sometimes those with left-of-center perspectives are pejoratively referred to as "communists"), there are many fascists. But in this case the term fascism loses all meaning.

Fascism, properly understood, is the complex of social, economic, political, and military policies practiced by countries such as Nazi Germany and Mussolini's Italy, and Spain during the 1940s. Fascism was an entire way of life.

There are, of course, a number of avowedly fascistic parties around the world—there is, after all, an American Nazi Party, as well as a similar group or groups in most Western democratic nations. However, without exception, these "parties" have no chance of attaining power and are composed almost entirely of misfits or thuggish youths. Occasionally, these groups may cause some property damage, engage in terrorism, or beat some people up (usually immigrants or minorities). They thus are reflective of and pose a social problem, but there is no chance that they will ever attain political power.

It is true that some rightist parties stressing immigration issues—most prominently the French National Front Party, led by Jean-Marie Le Pen—have achieved a level of electoral support that political parties espousing similar platforms did not achieve during the 1960s and 1970s. In Italian municipal elections in October 1991, the anti-immigrant Lombard League received the most votes in the city of Brescia; in Belgium's November, 1991 general election, the anti-immigrant Flemish Bloc received a quarter of the votes cast in Antwerp; and Le Pen's National Front Party won 14 percent of the vote in the March 1992 regional elections in France.

Germany deserves special mention, both because of its history and importance. Xenophobic, anti-immigrant, and racist sentiments are on the rise in Germany, as evidenced in a 1992 government report there showing that attacks on foreigners increased approximately tenfold between 1990 and 1991, to about 2,000 incidents. On the other hand, there are almost a million and a half assaults of all types on individuals in the United States each year: A foreigner in Germany still has less of a chance of being assaulted than he or she would have in the United States.

In 1992 German state elections, far-Right parties did increase their share of the vote compared to 1988, from 3.1 percent in Baden-Wurttemberg to 11.8 percent, and from 2.8 percent in Schleswig-Holstein to 7.5 percent. Over the same period, the far-Right vote increased in Berlin borough elections (in the western part of the city) from 7.5 percent to 9.9 percent. None of these figures indicate significant support, though, and German reunification and concomitant economic dislocation are responsible for much of the recent occurrences there.

The far-Right trends in a number of European nations are troubling, but more because they indicate general dissatisfaction with politics in these countries than because they show any nascent fascist organizations that have a real chance of obtaining power. As with David Duke in Louisiana, the success of these groups is aberrant rather than the norm. Moreover, in Europe, the small percentage increases in support for far-Right parties have been accompanied by similar rises in support for other extremist parties—either of the Left, representing absolutist environmental positions, or those advocating regional separatism. Furthermore, voting percentages for all of these political groups have been highest at regional, municipal, or special elections, indicating that their support is in large part a protest vote; at general elections, mainstream parties (whether Left or Right) continue to receive the overwhelming majority of support.

Moreover, the far-Right parties of today are not fascist, at least as fascism is understood here. They are not goose-stepping, fanatical Nazis, intent on transforming the world; rather, for the most part they are composed of individuals who believe that immigration to their countries is excessive. These people may or may not be racists; they probably harbor racist sentiments, but they generally are not totalitarian. Moreover, they do not officially practice or advocate violence, nor do they favor nondemocratic means of attaining power; they do not promote dictatorial government, nor are they usually militaristic; and, perhaps most importantly of all, for the most part they are not imperialist. While the fascist parties of old were largely outward-looking in their orientation—seeking to change the whole world as well as their own nations—the new far-Right parties are primarily inward-looking: They want to stop immigration, and in some cases deport existing immigrants and their children. These policies may or may not be correct, and they often certainly have racial overtones, but they are not of themselves fascist.

It has been argued that the policies of today's far-Right parties are pre-fascist, and that in time they could develop into fascism. This is potentially so—anything can happen, particularly in politics. However, it remains safe and accurate to say that the new Right parties of Europe are not now fascist, and that they have virtually no chance of achieving significant electoral success in the short to intermediate term running on their current platforms, much less would they have opportunities for electoral success on avowedly fascist platforms.

The true fascists of today remain what they have been since the end of World War II: small fringe groups capable occasionally of causing violence (as in the 1980 Bologna, Italy railway bombing by the fascist Armed Revolutionary Nuclei, which killed 85 people), but far from the political mainstream everywhere. Skinheads, rootless teenagers, white supremacists, anti-Semites, violent substance abusers—these compose the fascist, neo-fascist, Nazi, or neo-Nazi movements in most countries.

The example of the Armed Revolutionary Nuclei is instructive for the light it sheds on contemporary fascist movements. The group's heroes were Hitler, Mao, Muammar Qaddafi, and Juan Perón. Its slogans included: "Long live the fascist dictatorship of the proletariat" and "Hitler and Mao united in struggle." Clearly it was a confused entity. It is interesting to note the connection this group drew among totalitarians of all shades, for in truth such regimes, whether of the "Right" or "Left," are far more similar to one another than they are to the broad range of Right wing and Left wing parties.

There are those who have considered the military dictatorships in such countries as Argentina, Chile, and Greece during parts of the 1960s, 1970s, and 1980s to be semi-fascist. Such is not the analysis here, which sees such regimes as authoritarian military dictatorships. These countries were more similar to Francoist Spain in its latter days than to the Spain of the 1940s, much less to Hitler's Germany or fascist Italy. While they restricted political activity and were sometimes brutal, they interfered less with economic and social life, and were generally not too interested in mass support.

The progress that democracy made throughout the world during the 1970s and 1980s, and that it has continued to make during the early 1990s, has been genuinely significant. One country after another, particularly in Latin America, has shed military dictatorships for popularly elected governments. While a nation's move toward a democratic form of government does not mean it will stay there—as Alberto Fujimori's seizure of dictatorial powers in Peru in 1992 recently shows—neither does a departure from democracy indicate impending fascism.

Fascism was in part a last gasp of nineteenth century colonialism, which Paul Johnson has justly called "a cartographic entity"—that is, it was largely based on notions of domination that political control over large expanses of the globe gave to some nations. Hitler, and to a lesser extent Mussolini, sought such domination. The passing of the colonialist outlook also thus signifies poor chances for fascism ever again to become a factor in the future. As to the concept of economic fascism, whereby wealthy nations prey on less developed ones financially in a way that they once did militarily, this is misleading. There is a great deal of difference between militarily suppressing a country and investing in or trading with it.

The reasonably negligible chance that fascism has for a resurgence does not at all diminish the absolute centrality it had in shaping the twentieth century's political and economic circumstances. Nazi Germany mounted a ferocious challenge to Western democracies, and if its strategy had been a little different (in particular, if it had adopted an alliance with the Soviet Union), World War II could have turned out far differently than it did, with profound implications for the world. One of the lessons, thus, of the fascist experience is the fragility of democracy, and that democracy's success hinges as much on fate as anything else.

A further lesson of fascism is the pull that the irrational continues to exert in purportedly civilized life. Germany was among the most developed of European nations, and yet it was able to descend into a barbarism that would have been unimaginable in the nineteenth century. The Nazis were masters of the symbol, ritual, and mass rally, and the success they had in these areas has serious repercussions for the long-term viability of democracy. Good does not always triumph over evil, nor truth over falsehood, and the success of a form of government at one epoch in the world's history does not mean its permanent victory.

Fascism revolutionized the world by precipitating the collapse of colonialism, as European countries were not able to maintain far-flung outposts following the ravages of World War II. The collapse of colonialism, in turn, led to the birth of over a hundred new nations. Thus it is that fascism, which preached imperialism and racism, helped to contribute to the decline of both. Moreover, fascism moved the world's political dialogue decidedly in a leftward direction. Its defeat and demonstrated utter barrenness rubbed off in a negative manner on anything that could be labeled rightist.

Fascism rearranged the face of Europe. Perhaps most significantly, it led to a largely bipolar world for the forty-five years following World War II, in that its defeat subdued the positions that Germany, Italy, and Japan in the world, and wore out Britain, France, and other nations which had previously played a more dominant role in world politics. This left the United States triumphant and the Soviet Union strategically well-positioned, representing dichotomous ideological perspectives.

FOR FURTHER READING

ARENDT, HANNAH, *Origins of Totalitarianism*. New York: Harcourt Brace Jovanovich, Inc., 1966.

BRACHER, KARL DIETRICH, *The German Dictatorship: The Origins, Structure, and Effects of National Socialism*. New York: Praeger Publishers, Inc., 1970.

DE FELICE, RENZO, *Interpretations of Fascism*. Cambridge, Mass. : Harvard University Press, 1977.

EBENSTEIN, WILLIAM, "National Socialism," in International Encyclopedia of the Social Sciences, XI: 45-50. New York: Macmillan, Inc., and The Free Press, 1968.

FROMM, ERICH, *Escape from Freedom*. New York: Holt, Rinehart & Winston, 1941.

GALLO, MAX, *Spain Under Franco*. New York: E.P. Dutton, 1974.

————, *Mussolini's Italy*. New York: Macmillan , Inc., 1973.

HAMILTON, ALASTAIR, *The Appeal of Fascism: A Study of Intellectuals and Fascism 1919–1945*. New York: Macmillan, Inc. 1971.

HAYES, PAUL M., *Fascism*. New York: The Free Press, 1973.

LUBASZ, HEINZ ed., *Fascism: Three Major Regimes*. New York: John Wiley & Sons, Inc., 1973.

MARAVALL, JOSE MARIA, *The Transition of Democracy in Spain*. New York: St. Martin's Press, Inc. 1982.

NOLTE, ERNST, *Three Faces of Fascism*. New York: Holt, Rinehart, & Winston, 1966.

O'SULLIVAN, NOEL, *Fascism*. London: J.M. Dent & Sons, Ltd., 1983.

PAYNE, STANLEY G., *Fascism: Comparison and Definition*. Madison: University of Wisconsin Press, 1980.

SHIRER, WILLIAM L., *The Rise and Fall of the Third Reich*. New York: Crest Books, 1962.

4

Communism

Communism is the most important ideology to emerge during the twentieth century. Indeed, world history during the second half of the twentieth century is in large part the story of communist growth followed by communist decline. The monumental events in the former Soviet Union, Eastern Europe and elsewhere have irretrievably changed the face of the political world. While one-fifth of humanity remain members of communist regimes in China, Vietnam, North Korea, Laos, and Cuba, the forward practical advance of the ideology is at a full stop.

Continued study of communism is important for at least four reasons: First, because of its intrinsic significance. Second, because it provides a case history of a failed ideology. Third, as a result of the billion people who continue to live in communist systems. And fourth, perhaps most important of all, because the aftermath of communism will play a very significant role in world politics for decades, just as fascism influenced the world for years after its defeat.

MARXIST-LENINIST THEORY

The Economic Interpretation of History

Before Karl Marx, history was interpreted in several typical fashions. *Religious* interpreters saw history as the working of divine providence, and human development as but part of the unfolding of God's design of the whole universe. The main difficulties with this interpretation of history are that divine will is unknown and unknowable to our direct experience, and that there are many contrasting human conceptions of God and of divine plans for humankind.

A second dominant pre-Marxist approach to the understanding of human history was *political*: Great emperors, monarchs, legislators, and soldiers were viewed as the decisive forces in history; and historical writing was largely the record of monarchs, parliaments, wars, and peace treaties. This political emphasis tends to exaggerate the relative role that most people assign to government and politics in the total setting of their lives. It is natural that political leaders and political philosophers consider politics the most important single element in human relations, and political remedies the most important solution to human problems. But human nature and human problems are more intricate than politics; politics is only one approach—and not always the most penetrating one—among many others.

A third major approach, the *hero* interpretation of history, is closely related to the political viewpoint: Most heroes are conventionally chosen from great emperors, monarchs, generals, legislators, founders of new states, pioneering reformers, and revolutionaries. The hero interpretation, however, overstresses the role of the individual at the expense of the larger cultural, religious, social, and economic circumstances that form the background without which there can be no meaningful exercise of leadership. Although it is undoubtedly true that leaders mold events, it is no less true that events mold leaders.

A fourth pre-Marxist approach to the understanding of history stresses the impact of *ideas*: Ideas were conceived (by G.W.F. Hegel, for example) to be the principal causes of the historical process. The material conditions (social, economic, technological, military) of society were thought of as essentially derived from, and caused by, the great motivating ideas. This emphasis on ideas often also implied that history was evolving toward the realization of key ideas, such as freedom and democracy. While this theory undoubtedly contains much that is valid, the exclusive emphasis on ideas as the main driving force in history overlooks the fact that ideas not only generate events but also reflect them. Therefore, to isolate ideas as the chief agent of human action is to neglect the framework of circumstances; circumstances, after all, make some ideas possible and others not, and it is circumstances from which ideas derive their vitality and practical impact.

The study of history may also be focused on war: The phenomenon of conflict is present in all phases of human development; and the birth, rise, and decline of states are often directly connected with warfare. The shortcoming of the *military* interpretation of history lies in its failure to recognize war as the result, rather than the cause, of events. There is no doubt that war often marks a turning point in the life of nations and civilizations; yet the dramatic swiftness and decisiveness of war should not draw attention from the multitude of psychological, ideological, and material factors that lead to war and contribute to its complexity.

Marx's analysis of society was set forth in his *economic* interpretation of history: The production of the goods and services that support human life and the exchange of those goods and services are the bases of all social processes and institutions. Marx did not claim that the economic factor is the only one that goes into the making of history; he argued that it is the most important one, the *foundation* upon which is erected the *superstructure* of culture, law, and government, buttressed by corresponding political, social, religious, literary, and artistic ideologies.

Marx described the relations between people's material conditions of life and their ideas by saying that *"it is not the consciousness of men which determines their existence, but, on the contrary, it is their social existence which determines their consciousness."* In a nomadic society, for example, horses might be considered the principal means of acquiring and accumulating wealth. From Marx's viewpoint, this foundation of nomadic life is the clue to its superstructure of law, government, and dominant ideas. Thus, those who own the greatest number of horses in such a nomadic society would also be the political chieftains who make and interpret the law; they are also likely to receive the highest respect and deference from those tribe members who own no horses. The predominant social and cultural concepts would reflect the dominant economic position of the owners of the horses. Even in religion the impact would not be missing: God might be represented in the image of a swift and powerful rider, and the concept of divine justice and rule would be, in a sense, an extension and magnification of human justice as determined by the horse-owning nomadic chiefs.

In a settled agricultural society, the ownership of land would provide the clue to the political, social, legal, and cultural institutions and conceptions. In such a society, according to Marx, the landowning class governs state and society even if another formal organization of authority exists. Similarly, the landowning class would also set the predominant social standards and values.

Finally, according to Marx, *in the modern industrial society of the last two hundred years, the ownership of the means of industrial production is the master key*: The capitalists—the owners of the means of production—not only determine the economic destiny of society but also rule it politically (regardless of formal and legal façades to the contrary) and again set its social standards and values. The ultimate purpose of the law, education, the press, and artistic and literary creation is to maintain an ideology that is imbued with the sanctity and justice of capitalist property ownership.

The understanding of history has gained immensely from Marx's economic interpretation. It is virtually impossible to write history today without relating economic forces and conflicts to political, military, and international issues. Marx's economic interpretation suffers, however, from the same defect that afflicts all theories that pretend to supply the master key to history: *excessive generalization and simplification.* Whenever a single factor (be it the hero, war, religion, climate, race, geography, and so forth) is required to do the work of explanation and illumination that can only be properly done by several factors, its burden proves too heavy. No single factor has been predominant throughout history, and which factor is the most important in a particular situation is a question requiring empirical inquiry.

In any event or series of events, there is always a complicated pattern of many factors, and it is none too easy to disentangle them. It is difficult enough to identify precisely the component motivations of the actions of one person, because these actions are often mutually contradictory and logically inconsistent. It is even more difficult to isolate the determinant components in a single action of a small group. And it is virtually impossible to generalize about large-scale collective actions and processes throughout the whole of history.

To take a practical illustration: The Marxist interpretation of history holds that *imperialism* is caused primarily by economic interests and rivalries, that it is an essential aspect of capitalism, and that war in the capitalist era is the inevitable result of such imperialist rivalries among capitalist states. There have undoubtedly been examples of imperialism in history, ancient as well as modern, whose origins can be traced to economic factors—some of the colonial acquisitions of advanced capitalist nations like the Netherlands, Britain, and France in the eighteenth and nineteenth centuries can be attributed chiefly to economic forces. On the other hand, contemporary Western Europe and Japan provide examples of flourishing capitalist societies without empires or imperial ambitions, at least as traditionally understood.

Conversely, the examples of the former Soviet Union and to a lesser extent of China show there can be imperialism without capitalism. The Soviet Union annexed the three Baltic countries of Estonia, Latvia, and Lithuania in 1940, and helped itself to portions of Poland, Czechoslovakia, Romania, Finland, Germany, and Japan during or after World War II. In 1951 China occupied Tibet.

Russia followed a policy of imperial expansion before the coming of capitalism and during the capitalist era, and it followed this same policy during its communist stage of development. Indeed, it was only after communism collapsed in the Soviet Union that Russian imperial conquests over the centuries disappeared. Communist imperialism cannot be explained in Marxian economic terms, according to which imperialism is the last phase of an advanced capitalist economy with an abundance of capital that it seeks to invest in less developed areas. The former Soviet Union suffered from scarcity of capital rather than an abundance of it. Its imperial ambitions were motivated, as the imperial ambitions of other nations in the past and present, by a mixture of economic goals and noneconomic forces of national interest, expanding spheres of influence, and history.

Similarly, the Marxian economic explanation of *war* is neither wholly true nor wholly false and can account for only part of the historical reality. There have undoubtedly been some wars that have been primarily caused by economic interests and conflicts. Nevertheless, the economic interpretation misses the core of great and vital conflicts of history.

The Greeks fought the Persians 2,500 years ago not primarily to protect Athenian investments and trade interests in Asia Minor but because they knew that a Persian victory would mean the end of Greek civilization. Although a Persian victory would undoubtedly have entailed serious economic and financial losses for the Greek financiers, the main effect would have been the destruction of the Greek way of life.

To take more recent illustrations, the core of the conflict in the two world wars was not the protection of British investments in Africa or of American loans to Britain and France but rather the more fundamental issue of whether totalitarian militarism was to rule the world. Again, there is no doubt that a German victory in either war would have entailed profound economic losses for the vanquished, but the economic effects would have been relatively minor compared with the effects of forced conversion to a way of life based on a denial of Western tradition.

What the Marxist-communist interpretation misses in the analyses of major conflicts is (1) the element of *power* (which is often the cause rather than the effect of economic advantage) and (2) the clash of *value systems*, which are frequently more important to people than economic interests, whether the values concerned are specifically political, religious, intellectual, or—in the widest sense—the expression of an entire way of life.

In fact, when conflicts of interest are primarily economic, compromise may often be relatively easy. It is when more deeply felt values—individual liberty, freedom of religion, or national independence—are at stake that compromise becomes more difficult. Marx's fundamental error was that he posited a solely economic base to society when, in fact, it is founded on much else.

Dynamics of Social Change and Revolution

Before Marx, social change was usually thought to result from the work of great political leaders, legislators, and pioneering reformers. Marx rejected the traditional emphasis on the force of personality as the principal agent of important social change and looked instead for an explanation in impersonal economic causes. The two key concepts that he used in approaching the problem of basic social change are (1) the *forces of production* and (2) the *relations of production*. The clash between these two is the deeper cause of basic social change:

> At a certain state of their development the material productive forces of society come into contradiction with the existing productive relationships, or, what is but a legal expression for these, with the property relationships within which they have moved before. From forms of development of the productive forces these relationships are transformed into their fetters. Then an epoch of social revolution opens. With the change in the economic foundation the whole vast superstructure is more or less rapidly transformed. (Marx, *Critique of Political Economy*, 1859)

The Marxist conception of the forces of production expresses people's relation to nature and is essentially what today would be called *technological and scientific knowledge*. Marx's notion of the relations of production expresses the interpersonal relations that go into the productive process and includes all that today would be called *social institutions*. Seen in these more modern terms, what Marx roughly suggests is that in every social-economic system there is at first a balance between knowledge and social organization, but that gradually a disequilibrium or lag develops between available scientific knowledge and existing social institutions. *Scientific knowledge grows faster than social wisdom.* As a shift in the earth's plates deep beneath the surface of the ground causes changes in what happens far above it, so will a change in society's material-productive foundation cause a change in the superstructure of laws, traditions and customs—a social earthquake.

Thus, when new productive forces developed within the productive relations of the feudal system, social revolution therefore became—according to Marx—inevitable. The productive relations of feudalism (property relations, market controls, internal customs and tariffs, monetary instability) contradicted the newly developing productive forces of industrial capitalism.

According to Marx, the capitalist system, having run its cycle, now shows the same tendency to rigidity; and it is due to meet the same fate when its productive forces (the capacity to produce) have outstripped its productive relations (law of private property, production for private profit). Like the social systems preceding it, capitalism will eventually stand in the way of scientific knowledge and will not permit technological resources to be fully employed.

What has doomed all historically known forms of economic organization, according to Marx, is the fact that when new productive forces develop, the existing productive relations—that is, the existing social institutions—stand in the way of their proper utilization. Each system thus eventually becomes wasteful in terms of the creative potentialities that have developed in its womb but are not permitted to be born and to grow. The existing generation of institutions desires, as it were, no offspring.

Only public ownership of the means of production can, in the Marxist interpretation, bring into existence a new system of productive relations based on production for common use rather than for private profit that will match the tremendous forces of production actually or potentially known to humanity. People's capacity to produce will find full expression only in a social system in which production is limited only by scarce resources and incomplete knowledge, and not by such faulty social institutions as production for private profit based on the private ownership of the means of production—capitalism.

Marx's insight that people's knowledge of physical nature ("forces of production") grows faster than their wisdom in creating social institutions ("relations of production") is highly important in understanding a vital source of tension and conflict both between and within nations. In international affairs the capacity to produce nuclear weapons has been ahead of institutional arrangements for harnessing the atom for peaceful purposes. Within advanced industrial nations poverty testifies to the fact that the capacity to produce goods and services surpasses the wisdom to create institutions through which all have a fair share.

What distinguishes Marx from non-Marxists is his insistence that basic social change—caused by the excessive lag between advanced scientific knowledge and retrograde social institutions—can be brought about only by *violent revolution* Non-Marxists, on the other hand, affirm that necessary changes can be effected by peaceful means.

In the *Communist Manifesto* Marx explained why violent revolution is the only method of basic social transformation. When technological know-how begins to outstrip the existing social, legal, and political institutions, the owners of the means of production do not politely step aside and allow history to run its inevitable course. Because the ideology of the ruling class reflects the existing economic system, the owners of the means of production sincerely believe that the existing system is economically the most efficient, socially the most equitable, and philosophically the most harmonious with the laws of nature and the will of God.

Marx penetratingly denied that the individual feudal landowner or industrial capitalist obstructs social change out of selfish greed: The resistance of the ruling class to change is so obstinate—making revolution finally inevitable—precisely because it identifies its own values with universally valid ones. The ruling class will, therefore, mobilize all the instruments of the legal, political, and ideological superstructure to block the growth of the forces that represent the potentially more advanced economic system. For this reason, Marx stated early in the *Communist Manifesto* that the "history of all hitherto existing society is the history of class struggles"

Marx could find no instance in history in which a major social and economic system freely abdicated to its successor. On the assumption that the future will resemble the past, the communists, as the *Communist Manifesto* says, "openly declare that their ends can be attained only by the forcible overthrow of all existing social conditions." This is a crucial tenet of Marxism-Leninism, and one that clearly distinguishes it from democracy.

Marx had no clear-cut notion of how the political transformation from capitalism to communism would come about. Though in the *Communist Manifesto* as throughout most of his other statements on the problem, he spoke of the need for revolution, he was occasionally less dogmatic. Speaking in 1872 at a public meeting in Amsterdam, Marx conceded that the working class can travel on different roads in its quest for power: "We know that we must take into consideration the institutions, the habits and customs of different regions, and we do not deny that there are countries like America, England, and—if I knew your institutions better I would perhaps add Holland—where the workers can attain their objective by peaceful means. But such is not the case in all other countries." Marx never fully pursued the implications of this distinction, however, and the orthodox opinion of Marxism-Leninism has remained that fundamental social and economic change is impossible except by class war, violence, and revolution.

During the early 1830s there occurred two major peaceful social transformations that Marx failed to appraise properly. In 1832 the passage of the (political) Reform Act in England meant that the government of the nation would thenceforth be shared by the aristocracy and the middle classes, with the weight shifting in favor of the latter. At about the same time, Andrew Jackson's election as President of the United States effected a similar peaceful shift in class power by bringing the common person into American politics and successfully challenging the supremacy of the elites from Virginia and New England who had previously dominated American national politics.

These changes in Britain and the United States were more than just political victories: They commenced and were reflective of a permanent shift in the distribution of social and economic power in both nations, the kind of basic change that Marx had in mind. When revolution swept over Europe in 1848, England was spared because the aims of the revolution of 1848—winning for the middle class its proper share of social and political power—had already been peacefully obtained by the British middle class in 1832.

If Marx had given the political (as distinct from economic) factor its due weight, if he had fully grasped the importance of the Reform Act in England and the changes wrought by the Jacksonian era in the United States, he might have realized that socialism, too, might be accomplished without violence in countries that possessed democratic traditions strong enough to absorb far-reaching social and economic changes without resorting to revolution. A recognition of cultural and political factors in the equation of social change, however, would have amounted to a virtual abandonment of the central position of Marx: History is the arena of economic class wars in which ruling classes always defend their positions to the bitter end.

When Marx allowed, occasionally, that in countries like England, the United States, or the Netherlands violent revolution would be unnecessary in transforming capitalism into the classless proletarian society, it is obvious that what the three countries had in common was *political democracy*, providing the means for peaceful social change. This concession that in a few politically advanced countries revolution might be unnecessary has always been troublesome to communists. Lenin took up the question in *State and Revolution* (1918), his best-known and most influential political tract, claiming that by 1917 "this exception made by Marx is no longer valid"; England and the United States had developed bureaucratic institutions "to which everything is subordinated and which trample everything under foot." Between 1872 and 1917 both England and the United States broadened the suffrage and moved steadily in the direction of more political and social reform. In 1884, only one year after Marx's death, a British Liberal leader, Sir William Harcourt, stated, "We are all socialists now," indicating that all parties accepted basic social and economic reform.

Since the historical record of the years 1872–1917 seemed plainly to contradict Lenin's dogma, it was necessary to rewrite history. Far from admitting that Britain and the United States had moved toward greater political and social democracy and equality since 1872, Lenin maintained that both of the countries had become more repressive, authoritarian, and plutocratic.

During the twentieth century the United States has experienced a peaceful revolution of social reform: It started early in the century with Theodore Roosevelt's Square Deal and Woodrow Wilson's New Freedom, continued in Franklin D. Roosevelt's New Deal, and climaxed with Lyndon Johnson's Great Society. The experience in Britain has been similar. More recently, the partial departure in Britain and the United States from the welfare state shows that social reform can peacefully move in the other direction as well.

The communist insistence on violent revolution as the only way of basic social change vitiates Marxist doctrine at one central point. According to Marx, the conditions of one's existence determine one's consciousness, and social change is, therefore, not the product of mere will and free choice. Where the conditions of society permit peaceful change from private to public ownership of the means of production, the use of force is, in a deeply Marxian sense, un-Marxian.

The communist concept of universal revolution and dictatorship is in harmony with Marx's theory of consciousness only in societies in which the conditions of social and political life have created a general distrust in the possibility of peaceful change; it is out of harmony in nations whose democratic consciousness is real. By insisting on universal revolution and dictatorship as the one and only method of change, communists have in fact proclaimed the un-Marxian doctrine that regardless of historical, cultural, social, economic, and political conditions, a uniform consciousness—the creed of communism—can be imposed everywhere by sheer force.

Marx's Humanism and the Concept of Alienation

Marx's emphasis on class struggle and violent revolution as the conditions of basic social change proved a liability to the spread of Marxism in both communist and noncommunist countries. In communist countries, the experience of Stalinist totalitarianism showed more thoughtful people—particularly in the younger generation—that a doctrine of hatred easily leads to the practice of brutality, and that no true community can be founded on the perpetuation of hostility and violence. In noncommunist countries the experience of nonviolent and far-reaching social change has convinced many that Marxian class war and revolution are not only morally dubious but practically unnecessary, and that therefore desired changes can be accomplished better through gradual amelioration based on social cooperation than through sudden, fundamental changes based on revolution and class struggle.

In their search for a humanist basis for Marxian communism, liberal-minded writers in both communist and noncommunist countries have concentrated on Marx's early thought, particularly his *Economic and Philosophical Manuscripts*, written in 1844, when he was twenty-six. Interest in this early writing has been greatly stimulated by the fact that it focuses on the concept of "alienation" (estrangement), a concept that has become topical in contemporary thought as a result of popular works of social psychologists and existentialist philosophers.

The concept of alienation has many roots. In its Judeo-Christian origin, alienation signifies the separation of humans from God through sin. In early nineteenth-century German philosophy, Hegel formulated a more secular version of alienation that, though still tinged with religion, emphasized the individual's separation from his or her essence, spirit, the absolute. Marx rejected the concept of alienation as developed by the religious tradition, particularly in its Protestant Calvinist version, as well as in Hegel's metaphysical version, since both approaches seemed to him too abstract, too divorced from people in their concrete reality.

Further, the *romantic* doctrine of alienation greatly influenced the young Marx. Although in the early nineteenth century Romanticism was primarily a worldwide literary movement, its manifestation in Germany also had strong social and philosophical elements. In its social outlook, Romanticism was essentially a protest against the spread of industrial civilization. Romanticists felt that industrialism was destroying the natural and organic bonds of life that characterized preindustrial, medieval Europe. They lamented that people in industrial society were becoming "alienated" from nature, from their fellows, from family and nation, and—most important of all—from even themselves. In despair, some Romanticists felt that the only escape from the evils of industrial civilization was the return to agrarian life—a highly impractical proposal.

In this sense, communism can be seen as a partially conservative doctrine. It is to some extent a reaction against the Enlightenment and industrialism; this reaction was first signaled by Rousseau. In the *Communist Manifesto* Marx lamented the loss caused by the bourgeoisie of "idyllic relations." Also, the ninth measure he foresaw in the *Communist Manifesto* as being the likely course of development toward communism in most advanced nations is: "combination of agriculture with manufacturing industries; gradual abolition of the distinction between town and country, by a more equitable distribution of the population over the country." Because 1975 and 1978, over a million people died in Kampuchea (Cambodia) as the Khmer Rouge there attempted forcibly to implement this measure.

In the *Economic and Philosophical Manuscripts*, Marx shared the concern of Romanticists about alienation, but he arrived at a different conclusion because he saw the problem of alienation in a different perspective. Marx had the insight to see that industrialism in some form was here to stay and that it should be welcomed as the best hope of liberating humankind from the ills of material want, ignorance, and disease. While the Romanticists saw the evil in industrialism, Marx perceived alienation as the result of *capitalist* industrialism.

Under capitalism, Marx argued in the *Manuscripts*, people are alienated from their work, the things they produce, their employers, their fellow workers, themselves. Workers do not work, Marx wrote, in order to fulfill themselves and their creative potential, for their work "is not voluntary but imposed, *forced* labor." Their work does not satisfy their own needs but is merely a means of satisfying the needs of others—the capitalist employers who use them as an instrument for making profits. Capitalism thus dehumanizes the worker, who "sinks to the level of a commodity," and produces palaces for the rich but hovels for the poor. Workers are alienated from their employer, who appropriates the products of their labor and enjoys pleasures and freedoms denied the workers. They are also alienated from their fellow workers, with whom they compete for employment and favors bestowed by the employer. Money is the most visible symbol and expression of alienation under capitalism, the "visible deity" that transforms all human relationships—including love, friendship and family—into monetary relationships. Marx specifically affirmed the need for a society in which love cannot be bought, but can "only be exchanged for love."

Marx showed in his *Manuscripts* that the human condition includes ethical and psychological as well as economic elements. Postulating communism as the only solution to the human alienation engendered by capitalism, Marx defines communism in the *Manuscripts* without reference to hatred or class war:

> Communism is the *positive* abolition of *private property*, of *human self-alienation*, and thus the real *appropriation of human* nature by and for man. It is, therefore, the return of man himself as a *social*, that is, really human being, a complete and conscious return which assimilates all the wealth of previous development. Communism as a fully developed naturalism is humanism and as a fully developed humanism is naturalism.

In ambitious language born of youthful confidence, Marx also said that communism "is the solution to the riddle of history and knows itself to be this solution."

Yet this phase of Marx's humanistic and ethical concerns did not last long. In a crucial change of outlook, influenced perhaps by his growing familiarity with poor living conditions and struggles of the working class, he quickly abandoned the humanistic and ethical elements in his conception of communism. In *The German Ideology*, written jointly with Friedrich Engels in 1846, the ethical socialists were attacked for talking of "human nature, of man in general," rather than of people as members of the proletariat—the working class. The individualistic leanings of the *Manuscripts* were increasingly replaced by the concept of *class*, and the ideal of love and fellowship was replaced by that of class struggle and hatred.

In the *Communist Manifesto* (1848), Marx specifically ridiculed the philosophical socialists who talk about "alienation of humanity" or about the "philosophical foundations of socialism," conveniently forgetting that he himself had defined communism in the *Manuscripts* as "the true solution of the conflict between existence and essence, between objectification and self-affirmation, between freedom and necessity"—all philosophical terms taken directly from Hegel's vocabulary. In the *Communist Manifesto* Marx also attacked the ethical socialists as "utopians," because they reject revolutionary action and "wish to attain their ends by peaceful means, and endeavor, by small experiments necessarily doomed to failure and by the force of example, to pave the way for the new social gospel."

Marx was aware that in his *Manuscripts* he had expressed ideas similar to those of the ethical and philosophical socialists. He therefore decided not to publish what he later considered an insignificant juvenile aberration. In fact, the *Manuscripts* were not published during his lifetime, and after his death Engels, as his literary executor, also refrained from publishing them.

They were finally published in German in 1932; an English translation appeared nearly three decades later.

From the analytical and historical viewpoint, Marx cannot be transformed into a basically liberal humanist: From *The German Ideology* on, he saw in the humanistic, ethical, and liberal socialists the most dangerous enemies of communism. Most of Marx's polemical writings were directed not against avowed opponents of communist doctrines but against socialists who happened to disagree with him on what socialism meant and how it was to be achieved. This attitude of Marx was later repeated by Lenin and other communists who also saw as their chief opponents not capitalists, but socialists or even discredited communists.

From Marx to Lenin

The nature and deeper meaning of philosophical ideas can frequently be inferred from their appeal and impact. In the countries of Western Europe and North America, the inevitability of revolution as Karl Marx preached it had little impact; the democratic tradition in those countries kept the door open for peaceful change. Although many social reformers have agreed with some of Marx's indictments of society, they have refused to embrace a philosophy of class hatred and war to remedy social injustices.

In nineteenth-century Russia, conditions for the acceptance of Marxian ideas were more favorable. Of all the major states in Europe, Russia was first in illiteracy, economic backwardness, religious obscurantism, oppression of minorities, political despotism, and social inequality. Marx's prophecy, clothed in the language of scientific concepts, of the eventual liberation of humanity from bondage and oppression through revolutionary action made a strong impression on Russian radicals. *Das Kapital*, Marx's magnum opus, was translated into Russian before any other language; oddly enough, the czarist censors permitted publication of the work on the ground that it would not be read by many because of its difficult style.

Among the Russian followers of Marx, Vladimir Lenin (1870–1924) was both the leading theoretician and the most agile and effective practical politician. An important earlier contribution of Lenin's to the theory of communism is to be found in his pamphlet *What Is to Be Done?* (1902)—the concept of the *professional revolutionary*.

Marx, reflecting the nineteenth century's respect for people's capacity to think for themselves, had assumed that the working class would spontaneously develop its class consciousness in the daily struggle for economic existence, and that its leadership would come largely from its own ranks. Lenin had much less confidence in people, even if they belonged to the proletariat. Communist activity, Lenin believed, is to be carried on along two lines. First, workers are to form labor organizations and, if possible, communist parties, operating openly, legally, and as publicly as conditions allow. Second, side -by- side with such organizations, there are to be small groups of professional revolutionaries, patterned after the army and the police, highly select and entirely secret. Lenin did not care whether the professional revolutionaries were of proletarian origin as long as they did their job well. The organizations of the professional revolutionaries must be highly disciplined and centralized, he argued, and must constantly guide and supervise the communist-led economic and political associations—the labor unions, the party, and the rest.

Lenin also advised the professional revolutionaries to infiltrate and form cells in all existing social, political, educational, and economic bodies in society, be they schools, churches, labor unions, or political parties. But above all, he advised infiltration of the armed forces, the police, and the government.

Lenin made it clear that communists should engage in illegal work even where legal communist parties are permitted. He believed that legal opportunities should be utilized to the fullest extent, but he specifically advised communist activists to work through front organizations, constantly changing names and officers of organizations and always keeping the ultimate objective in mind: revolutionary seizure of power.

In particular, the secret nucleus of professional revolutionaries is responsible for the recruitment and training of spies, saboteurs, and agents for all other activities relating to intelligence, foreign and domestic. While there are bridges between the legal communist parties and the inner rings of spies and agents of the professional revolutionaries, since necessity often compels the choice of such agents from party ranks, ideally the two sets of organizations are to be kept separate.

Lenin always thought of himself as a faithful follower of Marx, yet as a person of action operating in Russia rather than in Western Europe, he was bound to modify Marxism in its practical revolutionary application. In his concept of the professional revolutionary, Lenin consciously introduced a new approach to class war and communist organizational strategy, which permanently changed the nature of Marxism as understood by communist parties. Other modifications by Lenin have created a body of ideas and attitudes, Marxism-Leninism, which combine some original ideas of Marx with their reformulations by Lenin.

In comparing Lenin with Marx, one is struck by the difference of temperament, background, and outlook. Marx was above all the scholar and polemicist, whereas Lenin was primarily the master organizer, politician and leader. Marx sought to change the whole world by his ideas; Lenin had one fixed, and more limited, goal: to seize power in one country, Russia, and reshape it according to his communist principles. Yet the most important difference between the two men is not found in explicit fundamental doctrine but in the differing implicit premises of their times. Marx was a product of the nineteenth century, and though he tried to envision and help create a society of the future, he always retained the world view typical of the nineteenth century. By contrast, though born in the nineteenth century, Lenin developed to maturity and stature in the twentieth century, and his deepest attitudes were typical of this century.

Marx's belief in the *primacy of economics over politics* not only resulted from his economic interpretation of history but also reflected a typically nineteenth-century bias. The prevailing view in the nineteenth century was one of almost unlimited faith in economic forces as the main engines of social and economic progress. Thus liberals in the nineteenth century confidently expected that the right economic policies would ensure domestic stability and progress, solve the problem of poverty, and lead to universal peace. Laissez-faire economic policies within nations and free trade among nations were the magic formula that would lead to a world without force and oppression. Marx's formula was different from that of his liberal contemporaries, but it was nevertheless an economic formula.

Lenin, by contrast, in typical twentieth-century style, believed in the *primacy of politics over economics*, although in terms of explicit doctrine he always considered himself a faithful follower of Marx's economic interpretation of history. Because of his deep commitment to the overriding importance of politics, Lenin spent most of his revolutionary energy building an organizational apparatus in czarist Russia. Although before the revolution he spent seventeen years abroad, mostly in Switzerland, he kept in close touch with the day-to-day activities of the Bolshevik group he led. His ability to maintain his leadership and the discipline of his revolutionary movement from afar for so many years testify to his political acumen and dynamic personality as a leader and organizer.

Because Marx was so committed to nineteenth-century economic thinking, he expected that the first communist revolutions would occur in Western Europe, with its advanced capitalist economies. Marx shared the general conviction of his century that the laws of economic development could not be interfered with, and that each country had to go through the various stages of capitalism before it became ripe for communist revolution. By contrast, Lenin looked at the problem from a more political viewpoint. The task of communist leadership and of professional revolutionaries, he believed, was to attack and destroy the existing social and political system where it was weakest—in the economically less developed areas of Europe, Asia, Africa, and Latin America. Lenin agreed with Marx that communist revolution was inevitable, but he asked: Why wait until capitalism has matured? Why not smash it where it is politically and organizationally weakest—that is, in economically backward Russia and in areas of Asia and Africa?

As a Russian, Lenin profoundly understood the weak social cohesion and low organizational energy that mark economically underdeveloped societies. In such countries the mass of population consists of poor peasants living in isolated villages, with inadequate means of communication. There are few or no independent labor unions and practically no middle class—the backbone of anticommunist resistance in economically more advanced nations. In his own country Lenin noticed that a comparatively small force of army and police could keep control over a vast—but unorganized—mass of people. Lenin therefore believed that with a relatively small but highly disciplined and well-organized counterforce, power could be wrested from the apparatus of the existing system. "Give us an organization of revolutionists," he wrote in *What Is to Be Done?*, "and we shall overturn the whole of Russia." By 1917, Lenin did have the organization he needed, and overturn Russia he did.

Lenin also had a deep understanding of the importance of the underdeveloped areas in the balance of world power. Marx shared the typical nineteenth-century conceit that Europe was the center of the world and that underdeveloped areas were merely colonial appendages of leading European powers. As a Russian, with one foot in Asia, Lenin was free of this European prejudice. He was the first important political figure in the twentieth century to see the world as more than Europe and, above all, to see the underdeveloped areas as an increasing factor in world politics. Many people in Western nations still do not grasp the crucial importance of underdeveloped areas; Lenin—with his genius for political analysis and organizational strategy—understood at an early date that communism must first be established in underdeveloped countries before the hard core of anticommunist resistance, Western Europe and North America, could be tackled. A master strategist, Lenin hoped that once the "soft underbelly" of world capitalism had been conquered by communism, Western Europe and North America would not put up too much of a resistance.

Both Marx and Lenin believed in the inevitable victory of communism throughout the world, yet this common belief was marked by significant differences. Marx expected that a communist revolution would lead to the *dictatorship of the proletariat*, an essentially economic entity, over the *bourgeoisie*, also a basically economic category. Marx even hoped that in such a temporary dictatorship of the proletariat there would be a variety of parties and groups, all united in the common goal of destroying the last remnants of capitalism but differing on lesser issues.

By contrast, Lenin's concept of dictatorship meant, in more political terms, the dictatorship of the Communist party over the proletariat, since he had little faith that the working class had the political understanding or spontaneous organizational ability to secure the existence and expansion of a communist state. In 1904 Leon Trotsky—then an orthodox Marxist critical of Lenin—predicted that the dictatorship of the party would be replaced by the rule of its Central Committee, "and, finally, the dictator will take the place of the Central Committee." Trotsky's prediction of Stalinism as the inevitable outgrowth of Leninism came true and was sealed tragically by Trotsky's own life experiences: In 1929 he was forced by Stalin to leave Russia, and after years of wandering from country to country, he was assassinated by a Stalinist agent in Mexico in 1940.

Marx believed that communism in a particular country would be preceded by internal economic crises, and that each country would develop its own revolutionary movements when conditions were "objectively ripe." Lenin, on the other hand, took a more activist and worldwide view, combining ideological universality with Russian national interest. Particularly after the success of the November Revolution of 1917, he saw that Russia would become the base and nerve center from which communist revolutions in other countries would be engineered.

Finally, Marx and Lenin viewed international politics from different perspectives. In nineteenth-century fashion, Marx took comparatively little interest in international politics, since economic forces and tendencies were presumed to determine world affairs. By contrast, Lenin saw every problem from its global perspective, both before and after he seized power in Russia. Even while Russia was still reeling under the devastating impact of military defeat, revolution, and civil war, while millions of Russians were starving, Lenin devoted much of his thought and political effort to organizing centers of communist activity throughout the world, particularly in Asia, which he correctly sensed would be the most fruitful area for eventual communist expansion.

COMMUNISM IN THE SOVIET UNION

The Early Years

The most important communist state was the former Soviet Union. Notwithstanding that communism was not a monolithic bloc—particularly as time went on—the Soviet Union's inspiration and influence were essential to the success that communism experienced.

The czarist regime in Russia was overthrown in a noncommunist bloodless revolution in March 1917. Before acquiring its new communist masters, it had seemed that Russia would have the opportunity to develop democratic institutions for the first time in its history.

The majority of Russians wanted political liberty as well as fundamental social change. Inexperienced in the conduct of public affairs, however, and failing to understand the nature and goals of the opposing communist forces, the new democratic government of Alexander Kerensky allowed the Bolsheviks, led by Lenin and Trotsky, to subvert and quickly destroy the new regime.

Between March and November 1917, the Bolsheviks (the party was not known as the Communist party until 1919) used three classic methods of gaining power. These methods were repeated later in almost identical fashion in other countries.

First, the Bolsheviks presented themselves in their propaganda as a people's party dedicated to liberty, democracy, and social justice, and opposed to all forms of reaction and social injustice. In an agrarian nation like Russia, the communists emphasized the need for agrarian land reform and encouraged the seizure of land by the peasants even before they were in control of the government. A generation later the Chinese communists proclaimed themselves no more than agrarian reformers, thus following the pattern of propaganda established by the Russian communists in 1917.

The second technique the Bolsheviks employed was infiltration of other political parties, trade unions, soldiers' councils, and local government. In particular, the communists managed to infiltrate and gradually disrupt the Social Revolutionaries, the largest party in Russia, dedicated to social reform and especially concerned with the circumstances of the peasants. This technique of infiltration was again employed by communists during and after World War II, when they tried to and did take over other socialist parties in a number of countries.

The third method used by the Bolsheviks in their revolution was force. In free elections in the summer and fall of 1917, the Bolsheviks polled about one-quarter of the total vote. Though this represented a far from negligible proportion, the Bolsheviks accepted the fact that in a free election they could not win. Thus, in November 1917, they seized the key positions of power in St. Petersburg and Moscow, and from there the revolution quickly spread all over Russia. Opposition to communist revolution sprang up in various parts of the country—aided by Western powers—and a civil war ensued that lasted until 1921.

The ravages of World War I, followed by the devastations of the civil war, made immediate social reform impractical. Lenin was realistic enough to see that the Russian people would starve to death if communist principles were imposed at that time. As a result, he inaugurated in 1921 the New Economic Policy (NEP), which permitted limited private ownership—this policy's main object was to maintain and increase production on the farms and in the workshops and factories by retaining the old capitalist incentives of efficiency and profit. The application of the NEP for seven years gave the Soviet Union a breathing spell, allowing the new rulers to consolidate their power and giving the Soviet people the temporary illusion that the bark of communism was worse than its bite.

The Economy

Lenin died in 1924. Of the Russian people, Winston Churchill wrote: "Their worst misfortune was his birth; their next worst—his death." In

1928 Joseph Stalin decided that the time had come to put communist principles into practice, and he withdrew the temporary concessions to capitalism made earlier by Lenin. The first Five-Year Plan, starting in 1928, aimed primarily at the rapid industrialization of the Soviet Union and secondarily at the collectivization of farming. In 1917 many peasants had sympathized with Bolshevism, not for reasons of theory or ideology, but because the Bolsheviks promised them the land that they and their ancestors had tilled and coveted for centuries.

The reasons that motivated Stalin to force collectivization on the peasants were manifold. First, the communist rulers felt that agricultural production would be increased by mechanization, and that this could be more easily done on large-scale, collectivized farms than on small, individually owned ones. Second, individual ownership and operation of farms denied a key principle of communism, namely that all means of production be transferred to public ownership. Collectivization would bring agriculture in line with industry, which was developed from the start on the basis of state ownership and operation. Third, the communist rulers saw in continued individual farm ownership a direct political and psychological threat to the acceptance of coercive political direction from the center.

The independent peasant had to be transformed into a dependent agricultural proletarian; as a member of a collective farm, the peasant was constantly working with others, talking to others, eating with others, and could thus be more easily supervised and regimented.

Another reason behind collectivization was the need for labor for the newly developing industries in the cities. The required labor force could be obtained only by mechanizing agriculture and thus saving human labor. Finally, collectivization had an important military object. In case of war, the collectives were to provide the nucleus for organized resistance behind the lines. During World War II these military expectations were largely fulfilled. The Germans were never completely able to suppress Russian guerrilla activities behind their military lines.

The cost of fundamental social and economic change in Russia was heavy. In the process of collectivizing the farms during the years from 1929 to 1933, about 7 million peasants lost their lives. Half that number died during the "collectivization famine," and the other half perished in slave labor camps in Siberia or the Arctic. To show their resistance to collectivization, the peasants slaughtered as much livestock as they could for their own use, so that by the time collectivization was accomplished, the number of livestock had greatly decreased. The number of cattle, for example, decreased by about one-half between 1928 and 1934, and did not regain its pre-1928 level until the 1950s and 1960s. As a result, there was widespread famine during the early 1920s, particularly in the Ukraine, where peasant resistance was strengthened by the force of nationalism. When the Nazis invaded the Ukraine during World War II, they initially were welcomed by many inhabitants, so great was the hatred of Ukrainians for Soviet policies. Years later in 1991, when the Soviet Union was in the throes of dissolution, Ukrainian nationalism was a major factor leading to its final fall.

The Soviet Union never renounced collective agriculture, and severe discontent with it—and low agricultural production—always remained. Peasant pressure ultimately forced the government to allow members of the collective farm to devote part of their time to a small plot of land under their own personal management; they could then sell the products of their own effort on the open market at higher prices than those paid by the government (which was able to buy farm products at artificially low prices, bearing little relation to the national forces of supply and demand). Although the peasants' own piece of land amounted to only an acre or so, it supplied them with nearly half of their income, and these dwarf holdings, amounting to only 3 percent of all Soviet farmland, accounted for about one-half of all Soviet production of potatoes, meat, vegetables, and eggs. There was not enough individual production to make a real difference, however; all grain production remained disastrously under collective control.

Agriculture was the Achilles heel of the Soviet economy. Not only did the agricultural sector absorb annually an exceptionally high proportion of investment funds that might otherwise have been devoted to producing additional consumer goods, but a series of poor harvests from 1979 through 1982 forced the Soviets to spend precious foreign currency to import large quantities of grain from abroad. The weather was partly to blame, but the roots of the failure went far deeper. The organization of Soviet agriculture in large-scale collective farms, and the artificially low prices for agricultural products mandated by Soviet planners to assure that food was available for everyone, lessened the incentive for individual farmers to work efficiently. Moreover, as agriculture depended increasingly on widespread use of complex machinery, it suffered from the general inadequacies of the Soviet civilian industrial sector—poor-quality machines, uncertain supply, and shortage of spare parts. As a result, despite the disproportionately high investment in agriculture, yields per acre remained far below Western standards.

In the field of industrialization, progress under Soviet communism at first was immense, as was first proven by Russia's ability to withstand the onslaught of Germany during World War II. Though the Soviet Union received some strategic supplies from the United States during the war, the bulk of the industrial production required to defeat Germany came from Soviet workshops and factories. Soviet industrialization, from the first Five-Year Plan on, was oriented primarily toward the power of the state. From a Marxian viewpoint, equitable redistribution of income should have been the main objective once the means of producing wealth were transferred to public ownership. However, the Soviet leaders were not only

Marxists but also realistic nationalists who regarded Soviet power and prestige rather than distributive egalitarianism as the top priority. As a result, industrialization was focused on heavy industry and military preparedness as well as on specific programs in science and technology in which—as later shown in the space program—Soviet power and prestige were vastly enhanced. Inevitably, the commitment of the Soviet leadership to these policy goals of industrialization led to considerable neglect of agriculture and consumer goods industries throughout most of the seven decades of communist rule.

Until the late 1950s appliances common in the American home were either unknown or extremely scarce in the Soviet Union. Through the 1970s, the Soviet economy then made some strides in meeting consumer demands for certain basic appliances and durables. However, the supply and range of such appliances always remained far behind other advanced industrial nations, partially because the latter often imported large quantities in addition to engaging in domestic production.

The Soviet Union's commitment to the economic needs and goals of a consumer society was reflected in the 1960s in its first program of mass production of several basic home appliances, such as television sets, refrigerators, and washing machines. The 1970s and 1980s were the first two decades of the personal automobile—the universally coveted symbol of the affluent consumer society. The Soviet Union was the only major advanced industrial nation in the world to have remained outside the automobile age. Both Stalin and his successor, Nikita Khrushchev, looked upon the automobile as a typical expression of capitalist frivolity and unrestrained individualism. Ironically, at the very time when the romance of the automobile began to lose its glow and glamour in Western nations because of traffic congestion and environmental concerns, Soviet policymakers decided, in response to intense and persistent consumer pressure, to enter the automobile age.

Declining productivity afflicted not only agriculture but also major segments of Soviet industry. In the 1950s Soviet industry grew at an average annual rate of 5 percent; by the 1980s this rate had fallen to 2 percent. Decline in industrial growth was paralleled by a slowdown in the growth of consumption. While Khrushchev promised Soviet consumers a dramatic improvement in living standards—pledging to overtake the United States by the 1980s—the reality under his successor, Leonid Brezhnev, proved very different. The relative downgrading of consumer goods in the Five-Year Plans under Brezhnev in favor of military and industrial development is reflected in the contrast between the amount of working time required for Soviet consumers to obtain particular goods as compared to the amount of working time required of consumers in Western Europe and the United States. Table 4.1 illustrates this contrast for a variety of familiar consumer items in the early 1980s.

TABLE 4.1 Retail Price of Goods Expressed as Work-Time Units, March 1982

ITEM	WASHINGTON	PARIS	MOSCOW
1 kilogram flour	5 minutes	6 minutes	28 minutes
1 kilogram pork	63 minutes	108 minutes	176 minutes
3.3 kilograms sugar	30 minutes	30 minutes	191 minutes
12 liters milk	72 minutes	96 minutes	264 minutes
18 eggs	14 minutes	23 minutes	99 minutes
1 kilogram apples	10 minutes	15 minutes	92 minutes
1 kilogram tea	10 minutes	17 minutes	53 minutes
1 liter vodka	87 minutes	187 minutes	646 minutes
120 cigarettes	54 minutes	48 minutes	90 minutes
TV set, black and white	38 hours	44 hours	299 hours
small car	5 months	8 months	53 months

Like the sources of inefficiency in agriculture, the roots of low productivity in industry lay deep in the structure of the Soviet economy. Not only were positive incentives lacking to improve efficiency but the system also encouraged practices that were wasteful and contradictory. For example, to assure that they could meet the quotas assigned to them under the national economic plans, managers at the plant and regional levels consistently overestimated their demand for labor and raw materials while at the same time underestimating their expected output. As a result, the entire planning process was permeated by misinformation that greatly complicated the task of allocating resources on the basis of actual need. Khrushchev's attempts to curb these practices by offering significant rewards for efficient management and imposing severe penalties for intentional wastefulness met with strong resistance from managers who felt threatened by genuine competition and differential treatment. To regain the support of these influential officials, Brezhnev later restored their former autonomy, and with it their habitual practices.

Popular dissatisfaction with the poor performance of both the agricultural and consumer sectors of the Soviet economy would undoubtedly have been far greater if not for the presence alongside the official planned economy of a thriving and expanding "second economy"—an informal network of private exchanges that offset the deficiencies of official structures by supplying for barter, bribes, or at far higher prices the goods and services that could not otherwise be procured. This second economy extended from personal items such as fresh meat and spare parts for automobiles to large-scale shipments of coal and other raw materials. While these operations were, strictly speaking, illegal and carried on outside the planned economy, Brezhnev ordinarily turned a blind eye to the second economy, since it did alleviate pressing shortages in consumer goods and serious bottlenecks in industrial production. Yet however useful it may have been in the short run, the second economy diverted goods and materials from the planned sector, thereby also undermining its legitimacy. Expansion of this second economy was telling evidence of the defects of a command economy.

The Soviet worker was subject to decisive managerial authority such as had not been known in most capitalist countries for more than two generations. The communist promise to liberate the worker from capitalist exploitation was partially fulfilled—the capitalist was eliminated—but this did not lead to the freedom of the worker, since the place of the capitalist was taken by a far more tyrannical state. The main function of Soviet labor unions was to promote maximum production as determined by state planners. In pursuing the goal of maximum production, the Soviet labor union enforced labor discipline within the plant and organized competitions to increase output. Basic conditions of work—wages and hours—were set by the government and could not be significantly changed by union pressure, since party members were expected to ensure that labor unions adhered to government policies. In addition to its role as an agent of government policy, the labor union had administrative and social welfare functions: Unions helped to enforce safety laws, administer the social insurance system, provide housing for workers, and supervise educational, cultural, and propaganda activities. The character of the Soviet labor unions as "company unions" was underlined by the fact that they included managerial personnel, since the managers directly represented the employer—that is, the government.

Freedom of job movement for Soviet workers was limited by various restrictions and disincentives. Until 1956 workers who quit their jobs without official permission were penalized by either salary cuts or prison terms. However, the penalties were increasingly ignored by the middle 1950s, and workers were finally legally permitted to change jobs, particularly since expanding industrialization opened up many employment opportunities in all parts of the country. In 1970 the Soviet government decided that productivity was suffering from excessively frequent job changes and imposed new restrictions. Workers who quit their jobs more than twice in one year had to accept employment in enterprises selected by government officials and could not receive higher wages than they earned before. Such "fliers" (as they were called in Russia) also lost various bonuses, vacation benefits, and other perquisites linked to seniority at the same enterprise. Another type of limitation on freedom of movement was imposed on graduates of professional, technical, or trade schools on the college or high school level: They were required by law to work for three or four years in assigned areas selected by authorities.

Of all the segments of the Soviet economy, services and housing were the most neglected. Complaints in the Soviet press revealed that it took three to four months to have shoes repaired, even longer to have a radio or television set fixed, and that it was next to impossible to get any laundering or dry cleaning done. Perpetual shortages of restaurant and hotel facilities not only limited domestic Soviet tourism but deprived the government of the eagerly sought hard currencies of foreign tourists. Shops and stores of all types were, and still remain, in conspicuously short supply. The Soviet shopper had to stand in line three times to purchase something. In the first line shoppers found out whether the item was in stock and what it cost. In the second line they paid the cashier and received a receipt. In the third line they exchanged the receipt for the merchandise. A few supermarkets and self-service stores opened during the late 1960s, and more appeared during the 1970s, but these made little dent in traditional Soviet methods of retailing.

The Soviet record in housing was even more unimpressive. In the pre-communist Russia of 1914, available per capita living space for the urban population was 7 square meters (1 square meter is equal to 10.76 square feet). In 1940, after a decade of communist industrialization and planning, per capita living space had dropped to 4.34 square meters. Until 1957 the figure still stood under 5 square meters. From 1958 on, the Soviet government made a determined effort to improve housing conditions, and by the end of the 1960s urban per capita living space finally reached 7 meters again—the level of 1914!

Since housing was perpetually scarce and most available housing was state-owned, the government allocated available space on the basis of social criteria as it perceived them. Thus, the primary consideration was not need but the contribution a person was considered to make to society, as expressed in this manner by a Soviet writer: "We consider it just to provide housing in the first instance to those who do excellent work." Outstanding scientists, scholars, and artists, high-ranking party and government officials, and military personnel with the rank of colonel and above received extra living space in recognition of their status and work. Need was recognized only in the cases of persons with certain types of illness who required some additional living space.

The main benefit for the Soviet citizen in state-owned housing was low rent, usually amounting to a mere 5 percent of monthly earnings. However, the Soviet citizen lived in cramped quarters, and Soviet housing often lacked the basic conveniences common in other industrial nations. Conveniences in urban housing were considerably upgraded during recent years, but rural housing changed little over seventy years of communist rule.

Since the government was unable to supply sufficient housing, the occupancy of one apartment by several families—each family living in one room and sharing the kitchen and bathroom facilities—was a vexing problem Soviet citizens with more money, initiative, and connections could escape state-owned housing in two ways: through private housing or cooperative housing. Citizens wishing to build their own house had first to obtain permission from the government to use a plot of land, since all land belonged to the state. Next, they had to obtain construction materials, either legally or through the black market. In the past, private homeowners were subjected to various forms of bureaucratic chicanery—being denied building materials, water lines, and other facilities; but in 1972 the government came out in support of private home ownership as a practical method of alleviating the perennial housing shortage, one of the most serious deficiencies in Soviet living conditions.

The second method of escaping state housing was through cooperative housing. In larger cities a minimum of sixty members was required, made up generally of fellow workers in a plant or families in a neighborhood who wanted better housing. In general, cooperative housing— accounting for 10 to 15 percent of new urban housing during recent years—was used mainly by the more affluent groups in Soviet society, since membership required a large downpayment for construction costs and monthly payments that were several times higher than rents charged for smaller and less desirable accommodations in state-owned housing.

The persistent housing shortage in the Soviet Union was reflected in Soviet law. No one was allowed to live in Soviet cities without registering with the police, and the police often rejected a request for residence in large cities because housing was not available. Illegal residents in major cities were subject to prison sentences, particularly if the offender was a person without officially sanctioned means of earning a living.

The Soviet launching of the first artificial earth satellite on October 4, 1957, came as a bombshell to those who still held the illusion that Russia was largely a country of illiterate peasants. This Soviet first was followed by many others: The Soviets sent the first man, the first woman, and then the first team of astronauts into space; they sent the first satellite past the moon and around the moon, and theirs was the first to land on the moon; and they accomplished the first "space walk" by an astronaut and the first link-up in space between two manned spacecraft. Although the successful landing of American astronauts Armstrong and Aldrin on the moon in July 1969 boosted American morale at home and American prestige abroad, this success does not lessen the importance and quality of the overall Soviet space effort.

Soviet failure to accomplish manned landings on the moon—in sharp contrast to repeated successful American manned landings between 1969 and 1972—was due to Soviet backwardness in computer technology. Manned spacecraft heading for the moon require vast computerized data-processing centers on earth receiving information from the spacecraft and guiding its course, and they also require microminiaturized computers on board the spacecraft that do not overload its space and weight. By the end of 1972, Soviet computer technology had not mastered either aspect of computerized data processing connected with lunar flights.

In market economies, investment flows toward areas of greater profitability, producers respond to the preferences of consumers, and prices fluctuate according to conditions of supply and demand. In the Soviet Union, however, all these basic decisions—which and how many goods to produce, what prices to charge, and where to direct further investment—were made, at least in the official economy, not mainly on the basis of economic criteria (such as consumer demand and actual cost of production) but primarily in light of political considerations, such as commitments to keep food prices low and to maintain full employment. As a result, the Soviet economy exhibited apparent anomalies that were sometimes difficult for Westerners to understand and that led to mistaken conclusions about Soviet economic performance. Most importantly, the Soviets invested heavily in some sectors of the economy while keeping other sectors relatively underdeveloped; instead of balanced growth, as tends to occur in market economies, the Soviet economy presented a seemingly incongruous mixture of backwardness in some areas combined with exceptional sophistication in others.

Historically, this disparity in levels of development was most striking in comparisons between the Soviet consumer economy—which was kept intentionally impoverished even by Eastern European standards—and the Soviet military and space programs—which in some respects surpassed Western achievements. Looking at the living standards of an ordinary Soviet citizen even in the major cities—at the variety and quality of goods and services available for everyday use—one might easily have concluded that the Soviet economy was underdeveloped and inefficient; yet if one glanced overhead at Soviet satellites and space stations, or watched a military parade of the latest Soviet tanks and missiles, just the opposite conclusion might have been reached. Western economies that produced advanced weapons and satellites also produced an abundance of consumer goods—cars, stereos, and especially food. The Soviet Union, through its command economy, allocated scarce resources to maintain an impressive space program and powerful military while at the same time neglecting the basic wants of its citizens. Backwardness and modernity coexisted in an amalgam unknown in any other developed industrial country.

Military Strength and Détente

During a period of sixty-five years, from the Russian Revolution of 1917 until the death of Leonid Brezhnev in 1982, only four men ruled the Soviet Union: Lenin, who died in 1924; Stalin, who died in 1953; Khrushchev, who was deposed in 1964; and Brezhnev. By the time he succumbed to heart failure in November 1982, Brezhnev had led his country for eighteen years, spanning the terms of five American presidents. Only Stalin held power longer.

Brezhnev emerged from World War II with the rank of major general in the Red Army, and his subsequent rise to power was supported by Soviet military leaders. Moreover, he assumed power not long after the Cuban missile crisis (October 1962), in which Soviet military weakness in confronting the United States was displayed before the world. Throughout his rule Brezhnev responded favorably to requests for more military spending. He assured his generals, "You will have everything you need." The Soviet Union devoted as much as 15 percent of their GNP to defense during the Brezhnev era, compared to about 6 percent spent on defense by the United States. Through such vast expenditures on the military, Brezhnev presided over the development of the Soviet Union as a global superpower, rivaling or surpassing the United States in military forces on land, sea, and in the air.

The Soviet Union's arsenal of missiles and nuclear warheads provided striking evidence of Soviet armed power. By 1983, Soviet nuclear forces could be compared to those of the United States as shown in Table 4.2.

TABLE 4.2   1983 Soviet and U.S. Nuclear Forces

	U.S.S.R.	U.S.
Land-based intercontinental ballistic missiles (ICBMs)	1,398	1,052
Submarine-launched ballistic missiles	989	989
Missile-armed manned missiles	150	376
Warheads in multiple independently targetable reentry vehicles (MIRVs)	4,872	6,774
Theater nuclear forces (TNF); missiles	860	108
Theater nuclear forces (TNF); bombers	880	218

These comparisons show that as regards intercontinental missiles, the Soviets had reached a rough parity with the United States—more than sufficient to assure nuclear devastation of the United States in case of an American attack; while in theater nuclear forces—the missiles and bombers that could be used in attacking or defending Western Europe—the Soviets had a clear preponderance. This preponderance was reinforced by Soviet superiority in conventional forces. In every type of weaponry except anti-tank missiles, the Soviets and their Warsaw Pact allies enjoyed a definite, and in some cases overwhelming, advantage over the United States and its NATO allies. This is shown in Table 4.3 on page 138.

Secure in the Warsaw Pact nations' military superiority over Western Europe, Brezhnev in his last years launched a determined campaign to prevent modernization and expansion of NATO forces. Capitalizing on widespread popular opposition to nuclear weapons and on doubts about America's commitment to defend Western Europe in a military showdown

TABLE 4.3   1983 Warsaw Pact and NATO Conventional Forces

	WARSAW PACT	NATO
Tanks	45,500	17,000
Artillery pieces	19,400	9,500
Antiaircraft guns	6,500	5,300
Surface-to-air missile launchers	6,300	1,800
Surface-to-surface missile launchers	1,200	350

the Soviets sought to prevent deployment in Europe of new American medium-range nuclear missiles, following their own introduction of such weapons into Eastern Europe. This would have altered the military balance between NATO countries and the Warsaw Pact nations. Under Gorbachev, both Americans and Russians subsequently agreed to abolish all intermediate-range and short-range nuclear missiles worldwide.

Even more notable than the Soviet buildup of missiles and land forces was the expansion of its navy. Starting with only limited naval forces under Khrushchev, under Brezhnev the Soviet Union developed into a leading sea power. Through an intensive program of shipbuilding, the Soviets surpassed the United States in important types of vessels, particularly attack submarines. Modern and heavily armed Soviet naval units became a familiar sight at political trouble spots around the world, from the Mediterranean to the Sea of Japan.

The massive Soviet arms buildup under Brezhnev reflected in part deep-seated Russian fears of foreign attack—fears fed by memories of three catastrophic invasions in less than 150 years. But the arms buildup also emboldened Brezhnev to project Soviet power around the world. In Latin America, Africa, the Middle East, and Southeast Asia, the Kremlin was always ready to fish in troubled waters. Soviet weapons found their way not only to Cuba but to Ethiopia, Syria, and Vietnam. As its military power expanded, Soviet foreign policy became increasingly aggressive, culminating in 1979 in the ultimately unsuccessful invasion of Afghanistan. This invasion, one in a series of armed interventions or threats of intervention in various countries, helped to undermine Brezhnev's major earlier initiative in foreign affairs—the policy of détente.

Détente referred to an easing of tensions between the United States and the Soviet Union, expressed most notably in a willingness of the two countries to reach agreements and to act together in areas of common interest, while retaining their differences. Among the most important of these common interests were arms control and nonproliferation of nuclear weapons.

The terrible danger of nuclear competition was brought home vividly to both sides in the Cuban missile crisis of October 1962. An attempt by the Soviets to place nuclear-armed missiles in Cuba was met by a strong response from President John F. Kennedy. Russian ships carrying missiles toward Cuba were to be intercepted by American naval units. For several days it was uncertain what Khrushchev would do next or how the United States would react. The world seemed to sway precariously on the brink of nuclear war. At last the Russian ships turned back for home. The crisis was over, but it helped convince both Washington and Moscow that a balance of nuclear terror was approaching. It was becoming evident that both superpowers shared an interest in regulating nuclear weapons.

The first fruits of this common interest in arms control were several agreements concluded during the 1960s that limited the sites at which nuclear weapons could be tested and deployed. These included the Limited Test Ban Treaty, the Outer Space Treaty, the Antarctica Treaty, and the Hot-Line agreement to speed communications between the White House and the Kremlin in case of a nuclear crisis. In 1968 both nations signed the Nuclear Nonproliferation Treaty. A still more significant step was taken in 1969, when negotiations began on the crucial issue of strategic arms limitations. The talks culminated in 1972 in a five-year interim agreement limiting the number of each country's offensive missiles and launchers (SALT-1).

By 1977, when SALT-1 expired, each nation still had at its disposal a destructive nuclear force a thousand times greater than all the bombs dropped during World War II. Yet both countries continued to strive for further advances in nuclear weaponry, and a SALT-2 agreement was delayed. In June 1979 the draft of a SALT-2 treaty was finally signed in Vienna, but support for détente was waning, and SALT-2 languished without formal United States approval.

Détente took other directions beside agreement on arms limitations. The most publicized was a series of summit meetings between President Richard Nixon (and later President Gerald Ford) with Secretary Brezhnev, beginning in 1972 and culminating in the Vladivostok agreement of, December 1974. At Vladivostok both countries pledged to expand their cooperation in many fields so that the process of improving relations "will become irreversible." Less than a year later (September 1975), a Conference on European Security was held in Helsinki, Finland. The Helsinki conference was the high point of Soviet–American détente.

The agreement reached at Helsinki covered several important areas: security and political stability in Europe; cooperation in economics, science, technology, and the environment; and joint efforts in humanitarian, cultural, information, and other activities. One section of the Helsinki accords— on respect for human rights—gained special significance after the election of President Jimmy Carter in 1976. The signatories, including the Soviet Union, pledged to "promote and encourage the effective exercise of civil, political, economic, social, cultural, and other rights and freedoms."

In line with the principles of Vladivostok and Helsinki, Soviet–American relations seemed to improve along a number of fronts. One of these areas was trade. In successive years of poor harvests, the Soviets purchased large quantities of American wheat, with options for more grain deals in the future. Negotiations also began for increased trade in a broad range of raw materials and manufactured products. In addition, cultural and scientific exchanges and joint ventures were conducted, culminating in the 1975 link-up in space of *Apollo* and *Soyuz* spacecraft.

Although heralded in the early 1970s by both sides as a historic new departure in Soviet–American relations, détente foundered during the later years of Brezhnev's rule, facing the obstacles of continuing conflicts of interest and ideological antagonism. At Vladivostok, Ford and Brezhnev pledged to work together in resolving outstanding international issues, yet as specific issues arose, notably in Africa and the Middle East, this pledge was ignored in the familiar struggle for political advantage. In a war between Ethiopia and Somalia, which erupted in 1977, the United States and the Soviet Union again found themselves on opposite sides, supplying sophisticated weapons and other assistance to each of the belligerents. Further, American peace-seeking efforts in the Middle East were hindered by Soviet support for extremist elements who opposed an Arab–Israeli settlement.

Another source of serious friction was the issue of human rights. At Vladivostok the two countries pledged to promote civil, political, and other basic rights. President Carter responded to this pledge by making violations of human rights a direct concern of American foreign policy— including the violations by the Soviet Union. Carter's criticism of Soviet repression and his encouragement of dissidents inside Russia reemphasized the fundamental disparity between an open and closed society. Insofar as the United States and the Soviet Union were committed to different types of society, promises of cooperation could hardly resolve the radical incompatibility between them. This issue surfaced at the conferences of European countries held in Belgrade (June 1977) and Madrid (November 1980), as successors to the Helsinki meeting. It was only by sidestepping the issue of human rights that the work of each conference could then proceed.

The move toward détente was an important innovation during the first decade of Brezhnev's rule, but the promise of détente faded as Brezhnev used the strong arm of military power to further Soviet interests both in Eastern Europe and around the world. By the time of Brezhnev's death, Soviet foreign policy seemed to vacillate between overtures for greater cooperation with the West and heavy-handed interventions that antagonized the West. Despite these inconsistencies in foreign policy, however, the unmistakable reality remained that the Soviet Union became a global superpower under Brezhnev, at least equal—if not superior—in military strength to the United States.

Party Control

Although he favored the Soviet generals, Brezhnev was first of all a man of the Communist party. Brezhnev understood clearly the opportunities and hazards of life in the Communist party —he himself had benefited from one of Stalin's bloody purges of party officials. Once in power, Brezhnev undertook to assure the loyalty of influential party leaders whose dissatisfaction had led to the ousting of Khrushchev in 1964. Under Brezhnev, party officials enjoyed a life of personal security and comfort such as they had never known before.

Brezhnev's peaceful accession to power—his predecessor, Khrushchev, moved quietly to private life—confirmed the ability of the party to manage the difficult task of political succession without violent disruptions. After Stalin's death the head of the powerful and quasi-autonomous KGB (secret police), Lavrenti Beria, had to be killed in order to assure a smooth succession controlled by party leaders. Beria's murder, arranged by Khrushchev, was the last such demise of a prominent Soviet leader during a struggle over political succession. In 1956 Khrushchev denounced Stalin to party leaders at the Twentieth Party Congress. This proved to be a turning point in Soviet internal politics. The bloody purges and pervasive terror that were an intrinsic part of Stalinist totalitarianism were renounced in favor of less violence means of institutional change and mass control. Khrushchev himself was then deposed in a bloodless maneuver by party leaders, opening the way for Brezhnev.

One factor in Khrushchev's downfall was his effort to shake up the organization and leadership of both the party and the bureaucracy in order to improve their responsiveness and efficiency. Influential officials were unceremoniously demoted or dismissed, leaving a trail of disgruntled and apprehensive party leaders. Brezhnev learned the error of his predecessor's ways. Once in power, he undertook to reassure party officials that their jobs were safe. Unlike the ruthless Stalin or the impulsive Khrushchev, Brezhnev avoided unnecessary disruption of the party apparatus, which grew not only complacent but notably corrupt. Safe from Stalin's purges and Khrushchev's unpredictable shake-ups, party leaders exploited their privileged position more confidently than ever.

The same sort of stability that Brezhnev fostered in the party also extended to the bureaucracy. By interfering less in the management of the bureaucracy, Brezhnev gained political support from another influential constituency. Like party officials, government bureaucrats enjoyed a welcome period of security; the result, however, was bureaucratic inflexibility and indifference to the public, ultimately paving the way to Soviet decline.

At the same time that Brezhnev solidified support among party officials and government bureaucrats, he cracked down on dissenters and dissidents. Under Stalin, opposition and dissent were controlled by the secret police with their characteristic methods of terror, purges, secret trials, and gulags. In 1956, in his famous "secret" speech on the crimes of Stalin presented at the Twentieth Party Congress, Khrushchev attacked the "era of the cult of personality"—the official Soviet term for Stalinism. Khrushchev believed that Stalinism could be disposed of by condemning its excesses as the crimes and mistakes of one man—an aberration from Soviet communism rather than its natural outgrowth. Brezhnev, by contrast, adopted the more consistently Marxist viewpoint that major social and political developments cannot be explained by the acts of one individual—monarch, president, or Communist party secretary—but must be perceived in the context of the whole system, that is, Soviet communism. From this viewpoint, intensive de-Stalinization would inevitably lead to decommunization, or at least to a loss of faith in the infallibility of Soviet communism and the Communist party hierarchy, which subsequently proved to be the case under Mikhail Gorbachev.

In effect, Brezhnev pursued a course of mild re-Stalinization, without the systematic terror of the Stalin era. Terror was replaced by less brutal, though no less repressive, methods. Dissidents who applied for emigration were sometimes allowed to leave the country, while others who refused to emigrate were forced into exile. The years of Brezhnev's rule witnessed a parade of renowned Soviet writers, musicians, and performers leaving their homeland for the West. In addition, Brezhnev added a new wrinkle to the techniques of suppression: widespread use of psychiatric hospitals and prisons for silencing political dissidents.

Although it remains uncertain as to exactly what extent psychiatric imprisonment was employed, certainly hundreds of individuals were consigned for long terms. No formal trial was needed for such incarceration, and "patients" could be confined indefinitely—until they confessed that they were sick when first "admitted" to a psychiatric prison-hospital and disavowed the actions that placed them there.

While prison, labor camps, and exile for political dissidents were not innovations of the Brezhnev regime, it used these penalties on a much broader scale than was seen during the Khrushchev years. Khrushchev's ambivalence toward repressing unorthodoxy was clearly shown in connection with the two greatest authors of the Soviet era, Boris Pasternak and Alexander Solzhenitsyn. When in 1958 Pasternak was awarded the Nobel Prize in literature for his novel *Doctor Zhivago* (which was banned from publication in the Soviet Union), he was compelled by the Soviet government to refuse the award. In addition, he was subjected to an organized campaign of vehement attacks and threats. However, in the early 1960s repressive controls on literature were relaxed, and the high point of this thaw was the publication of Solzhenitsyn's *One Day in the Life of Ivan Denisovich*—a story of life in a Soviet labor camp.

In 1969, following the publication in the West of *Cancer Ward* and *The*

First Circle, however, Solzhenitsyn was expelled from the Union of Writers, thus officially depriving him of the opportunity to publish in his own country. Yet in 1970 Solzhenitsyn was awarded the Nobel Prize in literature "for the ethical force with which he has pursued the indispensable renditions of Russian literature." Solzhenitsyn decided not to go to Stockholm to accept the prize in person when the Soviet government refused to assure him that he would be permitted to return to his homeland. Although wounded in World War II and twice decorated for bravery, he was accused of having collaborated with the Germans. His mail was examined, his apartment bugged, his wife lost her job, and his friends were shadowed by the secret police. The Soviet minister of culture, Yekaterina A. Furtseva, said, "Solzhenitsyn is opposed against our entire society, and that is why we treat him the way we do."

In 1973 Solzhenitsyn authorized publication in the West of *The Gulag Archipelago,* a damning indictment of Soviet slave labor camps, which had been in existence since the time of Lenin. The book had a powerful impact; it described in detail how the camps were run and who the victims were. For the Soviet authorities this was the last straw. In February 1974 Solzhenitsyn was suddenly deprived of his citizenship and expelled from the Soviet Union. After that time he traveled and lectured throughout the West, denouncing totalitarianism and calling for a return to spiritual values and more vigorous anticommunism.

In 1978 two prominent dissidents were sentenced to long terms at hard labor—Yuri Orlov and Anatoly Scharansky. Orlov was convicted of anti-Soviet agitation for his activities as a founder of the "Helsinki Watch Group," whose members reported on Soviet violations of the human rights guarantees contained in the Helsinki Agreement of 1975. Scharansky received an even harsher sentence for providing information on the treatment of Jewish "refuseniks," who were prevented by the Soviet government from emigrating. Both cases received widespread attention outside the Soviet Union not only because of the severe punishment the two men received but as a result of the courageous actions of relatives and friends in protesting the sentences.

The most renowned victim of Brezhnev's repression of dissidents was the renowned physicist Andrei Sakharov, "father" of the Soviet hydrogen bomb. A long-time advocate of greater freedom in the Soviet Union, Sakharov's international fame seemed to protect him from reprisals. But even this most eminent of Soviet scientists finally fell afoul of the regime, and Sakharov was banished to "internal exile" in Gorky, far from his Moscow home. While other major figures could be exiled abroad, Sakharov's knowledge of top-secret scientific information was given as the reason to keep him in internal confinement, which lasted until Gorbachev assumed power.

The most ironic fact about Soviet society was its increasing stratification into social classes. According to official claims, the problem of class had been solved in the Soviet Union, because from the Marxist viewpoint, there can be no class inequality except on the basis of the private ownership of the means of production.

Yet Soviet reality told a far different story. There were at least three distinguishable classes. In the first group—numbering a few hundred thousand families, perhaps as many as a million—were the top government officials, Communist party leaders, military officers, industrial executives, scientists, artists, and writers. Members of this elite group did not have to share their homes or apartments with other families; many benefited from padded expense accounts for travel and vacation for themselves and their families; some had town and country homes and official or privately owned cars; and a small privileged minority even enjoyed the luxury to travel to Western countries. The second class was made up of the intermediary ranks of civilian and military officials, collective farming managers, and some of the more affluent skilled workers and technicians in industry. This group—mostly party members—formed the middle class of Soviet society and numbered 4 million to 5 million families. The third class was made up of the bulk of the population, the mass of workers and peasants, numbering more than 50 million families. Thus the society that promised freedom and equality in fact delivered tyranny and inequality.

The Demise of the Soviet Union

Brezhnev's death on November 10, 1982 commenced the first act in the drama that saw communism repudiated in the Soviet Union and the dissolution of the Soviet Union itself. This startling change in world politics—the collapse of the Communist party in the USSR following a communist hard-liners' aborted coup in August 1991, and the subsequent dissolution of the Soviet Union—was preceded by two years by the equally shocking downfall of communist governments throughout Eastern Europe during 1989. These events are the most significant ideological occurrences in the world since the end of World War II.

For over two years after Brezhnev's death, both the political situation in and direction of the Soviet Union were unsettled. Brezhnev was replaced by the stern Yuri Andropov, who had served as Soviet ambassador to Hungary during the Hungarian uprising of 1956 and subsequently headed the KGB for fifteen years. Andropov's selection seemed to herald a toughening of Soviet policies at home and abroad. He called for more discipline in the domestic economy and condemned "any illusions about the possible evolution for the better in the policy of the present U.S. administration" in response to President Reagan's harsh criticism of the Soviet Union and policy of American military armament.

During his initial months in power, Andropov was able to replace a number of top Soviet officials, almost 25 percent of the Communist Central Committee. Before he could begin to implement much of a program, however, he became ill. Andropov died in February 1984, and was replaced by the already decrepit Konstantin Chernenko, a former Brezhnev crony, who himself died thirteen months later. Thus throughout the early 1980s, as the United States was led by a vigorous though aged President, the Soviet Union went through three leaders who were infirm: Brezhnev, Andropov, and Chernenko.

Mikhail Gorbachev succeeded Chernenko as General Secretary of the Communist party (the most important position in the former Soviet Union) immediately on the latter's death in March 1985; within four hours of the announcement of Chernenko's passing, it was announced that Gorbachev had replaced him. Gorbachev's ascension took top billing in the state-controlled *Pravda* newspaper the following morning; Chernenko's picture only rated page two! There was little disruption in the functioning of the Soviet government as a result of the change of leadership—the Geneva talks on European nuclear weapons (which had been scheduled to resume immediately following Chernenko's death as it turned out) went forward exactly as planned.

Gorbachev's succession had been agreed on in advance, before Chernenko's passing. Gorbachev had almost become party leader when Andropov died, but the Politburo old guard had been able to fend him off for another day. Another aging Soviet leader in ill health made the transfer of Soviet leadership to a new generation inevitable in this case. Gorbachev had chaired meetings of the Politburo first when Andropov, and then Chernenko, were unable to attend.

Because of the radical changes that Gorbachev wrought during his tenure, it is important to remember that there were three phases of his leadership. The first, during 1985 and 1986, was the period of conformity. Notwithstanding some change of rhetoric on Gorbachev's part compared to his predecessors, the impression of him was that he was simply a more refined version of those who had preceded him. The second stage of Gorbachev's leadership was the reform era, from about 1987 through 1989, when he attempted to implement significant changes in a Soviet Union that, in his mind, would remain communist and certainly united. The final phase of his leadership, from the uprisings in Eastern Europe during the fall of 1989 to his own resignation on December 25, 1991, was a time of disintegration and reaction. The reforms he unleashed grew out of control, culminating in the dissolution of the Soviet Union itself and the destruction of communism there.

There was nothing in Gorbachev's background to suggest he would be a radical reformer, and there was little at his ascension to power to suggest that the USSR was on the brink of radical change. Indeed, what was known of Gorbachev seemed to suggest just the opposite. Born of humble, peasant origins and trained as a lawyer, he joined the Communist party at the relatively young age of twenty-one. His patrons in the party had been hard-liners, first long-time chief ideologist Mikhail Suslov, then Andropov.

Once in office, Gorbachev immediately moved in classic Kremlin style to consolidate his power. In addition to being named General Secretary, he became chair of the defense council, controlling the Soviet military and in virtue of this exercising a great role in foreign affairs. Long-time Soviet Foreign Secretary Andrei Gromyko—who had officially nominated Gorbachev for General Secretary—was kicked upstairs to the presidency of the Soviet Union in July 1985, allowing Gorbachev to name his own foreign secretary, Eduard Shevardnadze. This gave Gorbachev even more of a free hand to run policy as he wished. Immediately on becoming General Secretary, Gorbachev named four members to the Politburo, increasing its size to thirteen members.

Gorbachev worked to remove adversaries from positions of power, starting with Leningrad party chief and Politburo member Grigory Romanov, who had been viewed as a potential challenger to Gorbachev for General Secretary, and who resigned from the Politburo for "health reasons" within four months of Gorbachev's ascension. By the time of the Twenty-seventh Party Congress in March 1986, Gorbachev had replaced close to half of all Central Committee members. Also, by the time of the Party Congress, only three voting members of the Politburo remained from the Brezhnev era. It is, in fact, partly because Gorbachev so thoroughly cleaned house at the top levels of the Communist party early in his tenure that he did not have more opposition subsequently when his reforms began to cause unimaginable and—from the perspective of the old guard— reprehensible results.

His reforms, however, were still in the future during Gorbachev's first two years, as he then appeared to be cut from the same cloth as his predecessors, only younger, more energetic, more charismatic, and more intelligent. The concern, indeed, of many Western strategists was that Gorbachev—as a result of his personality and skillful politicking and media relations—would lead a resurgent Soviet Union to more ably promote its interests in contrast to those of the United States. There was hardly any speculation about Gorbachev during his first two years that he would significantly liberalize the Soviet Union, much less lead it to its dissolution. An article on Gorbachev in a leading U.S. news magazine summed up the initial popular reaction to him: He was perceived as "a man who can appear genial and pragmatic, but who is also a tough true believer in the Soviet system" (*Newsweek*, November 18, 1985).

The early external focus of the Soviet Union during Gorbachev's tenure was nuclear arms control with the United States, in particular attempting to persuade Ronald Reagan to abandon the strategic defense initiative (SDI, for short, or pejoratively "star wars"). In 1983, Reagan stood four decades of nuclear thinking on its head by proclaiming that his goal for the United States was to develop a nuclear defense system. This was in stark contrast to the concept of MAD (Mutually Assured Destruction), which postulated that the way to make nuclear war least likely was to guarantee that its results would be unacceptable.

Regardless of the technical, political, and strategic merits or demerits of the strategic defense initiative, there is no question that it caused Soviet leaders extreme anxiety. Andropov, who was in charge at the time of Reagan's presentation of the proposal, called it "irresponsible" and "insane." Gorbachev's initial position remained essentially the same, although he toned down the rhetoric.

The Soviets had walked out of the Intermediate-Range Nuclear Force (INF) talks on reducing nuclear weapons in Europe following the West German Bundestag's vote in November 1983 to deploy Pershing II and cruise missiles. These nuclear reduction talks—which were of especially great importance to European nations—remained adjourned until January 1985, when at the end of Chernenko's brief tenure Soviet Foreign Minister Gromyko and U.S. Secretary of State George Shultz agreed that the INF talks should resume, in conjunction with talks on strategic arms and weapons in space. That the United States was willing to at least discuss the strategic defense initiative was essential to the Soviets' agreement to resume talks.

For the remainder of 1985 the USSR and the United States engaged in a fair amount of posturing to demonstrate that each was really the party interested in peace. Some of Gorbachev's concern to show his peaceful intentions was to divide the United States from West European nations, which had a much greater practical stake in the outcome of European nuclear arms reduction talks than did the United States, and which were under considerably greater domestic political pressure to work for European military disarmament. Gorbachev followed Andropov in trying to appeal to West European public opinion.

In November 1985, Gorbachev and Reagan met in Geneva for their first summit meeting. Though nothing much of substance was accomplished, at least the leaders of the United States and the Soviet Union were talking together again, and on a reasonably friendly basis. The Soviet media, which had previously referred to Reagan as a "cowboy" and "rabid militarist" who had adopted the "slogans and methods of Hitler," discontinued such vitriolic attacks, and Reagan gave up the harsh verbal assaults he had employed against the Soviet Union during his first term. At Geneva, Gorbachev and Reagan agreed to additional summits in the United States during 1986 and in the Soviet Union during 1987, renewed U.S.–Soviet cultural exchanges, established new consulates, improved airline safety, and put forward a general goal of a 50 percent reduction in U.S. and Soviet nuclear forces.

This partial thaw in the second Cold War required some time before the ice finally broke for good. During the first years of his tenure in office, Gorbachev seemed to increase efforts in some Soviet external endeavors, particularly in developing nations. Soviet aid and assistance to Afghanistan, Angola, Ethiopia, Libya, Nicaragua, Syria, and Vietnam actually increased during the first year or so of Gorbachev's leadership, as he attempted to project a more active role for the USSR in the world. The Soviet Union also backed a coup of hard-line Marxists in South Yemen. All of this was consistent with a view of Gorbachev that saw him as someone who intended to reinvigorate the Soviet Union, not reform it.

Furthermore, not withstanding some greater flexibility in nuclear weapons talks, the Soviet view on conventional arms during Gorbachev's early phase was uncertain. Former armed forces Chief of General Staff Nikolai Ogarkov, who had been demoted by Chernenko for saying that détente was dead and that arms negotiations were of no value, was reinstated by Gorbachev to commander of the Warsaw Pact. A somewhat lesser influence for the military had been signaled by Chernenko when Dmitry Ustinov, defense minister and Politburo member, died in 1984 and his successor as defense minister, Sergei Sokolov, was not made a member of the Politburo.

Nonetheless, the overall Soviet direction under Gorbachev was toward less emphasis on the military. The reason was simply economic: The Soviet military was bleeding the nation's treasury and resources—human and otherwise—dry. This was much of the reason for Soviet opposition to the strategic defense initiative; it promised to be a costly, and possible unsustainable, arms race for the USSR to maintain.

The Soviet Union at Gorbachev's advent truly was a nation with great difficulties. Alone among industrialized countries, life expectancy for males actually dropped during the 1960s and 1970s, from 66 years in 1964 to 62 years in 1984. Likewise, infant mortality grew. Alcoholism was rampant, among both men and women, and this contributed to the declining life expectancy and increasing infant mortality. Soviet workers lost three times as many days per year, on average, to illness as did workers in the United States. There were declining birthrates among the European peoples who made up the bulk of the Soviet Union, which was resulting in shortages of entry-level labor, and a change in the demographic composition of the Soviet Union from Russian predominance to Russian minority status and a larger proportion of Asians and Moslems. Soviet diets were poor and, most importantly, Soviet economic productivity was low, particularly in agriculture.

As a result of these problems, the Soviet economy had stagnated, and the economic gap between the Soviet Union and the West—far from diminishing or even standing still—was widening. By even official figures, the Soviet standard of living was only 40 percent that of the United States at the time of Gorbachev's ascension to power. Gorbachev's emphasis, accordingly, was domestic affairs, notwithstanding his international involvement. Indeed, his involvement in the outside world was in large part an effort to bring Soviet external affairs to closure and put them on a more even keel so as to be more able to resolve internal difficulties. This involvement did not at first include, as has been seen, a reduced Soviet presence in the world.

Gorbachev's initial domestic goal, as was his initial foreign goal, was to make the existing Soviet system work better, not to alter it fundamentally. He expressed a desire for less bureaucratic management systems, greater incentives for workers to produce, more capital investment, and increased worker output. At the same time, he was unable, unwilling or both to allow free market experiments or decentralized economic decision-making in the Soviet Union. During his first year in power, he spoke only of "perfecting" the economy; he did not use the word "reform." His major push was an anti-alcohol campaign, which was unpopular and often evaded.

Gorbachev did not at the start of his leadership have a specific economic program to implement his general goals. He did, however, early on announce a campaign of *glasnost*, which is Russian for "openness." Because of the larger connotations that this word later took on, it is important to recall that at first it only meant a slight relaxation of censorship to discuss economic problems more realistically. For example, as Gorbachev himself said: "Try to get a flat tire repaired. You will definitely have to find a moonlighter to do it for you. And he will steal the materials he needs from a construction site."

Glasnost did not originally imply a general political relaxation or ability to criticize the existing government (though some criticism of Brezhnev was permitted); it was more circumscribed than this. Demonstrating the limits of *glasnost*, when the Chernobyl nuclear power plant disaster occurred in April 1986, the first response of Gorbachev's government was, traditional Soviet secrecy, until radioactivity was detected by Sweden. Gorbachev himself did not publicly discuss the incident for eighteen days, and when he did he primarily used the occasion as a forum to discuss ongoing nuclear arms disagreements with the United States.

During 1986, Gorbachev's external focus was nuclear arms talks with the United States, with the goal in particular of heading off the strategic defense initiative. At a snap summit in Reykjavik, Iceland, during October 1986, Gorbachev revealed just how far his thinking had travelled regarding nuclear arms. While some details remain in dispute, Gorbachev apparently offered Reagan the complete abolition of nuclear weapons in exchange for a similar abolition—and the renunciation of the strategic defense initiative—by the United States. Reagan, in turn, was willing to go along with this, as long as testing in outer space of SDI would be allowed, to which Gorbachev would not agree.

Both leaders got ahead of their own nation's negotiating positions at Reykjavik, and this summit ended in a fair amount of acrimony. Nonetheless, the stage had been set for major reductions in nuclear arms.

Gorbachev expanded the *glasnost* campaign at about the same time as the failure of the Reykjavik summit. Leading Soviet dissident Andrei Sakharov, along with his wife, Yelena Bonner (a prominent dissident in her own right), were allowed to return to Moscow from internal exile in Gorky. Their return was without conditions; Sakharov would be free to speak his mind, which he did. This freedom granted to the 1975 Nobel Peace Price winner in December 1986 won kudos for Gorbachev around the world, and was a clear indication that this Soviet leader was qualitatively different from his predecessors.

The *glasnost* campaign continued to expand from this point forward. Over the next two years hundreds of dissidents were released from Soviet prisons and the "special" mental hospitals that were used to house those whose mental "illness" was to criticize the government. While some political prisoners remained, there was no question that a new political atmosphere now permeated the Soviet Union.

A large part of the *glasnost* campaign was more factual reporting in the press. The pages of *Pravda* and other state newspapers become more truthful, as opposed to merely propagandistic. When the government itself sanctioned the publication of information critical of it, it could hardly continue to hold in prison those whose criticisms of the system had been less than what was now appearing everyday in *Pravda*.

Much of the *glasnost* campaign, at least as practiced by the government, consisted of condemnation of the Brezhnev era, which became referred to as the "period of stagnation." Gorbachev denounced Brezhnev for complacency and cronyism. The anti-Brezhnev effort reached its peak in the 1988 indictment and show trial of a Brezhnev son-in-law for extortion and bribe taking.

Formerly taboo subjects came out into the open and were exposed to the light of full public disclosure: Stalin, life under the czars, and Jewish emigration, among others. Boris Pasternak's long-banned *Doctor Zhivago* was at last published in the Soviet Union, the works of Vladimir Nabokov were published in the land of his birth for the first time, and a film stunningly critical of Stalin, *Repentance*, was released. However, criticism of the military, the KGB, and the existing party elite were still not permitted for some time.

The great challenge to Gorbachev's reforms came not so much from the top Communist party leadership, because he had placed his own people in many leadership positions, but from the middle ranks of the party—the great central mass of the bureaucracy—which felt that it had much to lose in privileges and perquisites (legal and otherwise) if Gorbachev's program were successful. At a February 1987 Central Committee meeting he inveighed against "mountains of paperwork...disregard for laws, report padding, bribe taking and encouragement of toadyism" on the part of the bureaucracy.

Gorbachev's inability to get the middle ranks of the party to implement his reforms is what ultimately caused his downfall. It was not enough merely to place his own people in positions of leadership; to be successful he would have had to revitalize the entire party. But this he was not able to do, and it was perhaps an impossible task, given the party and the country as they had developed. Gorbachev's fundamental error may have been that he came to seek *reform* of a system that actually required replacement.

Partially as a response to the resistance he met from the central ranks of the Communist party, Gorbachev introduced some democratic election procedures in the Soviet Union during 1987 and 1988, which he called "control from below." At first, elections for party officials at the local and provincial levels, and for party secretaries of the Soviet republics, were by secret ballot with multiple candidates and open debate. While the Communist party still picked the candidates who could run, this was a monumental departure from previous Soviet practice.

During 1988, these same democratic election procedures were extended to the revamped Supreme Soviet—or parliament—which became the ruling body of USSR. Officials' tenure in office was also limited, to two five-year terms. The Supreme Soviet was elected by the people of the Soviet Union, not just by Communist party members, although all candidates were members of the party. Elections by the people were part of Gorbachev's effort to circumscribe party resistance. Among those elected to the Supreme Soviet were Gorbachev rivals Boris Yeltsin and Andrei Sakharov. Remarkable about the new Soviet parliament was not just its membership but its open debate and contested votes, all reported in the news media.

Notwithstanding his movements in the direction of democracy, Gorbachev also had a tendency to centralize power in himself, for which he was criticized by opponents who thought not that his reforms were going too far, but that they were not going far enough. For example, although he upgraded the Supreme Soviet, he also gave himself the power to issue decrees when it was not in session, having become president of the Soviet Union on Andrei Gromyko's resignation. Further, his replacements of officials within the Communist party continued unabated.

Gorbachev's reform program became twofold. In addition to its political component, *glasnost*, an economic component, *perestroika* (or "restructuring"), was announced. As time went on, it was the economic portion, *perestroika*, that received more attention.

Gorbachev's book *Perestroika*, published in 1987, caused a sensation and indicated just what a revolutionary thinker he was. It is a measure of how much the world has changed over only the past decade that the work was originally greeted in the West with a fair amount of skepticism. Many readers did not believe Gorbachev meant what he said, or that major change would soon characterize the Soviet Union.

Subtitled "New Thinking for Our Country and the World," *Perestroika* was just that. Although ostensibly written in a Marxist-Leninist framework and employing some of that rhetoric, *Perestroika* and Gorbachev's program as a whole had already become detached from their Marxist-Leninist moorings. Only a certain amount of form was left; the substance already pointed to something new. It was only a matter of time before either the reform program would break down, or the Marxist-Leninist theoretical substructure, now detached from its edifice, would do so. In the end, it was Marxism-Leninism that went.

The very opening of *Perestroika* is revealing for to whom the book is addressed, "the peoples of the USSR, the United States, indeed every country."Gorbachev spoke as much to the world as to his own country, and in particular he sought to help mold public opinion in the United States. The Soviets most often measured their deeds in comparison to the United States. The shedding of the bipolar outlook has been one of the greatest geopolitical changes that has accompanied the demise of the Soviet Union.

Gorbachev's candor regarding the Soviet economy in *Perestroika* was breathtaking. He pulled no punches.

> We first discovered a slowing economic growth. In the last fifteen years the national income growth rates had declined by more than half and by the beginning of the eighties had fallen to a level close to economic stagnation....Moreover, the gap in the efficiency of production, quality of products, scientific and technological development, the production of advanced technology and the use of advanced techniques began to widen, and not to our advantage.

This was different as he could be from Khrushchev's, "We will bury you (referring to the United States and West European nations)." Indeed, Gorbachev was saying what conservative American commentators had said for a number of years.

Other passages from *Perestroika* were revealing for the light they shed on both the Soviet system and Gorbachev:

> Creative thinking was driven out from the social sciences, and superfluous and voluntarist assessments and judgments were declared indisputable truths. Scientific, theoretical and other discussions, which are indispensable for the development of thought and for creative endeavor, were emasculated. Similar negative tendencies also affected culture, the arts and journalism, as well as the teaching process and medicine, where mediocrity, formalism and loud eulogizing surfaced, too.

> The presentation of a "problem-free" reality backfired: a breach had formed between word and deed, which bred public passivity and disbelief in the slogans being proclaimed.

Mass distribution of awards, titles and bonuses often replaced genuine concern for the people.

We need broad democratization of all aspects of society [emphasis in original]...*Perestroika* itself can only come through democracy.

The essence of *perestroika* lies in the fact that *it unites socialism with democracy* [emphasis in original].

We are not imposing our views on anyone. Let everyone make his own choice; history will put everything in its place.

Perestroika is a revolution.

Radical reforms.

The new atmosphere is, perhaps, most vividly manifest in *glasnost*. We want more openness about public affairs in every sphere of life.

Democratization of the atmosphere in society and social and economic changes are gaining momentum largely thanks to the development of *glasnost*.

As a result of his reforms, Gorbachev became recognized in the West as a break with the Soviet past. Former U.S. secretaries of state Henry Kissinger and Cyrus Vance had this to say about Gorbachev following their visit to the Soviet Union in 1987: He was "a totally new Soviet leader" (Kissinger); he was "interested in really radical reform" (Vance).

During 1987, Gorbachev made concession after concession on intermediate-range, and then short-range, ballistic missiles in Europe, which made possible a treaty banning these weapons on almost completely American terms. The United States first proposed the "zero-zero" option—whereby both the United States and the USSR would have no intermediate-range ballistic missiles in Europe—during 1981. Brezhnev turned down the offer. Subsequently, it will be recalled, the Soviets walked out of INF talks in 1983 under Andropov, and Gorbachev initially attempted to link any treaty on European nuclear missiles to American concessions on SDI.

During 1987, Gorbachev dropped the linkage between SDI and an intermediate-range ballistic missile treaty. He also agreed to eliminate all Soviet intermediate-range missiles worldwide (which the United States would also do), as the Americans had some concerns that Soviet intermediate-range ballistic missiles left in Asia could be transferred to Europe during a time of crisis. Gorbachev dropped an earlier insistence that French and British nuclear weapons should be considered in the equation before there would be any Soviet reductions. He agreed also to the elimination of short-range ballistic missiles in Europe, when the United States feared that their retention in Europe after intermediate-range ballistic missiles had been removed would upset the balance of forces. And he consented to, for the first time in a Soviet-American nuclear arms agreement, on-site verification procedures. As a result of Gorbachev's concessions, a nuclear arms treaty banning American and Soviet intermediate-range and short-range ballistic missiles was signed by the United States and Soviet Union in Washington during December 1987. This treaty called for the first significant destruction of nuclear weapons ever.

As Gorbachev's policy on nuclear missiles changed, so did his policies regarding Soviet involvement elsewhere. In Vietnam, Ethiopia, Angola, Cuba, Nicaragua, and North Korea, Soviet support and presence were cut back. Gorbachev wanted to free up resources that had been used in foreign ventures for use at home. Most significantly, in 1988 Gorbachev announced that the Soviet Union would be willing to withdraw from Afghanistan, a procedure that was then completed during early 1989. In addition, the Soviet Union refrained from involving itself in any new foreign endeavors.

Among the most notable of Gorbachev's initiatives was to give the Soviet satellites more independence. To Colombian novelist Gabriel Garcia Marquez he said: "We favor socialism, but we do not impose our convictions on anyone. Let everyone choose for himself, and history will eventually put everything in its place." This was a far cry from the Brezhnev Doctrine.

Gorbachev's period of reform in the Soviet Union raised high hopes in Eastern Europe; at last the USSR might ease its grip, and as a result local regimes might become less oppressive. The two hopes fed on one another and fueled considerable turmoil in Eastern Europe, most of all in Poland.

On the seventieth anniversary of the Russian Revolution (in November 1987) Gorbachev went on Soviet national television and stated that "the guilt of Stalin and his immediate entourage before the party and the people for the wholesale repressive measures and acts of lawlessness is enormous and unforgivable." This denunciation was in some respects similar to Khrushchev's speech to the Twentieth Party Congress in 1956, but Khrushchev's speech was originally secret and was given only to party leaders, whereas Gorbachev's was broadcast live to the entire nation. Gorbachev went on in the speech to become the first Soviet leader officially to utter Khrushchev's name in over two decades, and also mentioned "nonpersons" Trotsky (though in a disparaging light) and Nikolai Bukharin, another early Bolshevik leader who fell victim to Stalin's repression.

In the area of emigration, Gorbachev eased restrictions. Jewish emigration, which had reached a peak of over 50,000 in 1979, had declined to under 1,000 by 1984. Gorbachev again allowed Jewish emigration, also permitting emigration by certain other nationalities, for example, Germans. In foreign affairs, the Soviet Union reestablished consular ties with Israel, with whom diplomatic relations had been broken following the Six-Day War in 1967.

Gorbachev also permitted, most significantly, extensive freedom of religion. No longer were people suppressed for going to church, nor were church ecclesiastical organizations oppressed or placed under government control.

Gorbachev's reasons for his remarkable relaxation of Soviet policies at home and abroad are somewhat unfathomable, and to some extent must await the light of history. All along the way, particularly as he allowed more reforms, he was buffeted from two sides—from liberals who wanted him to go further and from conservatives who thought he had gone too far. Gorbachev's usual response was to split the difference, and move a notch further in the direction of reform, but without really acquiescing to reformers' desires. In this way, he ultimately lost the support of both groups and became a leader without a party.

There is no question that Gorbachev sought assistance—technological and financial—from Western nations. He saw his program partly as a way to secure Western aid to revamp the Soviet economy. In the aftermath of the Soviet invasion of Afghanistan, clamp-down in Poland, and continued mistreatment of dissidents, various Western nations (led by the United States) had placed restrictions of one sort or another on trade with the Soviet Union. These restrictions could only be relieved through changes in behavior on the Soviets' part.

Further, Gorbachev no doubt believed in his program (as distinct from pushing it for merely tactical reasons), although he surely did not foresee, as he did not countenance, its ultimate results. He did not recognize that a system built on terror cannot shed its worst aspects without also calling into question the system itself.

Perhaps the highlight of Gorbachev's tenure was his December 1988 address to the United Nations. There, following up on the European nuclear arms agreement with the United States the previous year, he announced that the Soviet Union would unilaterally cut its armed forces by 500,000 troops and 10,000 tanks over the next two years, including at least 50,000 troops and 5,000 tanks in Eastern Europe. He also used the occasion of his UN speech to reiterate positions he had taken earlier in his tenure, that "closed societies" do not work, that the Soviet Union did not possess "the ultimate truth," and that the "use or threat of force" is not a legitimate tool of foreign policy.

Among the responses to Gorbachev's announced military cutbacks were statements by East European nations that they, too, would reduce their armed forces. The Soviet bloc as a whole shifted its military posture to defense.

Gorbachev continued domestic relaxation during 1989. Foreign radio broadcasts beamed at the Soviet Union were no longer jammed. Mass posthumous amnesties were announced for the victims of Stalinist courts. The Soviet Union acknowledged for the first time that Stalin ordered Trotsky's murder. Jewish and other emigration were further eased.

Things really started to go wrong for Gorbachev during 1989. In February, a crowd of 100,000 Lithuanians demanded "independence," igniting the tidal wave of nationalism that quickly engulfed and destroyed the Soviet Union. Gorbachev himself acknowledged in his New Year's message for 1989 that conditions were not as he would have liked: "*Perestroika* gave rise to great expectations in society. But changes are not coming as fast as we would like them to" he stated.

In April, in the first free elections in the Soviet Union in over seventy years, the Soviet people delivered a sharp rebuke to Gorbachev and the Communist party by not electing thirty-four regional party secretaries and by defeating communists in some races who ran unopposed. Boris Yeltsin outpolled his official party rival in balloting to the Congress of People's Deputies by a nine-to-one margin. While, as a result of seventy years of organization, Communist party regulars were still able to win a majority, it was a Pyrrhic victory of sorts for Gorbachev and a diminution of stature for the Communist party.

New sessions of the Supreme Soviet were even more raucous than the old. Gorbachev was openly criticized,and ever more revolutionary proposals were put forward, including independence for the Baltic republics. In July, coal miners went on strike, and their placards bearing such slogans as "*Perestroika* in words, not deeds" were broadcast on television to the entire nation. Ethnic unrest was stirring throughout the Soviet Union, not just in the Baltics but in other republics such as Moldavia, the Ukraine, Armenia, Azerbaijan, Georgia, and the Moslem republics—indeed the entire nation.

Notwithstanding his deteriorating position, Gorbachev remained unchallenged (though not always supported) as General Secretary of the Communist party and President of the Soviet Union. During the spring of 1989 he was again able to demonstrate his dominance of the Communist party by forcing one-third of the 330-member Central Committee to resign—including long-term party stalwarts such as Gromyko and former Brezhnev-era prime minister Nikolai Tikhonov.

The monumental upheavals in Eastern Europe during the second half of 1989 shook the world's political systems and especially the Soviet Union to their core. The collapse of communism throughout Eastern Europe greatly influenced people in the USSR, especially now that the media was so much more free, and individuals were incomparably more able to show their dissatisfaction with the prevailing regime. The question of whether a communist regime was able to depart from communism had been decisively answered: Yes. This repudiated seventy years of Soviet doctrine.

Following a meeting with the Pope—the first ever by a Soviet leader—in December 1989, Gorbachev had this to say: "We have changed our attitude on some matters, such as religion, which admittedly we used to treat in a simplistic manner. Now we not only proceed from the assumption that no one should interfere in matters of the individual's conscience, we also say that the moral values that religion embodied for centuries can help the work of renewal of our country." This followed an equally striking and characteristic statement to Fidel Castro earlier in the year, breaking with another long-standing Soviet practice; the Soviet Union was "categorically opposed to...the export of revolution or counterrevolution." Gorbachev had profoundly different positions from his predecessors.

By the beginning of 1990 the Soviet Union was on the brink of collapse. In December 1989 the Lithuanian parliament voted 243 to 1 to end the Communist party's monopoly on power, an action that was followed in varying degrees by Estonia and Latvia. The Baltics were on their way to independence, which Lithuania declared on March 11, 1990. Gorbachev threatened the Baltics that he would not allow unilateral succession. He sent in tanks and troops and had jet fighters fly overhead before settling on an economic blockade—cutting off oil and gas—as the best way to restore control.

In March 1990, the Soviet constitution was changed to deprive the Communist party of its "leading role" in the Soviet Union. Henceforth, it would be one of a number of parties competing for power, not the driving force of the state. This followed a march on the Kremlin of 100,000 people in February demanding an end to party rule.

During this time Gorbachev's position began to weaken as a result of dissatisfaction on both the Left and Right. Also in March, the Supreme Soviet voted by only a 2 percent margin that it, rather than the people, would elect the Soviet president. This was a crucial vote for Gorbachev, because it was uncertain he could win a free election of the citizenry. The Supreme Soviet then elected Gorbachev president with only 59 percent of the legislators' support, additionally demonstrating his weakening general support.

The May Day parade of 1990, which in past years had been an occasion for proclaiming the virtues and strength of the Soviet state, was an utter rout for Gorbachev and his communist colleagues. Tens of thousands of spontaneous marchers passed through Red Square—under the viewing stand of government officials—holding banners with such slogans as "Down with the Empire of Red Fascism," "Communists Exploit the Workers," and "Freedom for Lithuania; Shame on the Imperialist President." Gorbachev and his fellow government ministers left the viewing stand after just a few minutes, to the chant of "Resign, Resign." Change had come to the Soviet Union.

The economy and other social conditions in the USSR deteriorated as the political situation did and as nationalism flourished. Crime increased by almost one-third in 1989, gross national product declined, and shortages, unemployment, and inflation grew.

In June 1990, the Russian parliament voted 907 to 13 that Russian laws take precedence over those of the Soviet Union. This was followed by a similar declaration by the Ukraine in July.

The Twenty-eighth (and last) Communist Party Congress of the Soviet Union during July was another disaster for Gorbachev. Rightists stepped up their attacks on his program, and Boris Yeltsin resigned from the party and walked out of the Congress following his address to it. The squeeze was on Gorbachev from both sides.

In October, Gorbachev at last seemed to adopt a reformist economic program for the Soviet Union that would lead it to a genuinely free market with a greatly lessened government sector. But economics was not his strong suit. Within weeks he backed off of the "500 days to a market economy" program that he had just announced.

As a result of the declining economy, Gorbachev's popularity plummeted in the Soviet Union, even as it remained strong abroad; indeed, he joked at times that he felt more at home in foreign capitals than he did in Moscow. During 1990, Gorbachev's approval rating in the Soviet Union, as measured by public opinion polls, dropped from about 50 percent to about 20 percent Abroad, he received the Nobel Peace Prize for 1990, which domestic difficulties prevented him from officially receiving until well into 1991.

In December 1990, Foreign Minister Eduard Shevardnadze resigned to "protest against the advance of dictatorship." In the early months of 1991 Gorbachev seemed to move to the Right, siding with conservatives who had criticized his policies. He picked rightist Gennady Yanayev (who would later be the front man for the coup against him) as his deputy, and approved army statements that further unrest would not be tolerated. Some of Gorbachev's original *perestroika* partisans were demoted, and he used force in the Baltics to quell nationalist demands there.

Gorbachev's major effort in the first half of 1991 was to draft and secure approval of a new union treaty for the Soviet Union, which would at once both assuage and contain nationalist sentiments ripping across the country. In this he failed, and this failure is what preceded the unsuccessful coup of August 1991.

Six Soviet republics boycotted a March 1991 vote on Gorbachev's new union treaty. While the measure passed in the remaining republics, many of the other republics added questions regarding national self-determination, which clouded the results. Among the questions also asked in the Russian Federation, for example, was whether it should have an elected president. This proposal passed, and in June Boris Yeltsin was elected president of the Russian Federation over five other candidates; he received 60 percent of the vote, greatly strengthening his position vis-à-vis Gorbachev.

Though Gorbachev tried to quell demonstrations, they continued. His attempts at control lost him support on the Left, and his inability to maintain order lost him support on the Right. The economy remained on its downward spiral, as inflation for the first three months of 1991 measured almost 25 percent on consumer goods, and coal miners remained on strike. In a revealing sign of the times, 55 percent of Leningrad citizens voted to change the name of the city back to its czarist appellation, Saint Petersburg.

The new union treaty was to be signed in August. Gorbachev stitched together only six of the fifteen republics for an initial signing—Russia, Kazakhstan, Uzbekistan, Kirgyzstan, Tajikistan, and Belorussia. Even this, however, proved too much for his new conservative allies in the Kremlin, who feared any devolution of power. On August 18, 1991, they struck, immediately before the new pact was to go into effect.

Gorbachev, vacationing in the Crimea, was placed under house arrest. The following morning Gennady Yanayev went on national and international television announcing that Gorbachev was no longer physically able to perform the his duties of president. The coup was supported by a number of party officials, government ministers, and military-industrial leaders.

The coup was not, however, backed by the Russian people or army, and it quickly broke down. The army would not fire on civilians or quell resistance by force, and hence when Yeltsin defied coup leaders and shouted resistance from atop a tank outside of the Russian parliament building, the balance of power moved decisively against the coup leaders. The Russian people had had enough of communism; they were willing to give something else a try. By August 21, the coup had collapsed, and the next day Gorbachev was back in Moscow.

The big winner of the aborted coup was Boris Yeltsin. His courageous defiance, at a time when Gorbachev was not on the scene, strengthened his position immensely. The big losers of the aborted coup were Gorbachev, whose weakness was now manifest; the Communist party, from which Gorbachev now resigned; and the continued existence of the Soviet Union itself, the centrifugal forces of which became completely unleashed.

The final act in the collapse of the Soviet Union occurred between the aborted coup and December 26, 1991, when the Soviet parliament voted the country out of existence. Yeltsin's new power was immediately demonstrated on August 23 when Gorbachev received a rough reception in front of the Russian parliament and was required to accept direction from Yeltsin. During the following days, countries around the world recognized the independence of Latvia, Lithuania, and Estonia; the Ukraine and Belorussia also declared their independence; and the Communist party was officially suspended.

On September 5, 1991, the Soviet parliament voted to create a much looser "Union of Sovereign States" to replace the Soviet Union, a considerably more extensive devolution of power than was proposed before the aborted coup—while still retaining union—but it was too late. A union of any sort was not what the peoples of the Soviet Union now wanted: They wanted independence.

Over the next three and a half months Gorbachev attempted to protect his position (and in so doing some semblance of the Soviet Union) but to no avail. Various configurations of union were proposed, but Gorbachev now lacked authority. The December 1, 1991, popular vote in the Ukraine, which confirmed its declaration of independence (by a margin of nine to one), was the Soviet Union's deathblow. A union of Soviet republics was impossible without the Ukraine, the second most important republic after Russia itself.

On December 8, Russia, the Ukraine and Belorussia announced formation of the "Commonwealth of Independent States," an intended European Economic Community-type organization of sovereign nations. Dissolution of the Soviet Union now proceeded apace. By December 22, eleven of the twelve remaining republics (excepting Georgia) announced their acceptance of the new entity, effectively ending the Soviet Union. Boris Yeltsin took control of the Kremlin and most ex-Soviet ministries. On December 25, 1991, Mikhail Gorbachev announced his resignation, and the next day he moved out of the Kremlin. The Soviet hammer and sickle was lowered and the traditional Russian flag was hoisted in its place.

Communism in Eastern Europe and Afghanistan

The Soviet Union's 45 year domination over the countries of Eastern Europe was imposed during and after World War II at the direction of Stalin. Milestones in opposition to Soviet control, before the 1989 uprisings, were Tito's declaration of Yugoslav independence in 1948; the East German uprising of 1953; the Polish Poznan revolt of 1956; the Hungarian Revolution of 1956; the Czech defiance of 1968; and, most importantly of all, the Polish Solidarity movement of 1980. During his long term in office, Brezhnev acted decisively in a number of crises, not only to reaffirm control of the satellites but to attempt to extend Soviet domination beyond Eastern Europe into Afghanistan.

Brezhnev's view of the proper role of the Soviet Union in relation to other communist regimes was expressed in the "Brezhnev Doctrine," formulated after the suppression of Czech independence in 1968. On August 21, 1968, Soviet troops invaded Czechoslovakia to end the experiment of "socialism with a human face" initiated by the popular party leader Alexander Dubcek. Speaking on November 12, 1968, at the Congress of the Polish Communist party in Warsaw, Brezhnev made plain that the action in Czechoslovakia was not an isolated incident but the application of a broader principle. Under this policy, the Soviet government reserved to itself the right to use military force in any communist country where, in its judgment, a threat arose to the cause of communism—"a threat to the security of the Socialist Commonwealth as a whole." Significantly, Brezhnev did not confine the application of his new doctrine to Warsaw Pact countries but spoke of "any socialist country" including, as it turned out in 1979, the USSR's neighboring state of Afghanistan.

The first challenge to Soviet control of Eastern Europe had come in 1948 from Yugoslavia. In that year Yugoslavia was more completely communized than any other communist state in Eastern Europe. Josef Tito's crime in 1948 was not in abandoning communism in favor of capitalism but rather in trying to regain national independence from Moscow for the people of Yugoslavia. The Soviet Union mobilized all its resources of propaganda and subversion to overthrow Tito and his brand of national communism. At the time, few people thought Tito could defy Moscow successfully. Yet the unlikely happened, and Yugoslavia became independent.

The next major explosion took place on June 16 and 17, 1953, in East Germany. Food conditions had steadily deteriorated under Soviet and East German communist management, and there was less food available than during World War II. Even bread and potatoes were scarce.

The spark that triggered the smoldering resentment of the people was a government announcement on May 28, 1953, that wages would be cut further unless workers produced at least 10 percent more than in the past. On June 16, building workers on Stalin Avenue in East Berlin staged a spontaneous strike and marched on government headquarters. The strike spread quickly throughout East Germany, and in many communities the workers were in command of the situation, occupying police offices, liberating political prisoners, and setting government and Communist party buildings on fire. Many members of the police force either took a wait-and-see attitude or even went over to the rebels. Before long the rebels demanded, in addition to more tolerable living conditions, free elections, free labor unions, and the end of Soviet domination.

Hesitating at first to intervene directly, when the Soviet government realized that the communist regime would soon be overthrown completely, Soviet tanks moved into the major strongholds of the rebellion, suppressing it in a few days. Several hundred Germans died in the uprising, hundreds were wounded, and about 50,000 were imprisoned.

Three years after the uprising in East Germany, the Poles revolted. On June 28, 1956, thousands of workers at the Stalin Steel Works in Poznan went on strike early in the morning and marched toward the center of the city—chanting "Bread, bread, bread," singing Polish national songs, carrying the old Polish national flags, and refusing to disperse despite the tank formations quickly brought into the city by the communist authorities. Before long the striking workers occupied the Communist party headquarters and the radio station and set the city prison on fire, after freeing the prisoners. In the ensuing battle with army and police, a battle that lasted for several days, about 200 Poles lost their lives, thousands were wounded, and many more thousands were arrested.

Militarily, the rebellion was successfully repressed, but politically it unleashed a chain of events that resulted ultimately in the Solidarity movement a quarter of a century later.

The events in Poland in 1956 immediately raised hope and passion in Hungary, just as in 1989 events in one Eastern European country influenced another. On October 23, 1956, university students in Hungary, quickly joined by thousands of industrial workers, held a mass meeting in Budapest's Parliament Square. Expressing their sympathy for the Polish fight for freedom and independence, they put forward a series of demands, including (1) the evacuation of Soviet troops from Hungary; (2) free elections; (3) free labor unions and the right to strike; (4) revision of workers' wages and a complete reorganization of the economy; (5) the immediate release of political prisoners and the return of Hungarians deported to the Soviet Union; (6) removal of statues of Stalin; and finally (7) reorganization of the compulsory system of farm collectives.

The political police turned a peaceful meeting into a rebellion by firing on the students and workers. The fighting quickly spread throughout the country. Workers declared a general strike, and the freedom fighters were soon joined by the regular Hungarian army and police. On the communist side the Hungarian political police were joined by powerful Soviet tank forces.

Yet the incredible happened. The freedom fighters won their struggle, and on October 29, 1956, Hungary was free. Political authority was exercised by the representatives of popular organizations, and almost at once dozens of democratic newspapers began publication. Communists were nowhere to be seen, statues of Stalin were publicly destroyed, and political prisoners were set free—among them Cardinal Mindszenty, who had been imprisoned since 1948.

However, this period of Hungarian freedom and independence lasted for only five days. On November 3, close to 200,000 Soviet troops and 2,500 tanks and armored vehicles moved into Hungary to suppress Hungarian freedom. After a week of heavy fighting, the revolution was put down. Prime Minister Imre Nagy was kidnapped by the Russians and later executed. Over 35,000 Hungarians were killed in the fighting, and many more were wounded. Many thousands were deported to Siberia, while more than 200,000 managed to escape to Austria. The physical destruction of towns was worse than that suffered by Hungary in World War II, when it was a major battleground for many months.

During the first years after the crushing of the Hungarian Revolution, many people inside and outside Hungary thought that the heroic effort of the nation had been in vain. The communist dictatorship was harsher than before the revolution, and for a while it seemed more Stalinist than the government of the Soviet Union itself. In the end this reasoning—an implied defense of inert submission to communist totalitarianism—proved wrong. The very fact that the revolution had occurred encouraged tendencies toward more national independence in communist states. Even Albania was able, from the late 1950s on, to defy the Soviet Union by enthusiastically siding with China in its conflict with the Soviet Union.

In Hungary itself the harsh government installed by the Soviet army after the repression of the revolution in 1956 gradually realized that Soviet tanks were not enough if the country was to regain some measure of political stability. Throughout the 1960s the movement to relax the most oppressive controls gathered considerable momentum; thousands of political prisoners were released under a general amnesty, and the government eased its stringent controls in industry and agriculture. Writers and artists were given greater freedom of expression, and noncommunists were appointed to important positions. While the previous slogan had been "He who is not for us is against us," the new official slogan became "He who is not against us is with us."

In 1968 Hungary embarked on a major reform of its economy, with the objective of creating market competition and incentives for managers and workers. Rigid centralized planning was relaxed in favor of more autonomy for individual enterprises, enabling them to decide what to produce and where to sell, and allowing them to keep a greater share of the profits. Instead of governmentally fixed prices for all goods and services, a new three-tier system was introduced: fixed prices set by the government, controlled prices allowed to fluctuate within a predetermined upper and lower limit, and entirely free prices set by the enterprise in accordance with competitive market forces. In addition, the government began to encourage private small-scale enterprise in the home-building, retailing, services, and handicraft industries. More imports of consumer goods were allowed, supplemented by direct foreign investments in tourism and other industries. As a result of these economic reforms, relations with Western nations greatly improved, travel to foreign countries was permitted on a larger scale, and the political environment inside Hungary moved in the direction of cautious liberalization, so-called goulash communism. By the early 1970s Hungary was, next to Yugoslavia, the most liberal communist state in Eastern Europe.

Romania was held up until the early 1960s as the model of a docile satellite of the Soviet Union. After this time, however, it showed an increasing independence in foreign policy. Although Romania continued its membership in the Warsaw Pact alliance, its policy veered in the direction of neutrality. It maintained active ties with both China and Albania, and refused to be a party to Soviet-led efforts at condemning China in its conflict with the Soviet Union. When Sino–Soviet border clashes were reported, the Romanian press—in the time-honored style of neutrality in wartime—published the official Soviet and Chinese communiqués, giving equal space to each side.

In its relations with the West, Romania was until 1972 the only member of the Warsaw Pact alliance—other than the Soviet Union itself—to maintain full diplomatic relations with both West and East Germany. At the outbreak of the Israeli–Arab war in 1967, all Warsaw Pact nations except Romania broke off diplomatic relations with Israel; Romania not only refused to join the other Warsaw Pact signatories in their anti-Israel campaign but maintained friendly relations with both Israel and the Arab states, and allowed over 300,000 Romanian Jews to emigrate to Israel.

Romania was the only Warsaw Pact country that refused to contribute troops to the Soviet-led invasion of Czechoslovakia in 1968, or to condone the act. Only a week before the invasion, President Nicolae Ceausescu had pointedly visited Prague and had signed a treaty of mutual help and assistance with the liberal Dubcek government there. After the invasion of Czechoslovakia, Ceausescu warned the Soviet Union that no foreign troops would be allowed to enter Romania, and he ordered the immediate creation of a "people's militia" of workers, peasants, and intellectuals for "the defense of freedom and independence" of his nation. Ceausescu condemned the Soviet aggression as "a grave mistake and a serious danger not only to peace in Europe but to socialism throughout the world." In 1984, Romania was the only Soviet-bloc nation to participate in the Los Angeles Olympics.

Communist rule in Czechoslovakia was established in 1948 through a coup of the Communist party aided by threats of Soviet military intervention. Czechoslovakia was the only country in central Europe that had a genuinely democratic and free tradition in politics, economics, and religion, and its standards of education and industrial skill compared favorably with those of its neighbors. The communization of Czechoslovakia in 1948 shocked the Western nations into a renewed awareness of Soviet imperialism, and the creation of NATO was the most significant response to that shock. From 1948 to the early 1960s, the communist regime in Czechoslovakia was rigidly Stalinist in its internal policy and docile in its relations with the Soviet Union.

From the middle 1960s on, a new generation of communist leaders began to reappraise the effects of communist rule on Czechoslovakia. In the economic field the country had fallen behind as a result of both domestic and foreign policy. Domestically, rigid central planning and bureaucratic routine had stifled the traditional initiative and enterprise of the highly skilled Czechs. In its foreign economic policy, the Czech economy had to adapt to the role assigned to it by COMECON, a kind of Soviet dominated Common Market. The Czech economy neglected the industries in which it had developed world-renowned skills and profitable markets in the West—such as textiles, glass, china, leather goods, and jewelry—and concentrated on basic industries that were not as satisfactory. Consequently, the growth record of the Czech economy was unimpressive, even when compared with the other communist states in Eastern Europe. In politics the democratic habits of the people increasingly reasserted themselves among workers, students, and intellectuals, as well as among growing numbers of Communist party leaders.

In January 1968 Antonin Novotny—the leader and popular symbol of Stalinist communism—was replaced by Alexander Dubcek, a liberal communist, as First Secretary of the Czech Community party. Under Dubcek's leadership, communism in Czechoslovakia embarked on a unique experiment in the history of communism: the transformation of totalitarian communism into *socialism with a human face* by peaceful means—that is, the combination of public ownership in the economy with political democracy in government.

One of the first acts of the Dubcek regime was to release from prison more than 30,000 victims of the Novotny regime and to abolish the secret police. Prominent victims of Czech Stalinism executed in the 1950s were rehabilitated posthumously. Old-line Stalinist communists were dismissed from their positions, but the new government was careful not to use force against them. This treatment, in line with the new emphasis on the rule of law, grew out of the conviction that the popular condemnation of Stalinist communists was so profound that no other penalties were needed. All travel restrictions on Czechoslovaks wishing to leave the country or foreigners wishing to visit it were lifted. This freedom to travel was an indirect blow at the Berlin Wall, since East Germans could visit Czechoslovakia and from there make their way to West Germany.

Freedom of speech, of the press, and of assembly spread spontaneously, as the government did nothing to discourage them. In fact, the government finally abolished all censorship of the press. Noncommunist newspapers were freely published, and criticism of communism was expressed. In the most famous document of the period—"2000 Words," a manifesto of intellectuals and workers—the following passage appeared: "The Communist party, which after the war possessed the great trust of the people, gradually exchanged this trust for offices, until it had all the offices and nothing else." The signers of the manifesto declared their commitment to socialism, but it had to be a socialism regenerated by democracy: "The regenerative process introduces nothing particularly new into our life. It revives ideas and topics, many of which are older than the errors of socialism." What many Czechoslovak communists wanted for their country was Marxism without Leninism. Some publicly stated that Leninism might be suitable for a country like Russia, but not for Czechoslovakia in its advanced stage of political and economic development.

Finally, the Dubcek leadership allowed the formation of noncommunist clubs and associations, and Wenceslas Square in the center of Prague became the Hyde Park of Czechoslovakia, where groups and individuals could freely express their views. The extent of the freedom enjoyed during the spring and summer of 1968 can be seen in the fact that a public opinion poll was taken on the question of allowing opposition parties. On June 27, 1968, the official daily of the Communist party reported the results of the poll: 90 percent of noncommunists favored the creation of opposition parties, and even more than half of the communists polled did so.

During the spring and summer of 1968, the Dubcek leadership was repeatedly warned by Brezhnev to give up the experiment in "socialism with a human face." The main fear of the Soviets—supported principally by East German and Polish leaders—was that the process of liberalization would undermine the monopoly of the Communist party in Czechoslovakia and that an opposition, once given freedom of organization and expression, might provide an alternative government some day. The Czech leaders defended themselves by arguing that they were fully confident that liberalization under communist leadership would strengthen the cause of communism, and that no political groups would be allowed that challenged the economic principles of public ownership of the means of production. In the area of foreign policy, the Dubcek regime repeatedly reassured Soviet leaders that Czechoslovakia would continue its membership in the Warsaw Pact.

The Soviet Union was unwilling to accept either possible outcome of the Czech experiment: If the experiment had led to the gradual elimination of communist influence in Czech politics and economics, it might have provided an example for other communist countries that communist rule was not irreversible and that a return journey to a noncommunist society was possible. Conversely, from the Soviet viewpoint, had the experiment in Czechoslovakia succeeded and the party maintained itself in a place of leadership by moral authority rather than by force, the repercussions of such a success might have been disastrous for the communist regimes in the Soviet Union and other communist states that relied on prisons and labor camps for the maintenance of communist rule.

The Soviet leadership decided that socialism with a human face had to be ended by armed force, since a voluntary return to a harder line in Czechoslovakia was out of the question. On August 21, 1968, some 200,000 troops—mostly Soviet but including East German, Polish, Bulgarian, and Hungarian contingents—invaded and occupied Czechoslovakia. There was sporadic individual fighting and a few dozen people were killed, but the Czechs decided not to resist the invasion with their armed forces. Swastikas were painted on Soviet tanks, and numerous inscriptions on buildings explained to the Soviet "liberators" that to the people of Czechoslovakia, German Nazism and Soviet communism were the same.

Soviet troops were to stay on Czech soil through 1989, and by the early 1970s Czechoslovakia was effectively subjected to a Brezhnev-type regime of spiritual and physical coercion. Writers, artists, teachers, and managers were induced or compelled to state publicly that they welcomed the Soviet military occupation of their country. Many formerly liberal communists were dismissed from their positions, and some were tried and sentenced to prison terms. The result, as a liberal communist leader who escaped abroad put it, was inevitable: "Of all Eastern European countries, the deepest depression, frustration, and feeling of hopelessness prevail in Czechoslovakia" (Eugen Loebl, "Spiritual Genocide," The New York Times, September 23, 1972, p. 31).

While the 1948 communist coup in Czechoslovakia was hailed by other communist states and parties as a victory for the cause of Marxism-Leninism, the Soviet occupation of Czechoslovakia in 1968 fragmented the communist world more profoundly than ever before. Three communist states—Yugoslavia, Romania, and China—sharply denounced the Soviet action, but the governments of Poland, East Germany, Bulgaria, and Hungary—who had themselves participated in the aggression—defended the Soviet Union. Not a single communist party leader in Western Europe supported intervention, and the large communist parties of Italy and France were particularly outspoken in their condemnation.

In 1979 Brezhnev took a bold step to expand the Soviet bloc in a new direction: He ordered Soviet troops into the neighboring country of Afghanistan to support a coup headed by Babrak Karmal, a pro-Soviet Afghan leader who had been living in exile in Eastern Europe.

Karmal's coup was the culmination of some two years of political turmoil in Afghanistan. A pro-Soviet regime that came to power through a bloody uprising in 1978 was itself overthrown in a matter of months. While still committed to a socialist domestic program, the new government tried to steer a more independent course in foreign policy. But the government was weakened by factional struggles inside the ruling People's Democratic party, and also by rebels within and outside the Afghan army who put their faith in Islam above their belief in Marxism. Resistance spread into the countryside, where Muslim rebels aided by the Islamic states of Pakistan and Iran began a guerrilla campaign that would soon embroil Soviet troops in a fierce, protracted struggle. Concerned that Afghanistan might veer further from its pro-Soviet course, and recognizing the vulnerability of the existing regime, Brezhnev acted to impose by force a puppet government headed by a dependable friend, Karmal. Proclaiming their desire to help restore political stability, the Soviets quickly moved 30,000 troops into Afghanistan—mainly into Kabul, the capital.

Like the United States in Vietnam, the Soviets in Afghanistan expected a swift and decisive victory. Instead, they became mired in a war lasting years, requiring greater commitment, and suffering heavy casualties. The Soviets greatly underestimated the tenacity of the guerrilla forces arrayed against them, as well as the intense nationalist feelings aroused by their presence as foreign invaders. Units of the Afghan army proved unreliable as allies, deserting in large numbers to the guerrillas, with whom they shared religious and political sympathies. Superior firepower and military organization enabled the Soviets to gain control of the larger cities and surrounding countryside, but in remote and forbidding mountain strongholds, the guerrillas continued to resist.

Brezhnev's invasion of Afghanistan, which marked a notable broadening of the Soviet sphere of control, provoked strong international reaction, expressed not only in almost universal political condemnation of the Soviet action but also in extensive aid sent to the rebels from many parts of the world. Moreover, the invasion brought the Soviet Union into direct confrontation with Islamic and nonaligned countries of the Third World. While Brezhnev's military interventions in Eastern Europe worked to keep the satellites within the Soviet orbit, in Afghanistan the Brezhnev Doctrine encountered resolute and costly resistance, and ended in ultimate failure with Soviet withdrawal from Afghanistan in 1989.

While its 1979 invasion of Afghanistan crystallized opposition to the Soviet Union from without its empire, the rise of the Solidarity labor movement in Poland during the early 1980s helped to foment opposition to it from within. While Solidarity was not initially successful in achieving its aim of a freer and more open and independent Poland, its example—though at first transitory—shone brightly in illuminating the way toward the revolutions in Eastern Europe and the Soviet Union that would occur within a decade.

The election in 1978 of Karol Wojtyla, Archbishop of Krakow, as the new Pope of the Roman Catholic Church—John Paul II—played a vital role in the rise of Solidarity (and through this the end of communism in Europe). Poland is 95 percent Catholic, and it is a country in which the Church grew stronger under communism, despite official persecution, because of its sole position as an organized body outside of the state. When John Paul II returned to his native land on a triumphal pilgrimage in 1979 the outpouring was fantastic. The complex task of organizing the Pontiff's week-long visit was left by the government in the hands of the Church, and Poles relished the novel experience of joining together as private citizens in a national network of information and practical arrangements to facilitate John Paul II's visit. This exceptional effort foreshadowed Solidarity's achievement a year later in mobilizing the workers of Poland into a national movement.

Moreover, the Pope left behind a pointed message: At his last public appearance, preaching to an audience of nearly 2 million, he exhorted his listeners to "accept the whole of the spiritual legacy that goes with the name 'Poland.' Do not be defeated. Do not be discouraged; never lose your spiritual freedom."

The founding of Solidarity at the Lenin Shipyard in Gdansk in August 1980 was preceded ten years earlier by a strike that turned into an uprising emanating from the same location. At that time, 1970, the long-time chief of the Polish Communist party, Wladyslaw Gomulka, was ousted in favor of Edvard Gierek. Although Gierek contained the immediate unrest, he was unable to solve the economic problems that were in large part its cause.

The specific incident that gave rise to the founding of Solidarity was the attempted firing of a popular crane operator, Anna Walentynowicz, from her job at the Lenin Shipyard. This led to a strike, which in a matter of days went far beyond "Mother Anna" (as she was affectionately called) to "21 Demands" for improved working conditions, greater participation in the political process, more civil rights, and, most importantly of all, the right to form an independent trade union with the ability to strike.

Surprisingly (though perhaps not so surprisingly, given the boost to Polish independence provided by the Pope), the government was willing to negotiate with the workers, and on August 31, 1970, the "Gdansk Agreement" was reached. In it, compromises were agreed to on a number of the workers' demands, and Solidarity was recognized as an independent union with the right to strike.

Solidarity's officially recognized independence was a momentous occasion because it was the first time that a communist state had so formally allowed a civil power in competition with itself to exist. While occasionally an accommodation would have to be reached with a religious body (as in Poland) or another body along these lines, never before had an independent trade union been allowed. The importance of this was that Solidarity was a crack in the communist monolithic view of societal organization, as an ongoing, independent body, with the capacity (through the ability to strike) to exert influence.

While Solidarity affirmed in the Gdansk Agreement the "leading role" of the Communist party, pledged not to act as a political party, and took a hands-off position on Polish foreign affairs, nevertheless the blow had been struck. Life in Poland, and ultimately other communist states, would not be the same again.

The Gdansk Agreement was attacked by hard-liners both among the workers, who saw it as too pacifying to the government, and within the Communist party, who denounced it as too lenient to the workers. Uncooperative officials reneged on specific agreements, and workers engaged in wildcat strikes as the Polish economy continued to deteriorate.

An early casualty of the continuing, see-saw struggle between Solidarity and the government was Party Secretary Gierek, who was replaced by Stanislaw Kania for being unable to control the situation. The charismatic leader of Solidarity, Lech Walesa, experienced a better fate; though he was criticized by some workers for being too moderate he was able for over a year to steer the way between a government clampdown and a union that could go out of control.

The response of the Soviet Union to events in Poland was uneven. While Soviet leaders sometimes expressed confidence in the ability of Poles to work out their own differences, at other times they warned of "fraternal assistance" to aid the Polish Communist party—a euphemism for armed Soviet intervention. During periods of greatest tension, Polish officials cautioned Solidarity to avoid a "national tragedy"—the code phrase for a Soviet invasion. Military maneuvers of Warsaw Pact nations were held along Polish borders and on Polish soil.

Solidarity's independence to a small extent spilled over into the Polish Communist party. In July 1981, for the first time, elections to the National Party Congress were conducted by secret ballot according to genuine democratic processes with competing (communist) candidates.

The high tide of Solidarity's initial phase came during September 1981 at its own First National Congress, a convention of delegates democratically elected from throughout the country. By this time Solidarity had 10 million members, in a nation of less than 40 million people, and there was also a Rural Solidarity with a half million agricultural members. But even as Solidarity celebrated its hard-won independence, storm clouds gathered. Confrontations between local officials and impatient workers continued to escalate; police brutality and work stoppages increased; no agreement on the economy was reached. Production of raw materials and manufactured goods fell; foreign debt continued to climb; food was in short supply.

In this deteriorating situation the more radical voices within Solidarity called for co-responsibility between workers and government in running the economy, and for extensions of grassroots democracy across the country. They finally proposed a national referendum on the issues of who should rule, how leaders should be selected, whether military ties with the Soviet Union should be continued, and what role the Communist party should have. These were provocative moves, to say the least. To head off the impending crisis, moderate leaders in Solidarity, in the Communist party, and in the Church urged compromise and cooperation. But the final act of the drama was already underway.

A month after Solidarity's exuberant National Congress, the indecisive Kania was replaced as party leader by General Wojciech Jaruzelski, the Minister of Defense. Unlike the party, which had fallen into disrepute in the eyes of most Poles, the army was still respected as a guardian of national independence, and General Jaruzelski enjoyed the prestige of a military man. He was also popular personally and regarded as a party moderate. But Jaruzelski had not come to power in order to preside over the dissolution of his country. As the crisis dragged on—shortages of the most basic commodities, including meat, soap, and vodka, were felt everywhere— General Jaruzelski, urged on by Moscow, resolved to act. On Sunday morning, December 13, 1981, moving with complete surprise and clockwork precision, the Polish army took control of the country.

Judging from its broad scope and efficient execution, the operation had clearly been planned weeks in advance. Thousands of Solidarity leaders were arrested, all internal and foreign communications were cut, and martial law was imposed throughout the land. Pockets of worker resistance in some of the large factories and mines were sealed off by the troops, while the actual mopping up was left to the ZOMO, the brutal internal security police that in every communist regime was the dependable strong arm of party rule. The voices of radicals and moderates alike were stilled. The process of "normalization" had begun.

General Jaruzelski's coup did not solve Poland's long-term problems; but it did end the stalemate between an increasingly militant Solidarity and an intransigent core of Communist party officials. Despite its own best efforts, the Catholic Church—a trusted institution outside the immediate struggle but with close ties to both sides—could not arrange a reconciliation. Many Poles agreed that General Jaruzelski acted from patriotic motives in order to avert a greater "national tragedy," even as they deplored the martial law he imposed on them. But a deadlock had been reached—an independent union claiming rights to economic self-management and political self-government could not coexist with a Communist party claiming its "leading role" in society.

The historic importance of Solidarity was reaffirmed in the spring of 1983 when Lech Walesa was awarded the Nobel Peace Prize. The award symbolized the support of the international community for the struggle waged by Solidarity to secure basic civil and political rights while avoiding the twin calamities of civil war and foreign occupation. Throughout the protracted crisis Walesa emphasized his commitment to nonviolence and peaceful negotiation. Pressured both by conservative opponents to all significant reform and radical advocates of a direct challenge to Communist party rule, he tried to steer a middle course between capitulation on essential demands and escalation of the conflict into bloody rebellion. Walesa's middle course initially failed, as Poland fell under the shadow of a military coup. Yet the courageous struggle was remembered and honored in the awarding of the Nobel Prize. And the lesson was once again confirmed that basic rights to free speech, religion, assembly, and to independent organizations, far from being outworn vestiges of "bourgeois democracy," are vital claims of free people everywhere.

Moreover, the long-term significance of Solidarity was immense. Not only did the union remain in existence underground, but it ultimately came back to lead the transition of Poland from a communist to a democratic state. Furthermore, by existing above ground for sixteen months it set a new example of what was possible in a communist regime. Finally, by the Soviet Union not directly intervening, potential limits were demonstrated to Soviet control over the satellites.

Solidarity retained influence even after its ban. Its flame flickered but did not blow out as discontent with the regime continued to build. In October 1984 members of the secret police kidnapped and murdered a popular pro-Solidarity-priest, Father Jerzy Popieluszko. It was a measure of the degree to which Poland had changed that the government found it necessary to bring the responsible secret police members to trial, although no higher-ups were implicated.

Lacking reform, the Polish economy continued to stagnate. On November 29, 1987, Jaruzelski held a referendum on his economic reform package. It was defeated, the first time in forty years that an Eastern European country had held a free election. Winds of change were altering events in Poland both from within and without. Solidarity and Lech Walesa reappeared, and externally the obvious changes in the Soviet Union influenced Poles as to what now might be possible politically.

Jaruzelski invited Walesa to participate in "round table" talks on Poland's future in August 1988. Walesa replied that Solidarity had to be legalized before he would attend. Over the ensuing months power shifted away from the government. It was forced to cede Solidarity's legalization, and then had to agree to free parliamentary elections.

The elections, which were held on June 4, 1989, were an utter rout for the government. Solidarity won 99 of 100 Senate seats, and all freely elected seats in the other house of Poland's legislature, the *Sejm*. Thirty-three of 35 communist candidates running unopposed on the ballot did not receive a majority of votes as most electors crossed off their names. According to Jaruzelski: "Our defeat is total." On August 24, Solidarity editor Tadeusz Mazowiecki became the first noncommunist prime minister in Eastern Europe since 1948.

The events in Poland were closely watched in Hungary, which had long been the most liberal of Eastern European communist nations. To some extent, the success of Hungary's flirtation with political and economic moderation fueled Gorbachev's hopes that reform of a communist state from within was possible. In the late 1980s, with news of *glasnost* and *perestroika* filling the already relatively free Hungarian media every day, the influence moved in the other direction: Hungary gave up all vestiges of communism.

In May 1988, Janos Kadar was replaced as General Secretary by reformer Karoly Grosz, who planned an orderly dismantling of the Hungarian communist system. Events overtook him, however, and within a year and a half Grosz found himself in unplanned retirement. He who had been a reformer became a conservative, so fast did communism evaporate.

Kadar had been kicked upstairs to be party president after he was replaced as General Secretary, much as Gromyko in the Soviet Union had been made president upon his replacement as foreign secretary. In May 1989, a mere year after he had left as General Secretary, Kadar retired as party president, paving the way for reformers even more progressive than him to take control of the party apparatus.

The pace of change now quickened—plans were made to eliminate remaining restrictions on the free market, freedom of expression was granted entirely, and free elections were contemplated. Most important of all, the remains of Imre Nagy and others who had participated in the 1956 uprising were exhumed and reburied with the prestige given a state funeral.

Over 100,000 Hungarians attended the funeral of the 1956 martyrs, and the rest of the nation watched transfixed on television, as eulogist after eulogist criticized the Soviet Union and the regime it had installed. This was the first great demonstration of the "people's power" that transformed countries in Eastern Europe during 1989.

In May, Hungary had dismantled the remaining barbed wire on its border with Austria, so rusted had the Iron Curtain become. Thousands of East Germans were then emboldened to travel to Hungary (to which they could travel legally) in the hope that they could escape to the West over the now open boundary.

The thousands became tens of thousands, and by August Hungary filled with East Germans seeking to cross over to the West. On September 10, with no guidance from the Soviet Union, Hungary lifted all restrictions on travel to the West by foreigners in its midst. The dam now broke.

East Germany, whose existence most symbolized the division of Europe, stood on the brink of disaster, much as it had in 1961 prior to the building of the Berlin Wall. Now, as then, East Germans were voting with their feet in place of the franchise that was denied to them. Unless East Germany could stop its hemorrhaging, it would lose legitimacy as a nation, as well as potentially millions of its members.

The year 1989 was not to be a repeat of 1961, however. The East German people were no longer willing to be cowed into submission; neither was the Soviet Union now willing to militarilily intervene.

Party secretary Erich Honecker attempted to stop travel by East Germans to Hungary once it opened its borders to the West, but this proved ineffective. East Germans now besieged West German embassies in Czechoslovakia and Poland, hoping to gain access to the West via one of these routes.

On October 7, 1989, East Germany "celebrated" its fortieth anniversary as an independent state. Eleven days later Honecker resigned as party leader, and was replaced by Egon Krenz. The situation was now out of control. Tens of thousands were taking to the streets in Leipzig, Dresden, and East Berlin. In Helsinki, on October 25, Gorbachev spokesperson Gennadi Gerasimov announced the "Sinatra doctrine"—each Eastern European nation would be free to go its own way.

On October 30, some 300,000 East Germans demonstrated in Leipzig, and on November 4 half a million demonstrated in East Berlin. On November 7 and 8, the government and Politiburo resigned, and on November 9 the Berlin Wall fell—electrifying the world.

Events in East Germany propelled change in Czechoslovakia, which had been steadfastly pro-Soviet following the invasion of 1968, but by 1988 the Soviet Union itself had gone beyond where Czechoslovakia had been twenty years earlier.

On November 17, 1989, a week and a day after the Berlin Wall fell, 25,000 students demonstrated in Prague—the first significant public expression of how Czechs felt since 1969. Three days later the crowd grew to 200,000 and called for the government's resignation.

Leader of the Czech opposition was Vaclav Havel, the playwright who was the primary author of "Charter 77," a statement of principles that called on the government to implement the human rights sections of the Helsinki Agreement of 1975, and who had spent five years in jail for opposition to the regime. Havel led daily rallies in Prague's Wenceslas Square, and by November 29 some 500,000 Czechs jammed into the square to hear Havel and Alexander Dubcek, who appeared before a Czech audience for the first time in over twenty years. That night, the government resigned.

Coincident with change in Czechoslovakia was change in Bulgaria, usually considered the most compliant of satellites. On November 10, Todor Zhivkov, longest-serving of Soviet bloc leaders, was dismissed as president and Party General Secretary by reform-minded communists. A week later laws prohibiting political expression were eliminated, and on November 18, demonstrations began in the Bulgarian capital, Sofia, as had occurred in other East European cities.

This left Romania. Notwithstanding its maverick status within the Warsaw Pact in the area of foreign policy, Romania by 1989 was the last truly Stalinist nation left within the alliance when it came to domestic policy. Moreover, Ceausescu was the last communist leader to practice a "cult of personality" on a grand scale. He regularly had himself referred to in the media by such appellations as the "Enlightened One," "Great Conductor," "Genius of the Carpathians," and "Danube of Thought." He meant to hold onto power.

Ceausescu's regime was particularly oppressive. Contact with foreigners was virtually prohibited; typewriters were registered with the police. Ceausescu also had brutal population policies (to increase population)—birth control and abortion were illegal, and every three months women were checked by the so-called menstrual police to ensure that these policies were being practiced.

On December 14, 1989, rioting began in Timisoara, and Ceausescu responded in classical form, ordering the army to "shoot to kill." A week later, he found himself being yelled at on national television, at a rally he had called to demonstrate support for himself. At this point, the revolution erupted.

The army sided with the people, who massively and spontaneously rose up. Ceausescu's *Securitate*—the dreaded secret police—remained loyal to him, and for several days a battle waged. On December 22, however, Ceausescu and his hated wife, Elana, were captured by the army and turned over to the Council of National Salvation for trial. Their execution on December 25, 1989, especially after their corpses were shown on television, halted effective opposition to the revolution.

Albania and Yugoslavia, communist though not part of the Soviet bloc, were unable to resist the winds of change as 1990 and 1991 progressed. In Albania, President Ramiz Alia began a program of democratization, restoring freedom of travel and religion, and thousands of particularly young people attempted to flee to Italy. In Yugoslavia, Slovenia's and Croatia's declarations of independence in 1991 ignited civil war there, which occupied much international attention during the latter part of that year and through 1993, as Serbia attempted to establish a greater Serbia in remnants of Yugoslavia, particularly Bosnia.

CHINESE COMMUNISM

With the collapse of the Soviet Union, the People's Republic of China is the most important communist state in the world today. Among the major revolutionaries of the twentieth century—including Lenin, Trotsky, Mussolini, and Hitler—none had so long-lasting and far-reaching an effect on his country as Mao Zedong. Lenin died in 1924, during the formative years of Soviet communism, warning from his deathbed against the scheming and ruthless Stalin; Trotsky founded the Red Army, which won the civil war that followed the Russian Revolution, but he was exiled from the Soviet Union in 1929, a victim of Stalin's enmity; Mussolini led his March on Rome in 1922, pledging to restore the glories of the Roman Empire, but he was executed ignominiously in 1945 amid the ruins of a lost war; and Hitler's promised Thousand Year Reich ended in flames after little more than a decade.

For his part, Mao Zedong helped found the Chinese Communist party (1921); he guided it through two civil wars and a foreign invasion; he led it to power in a national revolution (1949); and then for more than a quarter of a century—until his death in 1976—he presided over the reconstruction and transformation of Chinese society and politics. For forty years, from the time he became chairman of the party in 1935 until he died at the age of eighty-three, the person of Mao Zedong and the cause of Chinese communism were inseparably linked. His prescriptions for how to think and act, published as *The Thoughts of Mao Zedong*, became for millions of Chinese a modern equivalent of the ancient *Sayings of Confucius*. Until his death he remained the predominant theorist, leader and symbol of Chinese communism.

Proclamation of the People's Republic of China on October 1, 1949, was the culmination of a long and arduous journey for Mao and the Chinese Communist party. When the journey began, China was weak and divided, poor and semifeudal, prey to periodic famines, ruled by reactionary warlords, and at the mercy of foreign powers who exacted economic and political concessions from an ineffective central government. When Mao died, China was unified and independent, rid of the excesses of political corruption and mass starvation, and moving toward economic development. Further, it was a world power wielding nuclear weapons and serving as a base of support for other communist regimes as far away as Albania. The achievements were prodigious, but the costs were enormous. If Mao can be credited with extraordinary achievements, he is also responsible for their exceptional costs.

The Early Years of Chinese Communism

Mao was born in 1893 into a relatively comfortable "middle peasant" family that provided him with the basic education that was essential for further advancement. By his own account, he was in continual conflict with his father, whom he regarded as harsh, unreasonable, and philistine. At the age of sixteen, Mao defied his father by leaving his native village to attend school in a nearby town. His studies there were interrupted by the Revolution of 1911, which overthrew the reigning Manchu dynasty and inaugurated the Chinese Republic, welcomed enthusiastically by Mao. After a brief stint in the pro-Republican army, he entered the Teachers' Training School in Changsha, capital of his native province of Hunan. During the five years he spent at this school (1913–1918), Mao encountered the personalities, ideas, and activities that soon launched him on his revolutionary course.

Mao's revolutionary impulses turned toward communism after he moved to Beijing University to work as an assistant in the library. There he joined a Marxist study group and took part in the momentous May 4th Movement (1919), a violent demonstration against the government's acquiescence in territorial concessions to Japan. This explosive display of nationalist fervor was later celebrated as the beginning of communist activity in China. Observing the condition of China during these years, Mao felt deep disillusionment over the results of the Revolution of 1911, a feeling shared by his radical teachers and fellow students. The leader of that revolution, Dr. Sun Yat-sen, was a Western-educated physician who had been agitating for years against the corrupt and ineffective rule of the Manchus. In 1905 he formulated his program as the Three Principles of the People: People's Rule (nationalism), People's Authority (democracy), and People's Livelihood (socialism). These principles, always ambiguous and never directly applied to the specific problems of the time, became the main ideological guide for reform groups until Mao himself adapted Marxism-Leninism to the conditions of Chinese society.

Dr. Sun's efforts bore fruit in 1911 when with the aid of the influential general Yuan Shih-k'ai, the boy emperor was deposed and a republic proclaimed. For Mao, as for all progressive-minded Chinese, this was an exciting time. But hope soon turned to bitter disappointment as General Yuan, now president of the republic, betrayed the revolution. He aimed to install himself as a new emperor, which he hoped to accomplish through alliances with provincial warlords whose military power would be the basis of his government. Yuan died in 1916 before his plans could succeed; he left as his legacy, and thus as the legacy of the Revolution of 1911, a divided country ruled by autonomous warlords.

The ensuing period was a time of intense intellectual ferment and equally intense political frustration. Reforms of all sorts were proposed and attempted, but it became increasingly clear that without some fundamental change in the governmental structure, no permanent progress could be achieved. The violent demonstration of May 4, 1919, was an expression of growing dissatisfaction.

The revolutionary forces that won an inconclusive victory in 1911 produced two heirs; the Nationalist party, later renamed the Kuomintang (National People's Party), and the Communist party, founded in 1921 by a small group of Marxists, including Mao, in the main industrial city of Shanghai. For a time the two parties worked in collaboration, thanks largely to the urgings of the Soviet advisers who counseled and aided both groups. This collaboration culminated in the successful military campaigns of 1926–1927, in which the warlords were defeated and China seemed on the verge of reunification. But even during the years of collaboration, a serious rift was developing between the Kuomintang, now led by Chiang Kai-shek, and the communists. In 1927 the struggle broke into open civil war.

The sources of this rift, which was to have the most fateful consequences for the future of China, were deep-rooted. At issue were alternative visions of the way to a modern China. Although he had started out as a nationalist revolutionary, Chiang's views and policies grew increasingly narrow and conservative. Consolidating the power of the Kuomintang became his primary purpose, overriding a concern for major economic and social change. Married to a daughter of the wealthy and Westernized Soong family, he converted to Christianity and moved closer to the propertied urban merchants and rural landlords who provided his main support and whose interests he protected. Instead of basic political and social reform, he advocated traditional Confucian morality and rigorous military discipline. In a critical decision he determined to make extermination of the communists his first priority, before turning either to domestic reform or to the looming menace of Japanese aggression.

Mao, on the other hand, envisioned a fundamental transformation in the entire base of agricultural China. His early major work of social analysis, "Report on an Investigation of the Peasant Movement in Hunan" (1927), revealed both the unorthodox bent of his communist theory—he placed primary emphasis on the revolutionary potential of rural peasants rather than urban workers—and also the very radical implications of his call for revolution in the countryside. China was an overwhelmingly agricultural nation, and Mao was attacking the fundamental institutions of traditional Chinese society.

Chiang's war against the communists went well; before long his Kuomintang armies controlled most of the country. Assaulted in their main base in east-central China (Kiangsi province), the communists resolved on a daring escape to a remote region of the northwest (Shensi province) where they would be safe against attack. The "Long March" (1934–1935) became a legend in the history of Chinese communism. The tortuous route covered nearly 7,000 miles; of some 100,000 people who began the march, less than 30,000 survived to the end. But this remnant, which became the core of victorious communist armies a decade later, consisted of tough, disciplined, dedicated cadres, politically united under their newly elected chairman, Mao Zedong.

Mao's Doctrines

During the period Mao spent in the north at his capital of Yenan, he formulated his theoretical views and initiated the policies that would later be imposed throughout the country. Mao's theories are not always internally consistent, nor did they remain the same through the years. On the contrary, his thought underwent many modifications, even in basic emphasis. Although he was a self-proclaimed disciple of Marxism-Leninism, and important parts of his thought are orthodox Leninism, from the very beginning his views reflected the specific conditions of Chinese society as well as the particular circumstances of his own rise to power. A number of themes emerge that are distinctly Maoist:

1. Cities are secondary to the countryside.
2. Mass action is secondary to the Red Army.
3. Revolutionary fervor is more important than efficiency.
4. Objective realities are secondary to subjective forces.

Cities are secondary to the countryside   Mao's first efforts as a communist organizer were spent in the villages of his native Hunan, and this experience opened his eyes to the revolutionary potential in rural areas. Lenin too had recognized the revolutionary role of peasants in underdeveloped countries as allies of the industrial workers, but his belief that the more active part would be taken by the better-organized urban proletariat was closer to Marx's original view that the leading revolutionary force in capitalist society was the industrial working class. At first Mao may also have shared this belief; however, he became convinced that the peasants must act not merely as an ally but as the main force in the revolutionary struggle, and that leadership in the struggle must also come from the peasants. Although Mao's view accurately reflected Chinese realities, it was a significant step beyond Lenin.

Mao's determination to base the communist movement in the countryside rather than in the cities was confirmed during the Long March. Not only had earlier attempts by the Red Army to capture Kuomintang-dominated cities failed, but in their long trek northward the communist forces found welcome aid in the villages along the route. By the time Mao reached Yenan, he was convinced that control of the countryside was the key to success. With the active, or at least passive, support of the local peasants, the communist forces could operate effectively in the countryside, interrupting communication and supply routes, choosing favorable occasions to engage and defeat the troops sent against them, and eventually reducing the cities to submission.

Guerrilla warfare became Mao's overall strategy: Communist armies would move through the countryside like fish in the sea ("The People are the Sea; We are the Fish"), ultimately to encircle and conquer the major urban centers. It was a strategy applied by Mao and his trusted comrade-in-arms, General Lin Piao, to the revolutionary struggle—both internal and international. Just as control of the countryside would lead to conquest of the cities, so control of former colonial areas would lead to strangulation of the capitalist heartland in Europe and America. In both respects Mao had reversed the original Marxist priorities: Revolution would succeed in the countryside before the cities, and in underdeveloped countries before the industrialized centers. Mao was adapting Marxism to the conditions of the developing world.

Mass action is secondary to the Red Army   The success of Mao's strategy depended not simply on the support of the local population but mainly on the effectiveness of the Red Army as a military organization. Protracted revolutionary warfare, extended over decades, could not be won by the people; only the army could win such a struggle. This is the basis of Mao's statement that "viewed from the Marxist theory of the state, the army is the chief component of the political power of a state. Whoever wants to seize and hold onto political power must have a strong army."

In fact, military and Communist party operations were virtually indistinguishable throughout these years. Mao and his most faithful lieutenant, Zhou Enlai, were generals before they assumed key political and administrative roles in the People's Republic, and the same was true of other major leaders from the older generation. The Red Army had played an active part in the revolution since 1927, when General Chu Teh founded the People's Liberation Army by leading a rebellion against the Kuomintang in the city of Nanking. General Chu and his troops subsequently joined Mao on the Long March. The survivors of this ordeal formed the nucleus of the armies that fought first against the Japanese invaders (1937–1945) and then for four years more against the Kuomintang forces.

After the People's Republic was established in 1949, the military continued to play a vital role in Mao's regime, both internally and internationally. At the outset the victorious armies served as the de facto administrative units for the entire country; then in a series of military operations they proved themselves defenders of Chinese perceived national interest. They fought against the United States in Korea (1950), against India on the borders of Tibet (1962), against the Soviet Union on the borders of Mongolia (1969), and against Vietnam (1979).

The most dramatic intervention of the military in internal politics during the Maoist era came with the Cultural Revolution of 1966 to 1969. Mao made exceptional use of the army during this period, first in moving the groups of youngsters who were the agents of the Cultural Revolution from one part of the country to another, and then in suppressing these same groups when their organizations of Red Guards proved uncontrollable. Later, this same pattern of reliance on the military was repeated in the 1989 armed suppression of the Tiananmen Square uprising.

From the early years of communist activity and throughout Mao's reign, the Red Army was a direct partner of the Communist party as revolutionaries and rulers. Unavoidably, the partnership suffered periodic strains as struggles for power developed within the leadership. The proper relationship between the army and the party, as Mao saw it, was that "political power grows out of the barrel of a gun. Our principle is that the Party commands the gun; the gun shall never be allowed to command the Party." Although the army, wielder of the gun, is the foundation of the communist state, ultimate control must lodge with the Communist party, if only because the party has the final say in applying communist ideology to present conditions. The supremacy of the party is a fundamental tenet of Leninism, which Mao embraced wholeheartedly and which was endorsed by all loyal communists including the generals who were themselves members of the party. But ideology is one thing, and the urge for power is something else. A major challenge to Mao's leadership was exposed in 1971 with the mysterious death of General Lin Piao, Mao's chosen successor.

The Lin Piao affair illustrates special difficulties of understanding China. Government control of information and travel has been so tight that significant events have been entirely concealed, as in the death of General Lin. When the official report was made almost a year after the event, it was so sketchy that some of the most troublesome questions remain unanswered to this day. General Lin had been one of Mao's oldest and closest comrades: His military exploits were renowned; he made contributions to

Maoist ideology; as Minister of War he reorganized the army according to Mao's directives and published the famous *Little Red Book*, containing the thoughts of Mao, which became required reading throughout the army and the country; he helped facilitate and then terminate the Cultural Revolution; and finally, in 1969 he was named successor to the aging Chairman Mao. The long-term collaboration between Lin and Mao seemed to confirm the partnership between the army and the party, which Mao celebrated in his writings. But Lin was ambitious and impatient. According to subsequent accounts, he organized a conspiracy to assassinate Mao, and when the plot was uncovered, he attempted to fly to the Soviet Union. The plane crashed, and Lin was killed.

The official story leaves many loose ends, but the undeniable conclusion is that Mao perceived a threat to his rule and acted decisively to end it. Nonetheless, despite the death of General Lin, the army remained a dominant force in the regime. To this day, military officers are a privileged elite in China. The gun out of which political power grows is well polished.

Revolutionary fervor is more important than efficiency   Mao's vision of communism extended beyond changes in ownership of property, class relations, and social institutions. He envisioned the emergence of a new type of person with distinctive attitudes, motives, and behavior. According to Mao, a genuine communist is not removed from but directly involved with the masses, listening and responding to their needs, participating in their work and culture. Mao held up an egalitarian and communal ideal in which the usual divisions between rural and urban, worker and manager, citizen and official, thinker and doer, elite and mass would be obliterated. All would join the same activities, share the same values, follow the same morality, enjoy the same art. To create such a truly communal society was the revolutionary goal toward which communists must actively strive. Mao expressed the ideal of a close and continuing interaction between leaders and masses in his doctrine of *the mass line*: "In all the practical work of our Party, all correct leadership is necessarily from the masses to the masses."

But implementation of this revolutionary ideal encountered serious obstacles, which Mao repeatedly denounced and resisted. One obstacle was the all-too-human reluctance of individuals who have achieved some success and influence to share the ruder life of factory and farm. Like people elsewhere, many Chinese preferred the perquisites of higher office to the rigors of physical labor.

The ambitious goals of reconstruction, development, and social mobilization that Mao set for China posed immense organizational challenges—affecting the army, economy, schools, communications, government, and the party itself—that could only be met by growing specialization, stratification, and bureaucratization. Well-trained, competent people would only work efficiently in an atmosphere of personal security, institutional stability, and material incentives—in short, in conventional, stratified organizations. In every sector of society, leaders emerged who welcomed the tendency toward specialization and stratification as the necessary conditions for effective performance of the great tasks that needed to be done. But this tendency went directly counter to Mao's revolutionary ideal of a communal society. The problem came to be expressed as the contradiction between "Red and Expert."

Expert referred to those individuals with special skills or knowledge who remained preoccupied with their work instead of turning to the masses as Mao prescribed. They were less concerned with Maoist ideology than with doing a competent job, whether as scientist, teacher, engineer, or factory manager. Mao derided these people with choice epithets such as "formalists" and "bureaucrats." The individual who came to personify the tendency toward Expert, and who became the main victim of the Cultural Revolution, was Liu Shaoqui.

Liu was a long-time associate of Mao's whose special province was the organization of the Communist party. It was Liu who supervised recruitment of new members, promotion of party officials, and internal administration. He was, together with Lin Piao and Zhou Enlai, one of the preeminent leaders next to Mao himself.

But unlike Mao, Liu was far more of a practical administrator than a revolutionary zealot. He saw the need for building stable institutions rather than instigating further radical change. This attitude, exemplified by Liu but of growing importance in all major sectors of society, posed a threat to Mao's supremacy as ideologue and perhaps also as political leader. Mao prepared the ground carefully, and when the time was ripe, he struck against Liu and all the other Experts.

The "Red and Expert" issue is one aspect of a more general problem that has plagued all communist societies: the emergence of what the Yugoslav communist Milovan Djilas called "The New Class." Despite their commitment to egalitarian ideals, communist societies have produced a distinctive ruling class based on inequalities in status, privilege, and power. Djilas formulated his heretical view after observing developments in Yugoslavia, but it has particular significance in China, since traditional China was the home of one of the most enduring and distinctive of all ruling classes: the mandarins.

The mandarins comprised an elaborate hierarchy of governing officials in the Chinese empire. They were recruited through an arduous process of formal examinations, which produced a self-conscious elite remote in education, attitudes, social position, and even language from the ordinary population. The mandarins were about as far removed from "the mass line" as any ruling class could be. Mao was well aware of this historical phenomenon in Chinese politics, and his emphasis on revolutionary fervor, which exploded in the Cultural Revolution, was ultimately directed against the reemergence in China of another such ruling class and toward the creation of a Chinese classless society.

As events since his death suggest, he failed.

Objective realities are secondary to subjective forces   The most distinctive element of Maoism is its emphasis on the possibility of achieving revolutionary change through the application of character, will, and "correct thought" in a variety of historical circumstances. The voluntaristic element in Marxism—that is, the view that change is the result of intentional human rather than objectively determined social conditions—had been developed by Lenin, but Mao carried it much further, as is apparent in his discussion of which groups in society could become part of the revolutionary movement.

Marx's position on this central question was based on his rather clear-cut analysis of class relations and the role of particular classes in successive periods of history. Each period revealed a progressive class, whose interests and actions would advance the course of social development, and a reactionary class, which resisted this development. Under capitalism the progressive class was the proletariat, whose actions would "redeem mankind," while the reactionary class was the bourgeoisie, whose opposition to the socialization of private capital must be overcome through revolution.

With Mao, the Marxist analysis of class gives way to a far more ambiguous categorization of groups—including poor peasants, middle peasants, rich peasants, farm laborers, rural vagrants, enlightened gentry, landlords, and liberal bourgeoisie, as well as the proletariat. In the end, Mao appealed not to a particular social class but to "the people," which could include individuals from the most diverse social origins, united by their support of communism and adherence to the "Thought of Mao." In 1949 he wrote: "Who are the people? At the present stage in China, they are the working class, the peasantry, the urban petty bourgeoisie, and the national bourgeoisie" ("On the People's Democratic Dictatorship"). Mao's net was cast wide.

In the last decades of his life, when he was venerated as the "Great Helmsman" and his *Thoughts* were revered as gospel, Mao became less a communist theoretician and more a Confucian sage. His prescriptions for how to be a good communist touched upon all matters of personal conduct and positive thinking. But ideological flexibility and personal exhortation were always a central part of Mao's approach. In a youthful essay on physical education, Mao remarked, quoting a line from Confucius: "When one's decision is made in his heart, then all parts of the body obey its orders. Fortune and misfortune are of our own seeking. 'I wish to be virtuous, and lo, virtue is at hand.'" Perhaps this was Mao's most enduring belief.

Despite his adaptations and modifications of Marxism-Leninism, Mao remained an orthodox Leninist in at least two basic respects: his emphases on the role of the Communist party and on the importance of the dictatorship of the proletariat (or People's Dictatorship). For Mao, as for Lenin, the party was the central dominating organization, first in carrying out the revolution and then in governing the country. He stated just before the final communist victory: "If there is to be a revolution, there must be a revolutionary party. Without a revolutionary party, without a party built on the revolutionary theory and style of Marx, Lenin and Stalin, it is impossible to lead the working class and the broad masses of the people to defeat imperialism and its running dogs...The Communist Party of China is a party built and developed on the model of the Communist Party of the Soviet Union." In the late 1950s, under Liu Shaoqui's direction, the party had moved away from Mao's control; and in the Cultural Revolution of the late 1960s, Mao instituted a far-reaching purge of the party that threatened to destroy the entire organizational structure. But afterward the party was restored to its central position, and following the death of Mao, many old figures and practices reappeared.

Dictatorship—People's Democratic Dictatorship—was also a firm Maoist tenet. In 1949 he wrote:

> Our present task is to strengthen the people's state apparatus—mainly the people's army, the people's police, and the people's interests....The people's state protects the people. Only when the people have such a state can they educate and remold themselves on a countrywide scale ("On the People's Democratic Dictatorship").

Mao presided over the institutionalization of a remarkable totalitarian system. The goal was not only to suppress opposition but to indoctrinate the entire population into prescribed ways of thinking and acting. Not force and terror but self-criticism, public confession, brainwashing, and social pressure were the instruments of control. Despite some notable reverses, Mao pursued this goal to the end. He created in China, a country long renowned for the colorful diversity of its regions, a society marked by striking uniformity and conformity—at least outwardly. This veneer of uniformity has diminished in the recent years following his death.

Communist Victory

During the lean years in Yenan, safe from the conquering armies of the Kuomintang, Mao Zedong instituted the policies that became the basis for his popular support. These policies included agrarian reform, nationalist appeals to resist foreign invasion, mass recruitment to the communist cause, and intensive political training.

During these difficult years Mao displayed tactical flexibility and a lack of dogmatism. He adjusted his policies to fit the circumstances. For example, his program of agrarian reform was moderate and cautious so as not to antagonize the peasants whose support he needed. He recruited soldiers for the Red Army and members for the Communist party wherever he could find them, even among vagrants whom Marx would have dismissed as social flotsam. He insisted that his troops treat the local population with scrupulous honesty, a sea-change from the plundering and corruption of the warlords, the Japanese, and the Kuomintang. Goods taken by the soldiers were always paid for—with script that would be redeemed after the revolution. In this way a large part of the rural populace developed at least an indirect interest in a communist victory.

To mold his diverse recruits into a unified force, Mao relied on two potent forces: appeals to nationalism and intensive political training. While Chiang Kai-shek denounced the communists as his main enemy, Mao warned against the danger of foreign invasion. This nationalist appeal won wide support among people of all social classes. When the Japanese invasion came, Mao was ready to join with the Kuomintang in a war of national defense. At the same time, he also made strenuous efforts to train and indoctrinate new party members as effective cadres—that is, as dedicated and disciplined party activists. When discipline and dedication seemed to wane, Mao instituted a purge of the party—a practice he came to employ periodically in maintaining control—in which officials were transferred to remote areas, denounced for ideological deviations, or expelled from the party.

With the defeat of Japan in sight, the old struggle between the Kuomintang and the communists resumed. This time the communists were in a much stronger position than before; they were in control of large territories in northern China, with experienced guerrilla armies, tested strategies and policies, and broad popular support. China was in effect divided in two— with two armies, two governments, and two contending leaders.

Into this difficult situation the United States, formally allied with Chiang's Kuomintang government, sent a mediation mission headed by General George C. Marshall. The two sides came together under Marshall's auspices, but their meetings only confirmed the depth of the conflict between them. Chiang insisted that the communists recognize his position as the legitimate ruler of all China; the communists demanded participation as equal partners in a coalition government and a unified army. General Marshall left, unable to resolve the impasse. In 1946 violence again erupted in the war-weary country. By 1949 the Kuomintang forces had collapsed and Chiang Kai-shek retreated to the island of Taiwan (Formosa), to preserve there the remnant of resistance to communist rule.

Mao's decisive military victory over the Kuomintang produced a traumatic effect on the United States. Chiang was a wartime ally, he had influential friends both inside and outside the government, and he had relied on American aid and encouragement in his anticommunist struggle. Now in the United States the bitter question was raised: Who "sold out" Chiang and "lost" China? A search for the guilty began. In the harsh atmosphere of the deepening Cold War, a grim hunt got underway for communists and communist sympathizers in the U.S. State Department, the media, the universities, and among liberal groups.

Congressional investigations were launched, loyalty programs were enacted, accusations of treason were made and repeated—all fueled by frustration over the "loss" of China. In retrospect, it is clear that no traitors were to blame; only a thorough reorganization of the entire Kuomintang governmental structure, leadership, doctrine, and policies could have preserved China from communism. The United States would learn a similar lesson, at far greater cost, in Vietnam.

The People's Republic

In the years between the founding of the People's Republic in 1949 and Mao's death in 1976, Chinese domestic policies underwent striking alterations and reversals, reflections of Mao's ideological commitments as well as changing economic conditions and shifts in power among the leaders. Achievements during some years were notable, but the failures at other times were no less remarkable.

The initial tasks facing the new regime were to establish a national administrative structure and restore the war-shattered economy. The object was to put China back on its feet as a first step toward the more ambitious goals of development and socialization. The approach during these years (1949–1952) was pragmatic rather than ideological. Land-reform policies that had been tried in Yenan were extended throughout the country; planning agencies were established to direct economic activity on a national scale; industrial production was revived, in many cases to pre-1949 levels.

At the same time, the first of the nationwide mass propaganda campaigns was introduced. These campaigns were to become a characteristic communist method for introducing new policies and mobilizing popular support behind particular programs and leaders. The ground was being readied for the next stage of industrial expansion and the collectivization of agriculture.

In the first Five-Year Plan (1953–1957), China began to move in earnest toward industrialization and collectivization. The model for this effort was the Soviet Union. The Chinese adopted a number of practices familiar from Soviet experience: highly centralized economic planning with strict controls over all phases of production, distribution, and consumption; priority on industry rather than agriculture, and on heavy industry rather than consumer goods; significant differentials in income as incentives for a maximum effort toward economic growth; and collectivization of agriculture as the means to control investment, production, and marketing in the agricultural sector. The Russians provided not only an example but also substantial aid, in the form of development loans and technical assistance, for which the Chinese were obliged to pay heavily in their trade with the Soviet Union.

Results of the first Five-Year Plan were impressive. China had taken a major stride toward industrialization and had achieved a significant rate of economic growth. But the forced pace and direction of development also led to serious problems, which became a source of controversy among the leaders. Some problems were obvious: lagging agricultural output, growing urbanization and urban unemployment, and balance of payments deficits in foreign trade. Beneath these overt economic difficulties were deeper issues of the underlying social and ideological implications of Soviet-style development.

Although Mao himself launched the program of rapid industrialization and collectivization, against the advice of other leaders who urged a more gradual course, he now came to oppose many of its consequences. Centralized planning reduced local initiative and popular participation in decision making; differential incentives produced inequalities of income and status; bureaucratic agencies spawned a new stratum of technicians and "experts," removed from mass attitudes and experiences; and Soviet assistance led to growing dependence on Russian personnel and technology. The distinctive features of Mao's vision of a communist society were being undermined in the reality of an industrial, bureaucratic, materialistic system increasingly removed from egalitarian and communal values. In a momentous decision Mao resolved to abandon the Soviet model of development and strike out along a new and radically different path. The result was the Great Leap Forward.

The Great Leap Forward (1958–1960) involved a reversal of earlier policies and the introduction of a whole series of innovations in industry, agriculture, and administration designed to solve the problems of the first Five-Year Plan and at the same time to set China on a distinctive, Maoist path. As he would do again a decade later in the Great Proletarian Cultural Revolution, Mao intervened in the name of revolutionary ideology to impose a set of policies that were highly controversial, strongly resisted by other leaders, deeply disruptive of existing practices, and largely damaging to further development.

The Great Leap Forward was part of a cycle of alternating tendencies that characterized the entire era of Mao's rule: radicalization versus moderation, ideological fervor versus practical flexibility, mass mobilization versus elitist bureaucratization, "politics in command" versus "economics in command," and Red versus Expert. In the Great Leap Forward, Mao initiated many untried practices that proved unworkable as a basis for sustained economic growth, and in so doing he opened the door to his own temporary political eclipse. In a few years of far-reaching and ill-conceived innovations, Mao inflicted severe suffering upon the Chinese people.

Among the many innovations of the Great Leap Forward, several are especially noteworthy: in overall strategy, the policy of "walk on two legs," or emphasis on agriculture as well as industry; in agriculture, introduction of the communes as a new institutional structure for organizing the entire rural sector of society; in planning, decentralized decision making with broad initiative at the local and provincial levels; in incentives, reliance on ideological motivations rather than on material rewards; in the general organization of economic activity, intensive utilization of cheap labor in place of expensive technology and expertise; and in the development of the country's resources, self-reliance rather than dependence on foreigners.

An example that in some ways epitomizes the entire Great Leap experiment was backyard blast furnaces, a quixotic attempt to produce steel not in complex, technologically sophisticated, competently managed steel mills but rather in rudimentary furnaces tended by ordinary people in their own neighborhoods. The backyard blast furnaces, like other ambitious but ill-considered policies of the period, were a disaster. Combined with a series of bad harvests, the Great Leap Forward resulted in a giant step backward for Chinese economic development. The years that followed were spent repairing the damage resulting from Mao's innovations.

One other innovation deserves special mention: the communes. Introduction of communes—large-scale organizations to plan and manage the whole range of economic, educational, and political activities on a communal basis within countywide territorial units—was a triumph of ideology over practicality. Communes were viewed as a higher stage of social organization, in which all private, self-interested behavior would be replaced by community-oriented, socially beneficial, planned activity.

The commune movement was an attempt to implement literally the ideal "from each according to his ability, to each according to his need." The peasants' ownership of small private plots was a particular target. Although private holdings amounted to only a small part of the total land in production, they accounted for most of the actual output. This survival of private enterprise was eliminated in the communes, where all land was held in common. People were expected to work hard not for private gain but for the common good, and in return they would receive from the community whatever they needed, including free food.

Chinese peasants were not ready for this experiment in altruism: They gladly ate the free food, but avoided the hard work. It is still unclear which contributed more to the shrunken harvests of those years—the natural disasters of floods and drought, or the human-engineered disaster of the communes.

The years from 1961 to 1965 were a time of readjustment in which the failed innovations of the Great Leap Forward were undone and the country moved toward recovery. The pendulum swung from ideology back toward practicality. Private plots were restored, and the communes disappeared in all but name; material incentives were reintroduced, and technical expertise was rewarded; technological innovation was emphasized rather than mass mobilization—for example, by intensive use of chemical fertilizers; central planning was revived, and extreme decentralization reversed. Mao's policies, and Mao himself, gave way to the more conventional approach of the Experts.

The readjustments had their effects. Despite continuing problems, such as high population growth, the economy recovered. Moreover, the recovery was achieved without Soviet aid; self-reliance had become a reality. But Mao still had to be reckoned with. Behind the scenes he began preparing the most radical of all attempts to revolutionize Chinese society: the Great Proletarian Cultural Revolution.

The Cultural Revolution

Although the Cultural Revolution (1966–1969) broke like a bombshell on the outside world, within China it was the outcome of a political struggle that had been going on for several years. Factions in both the party and the army had been jockeying for power, but not until 1966 did Mao feel strong enough to launch his new campaign. When it came, the shocks were felt throughout Chinese society. While the Great Leap Forward had its principal effects in the economy—although innovations were also attempted in other areas—the Cultural Revolution aimed at transforming all major sectors of society: the party, the army, government, factories, schools, culture, arts, family, and the role of Mao himself.

The heart of the Cultural Revolution was the "publicization" of all social activities, so that no place—schoolroom, laboratory, office, workshop, concert hall, temple, library, or household—was immune from intrusion and interruption in the name of the people's revolutionary consciousness. The initial personification of this consciousness was in swarms of teenage youths whom Mao unleashed as the agents of social transformation. These youths, transported from place to place by the army, converged on cities and towns, confronting teachers in their classrooms, bureaucrats in their offices, managers in their factories, writers in their studies, and demanding adherence to revolutionary egalitarianism.

Mao got more than he wanted. The youths, organized into brigades of Red Guards, took over government agencies, terrorized the cities and foreign delegations, and started battles among themselves. Mao had to replace them, first with revolutionary committees of adults, and eventually with many of the same officials who had been removed in the first place. But the young people were reluctant to give up their new-found power. To put the genie back into the bottle, Mao again called upon the army, this time to disband the Red Guards and disperse their members throughout the country.

Primary targets of the Cultural Revolution were the agents of socialization—those institutions that directly shape people's values and beliefs. Some of the most radical effects occurred in the schools and universities. Conditions sometimes dreamed about by students became reality: no standards for admission to college, no demanding academic requirements, no discipline in the classroom, no examinations, no failing grades. The result was a nightmare. Teachers could not not teach and students would not learn. Aside from the loss to society as a whole—it is estimated that during the Cultural Revolution China lost a million potential doctors, engineers, teachers, and other professionals—one can only imagine the personal misfortune for those young people who instead of embarking on promising careers were left ill educated and ill trained in an increasingly modernized society—victims of Mao's devotion to revolutionary egalitarianism.

Although dramatic effects were felt in education and the arts, the most politically significant changes occurred in the Communist party itself. Mao instituted a massive purge of the party, which came close to destroying the entire structure that he himself had forged over a period of thirty years. In cities and provinces long-term party officials were vehemently denounced, removed from office, and sent far from home. They were replaced by inexperienced but ardent youngsters who were often incapable of managing the party's tasks. Mao was creating an organizational vacuum in which the army would become the dominant political institution. For a time this actually happened, but with the death of General Lin Piao in 1971, the threat of a military coup was thwarted. The party was gradually rebuilt and restored to its central role.

The Cultural Revolution was Mao's last great effort to transform Chinese society according to his egalitarian and communal vision. Dismayed at the trend toward bureaucratization and elitism, which seemed the unavoidable accompaniment of political stability and economic development, Mao intervened decisively, like the Chinese emperors of old, to change the course of his regime. He drastically disrupted the conventional practices and regular personnel in every sphere. The resulting chaos set back the clock in many fields, from the arts to the economy. Moreover, the process got out of hand even for Mao, and he was forced to suppress the very people he had first enlisted in his cause. Although many extreme practices of the Cultural Revolution were subsequently modified, and many individual victims returned to their former positions, its effects continued for years. Until Mao's death, China remained in the shadow of the Cultural Revolution.

The Deng Era

Mao Zedong died on September 9, 1976. His passing had been preceded within a year by the deaths of Zhou Enlai, who was the chief executive of the government departments, and Chu Teh, founder of the Red Army, who was formally chief-of-state. Thus, a triumvirate of founding fathers passed from the scene together. An era had ended.

The death of Mao brought into the open a struggle for power within the Communist party that had been smoldering beneath the surface during the last several years of Mao's rule. Several factions vied for dominance: the radicals, led by Mao's widow, Jiang Qing, consisting of young cadres who had emerged during the Cultural Revolution dedicated to a continuation of Mao's uncompromising revolutionary program; the moderates, of whom the most prominent was Deng Xiaoping, consisting of established party and government officials who had been victims of the Cultural Revolution but who were regaining their positions; and a "Center-Left" faction somewhere between the other more extreme groups, led by Hua Guofeng, the prime minister and newly appointed chairman of the party.

Similar factions were also present in the army, and it was to the Center-Left elements in the army that Premier Hua owed much of his strength. Before Mao's death the radicals seemed to gain the upper hand, deposing the moderate leader, Deng, from his government post and conducting a vigorous campaign against the "capitalist-roaders." Violence erupted as the radicals moved to secure control of the party organization. But they were not strong enough, and the tide began to turn. Deng was rehabilitated, and a new campaign was begun against the radicals themselves—the notorious "Gang of Four" (Jiang Qing and three other leading radicals).

The inability of the radicals to win control of the party cleared the way for Deng to consolidate his position. The "Gang of Four" was denounced, subjected to a campaign of vilification, and finally arrested. The radical challenge had been crushed.

Relief at the demise of the "Gang of Four" swept across the country. Far more was involved than a struggle for power among ambitious individuals: The character of the regime and the direction of future policy were both at issue. In the campaign against the "Gang of Four," accusations were made covering a broad range of basic domestic and foreign policies. The arrest of the four radicals signaled a repudiation of the main thrust of the Cultural Revolution and a reaffirmation of the more conservative approach against which the radicals had struggled.

The swing of the pendulum away from the doctrinaire ideology of Mao and toward a more pragmatic approach to development is epitomized in Deng's Four Modernizations, announced in 1978: modernization of China's industry, agriculture, science and technology, and national defense. The emphasis of this program was on practical results, not ideological orthodoxy. Deng's long standing pragmatic bent is expressed in his provocative comment, "What does it matter if the cat is black or white, as long as it catches rats." While this policy has resulted in significant economic progress for China, much political liberalization has yet to occur, and China has at times moved away from greater political freedom.

A critical part of the Four Modernizations is reliance on market mechanisms in conjunction with state planning as the means for stimulating production and improving efficiency. Like Lenin's New Economic Policy, adopted in the aftermath of a devastating civil war, Deng's Four Modernizations, adopted in the aftermath of the debilitating Cultural Revolution, involve a retreat from socialism in the direction of increased competition, differential incentives, greater independence for farmers, more autonomy for management, and broader scope for small-scale private enterprise. In place of the socialist ideal "to each according to his need," people are rewarded "to each according to his work."

Deng justified the move toward market socialism in the following terms:

> We should like to expand the role of the market economy as we develop further. This has led some to question whether China is moving in the direction of capitalism. We are not. It is incorrect to assume that a market economy can exist only under capitalism. Under socialism, a market economy can exist side by side with a planned production economy and they can be coordinated. If there are similarities between a market economy under socialism and under capitalism, there are also crucial differences. Under socialism, the market economy operates in the context of a two-sector system...but the common basis is still socialist ownership. By nature a socialist society is designed to enrich the whole population; an exploiting class will never arise.

Within the framework of collective ownership of the means of production, individual initiative is given scope through competition between enterprises, wages geared to productivity, personal marketing of agricultural products grown on private plots, and limited entrepreneurial ventures.

The goal of the Four Modernizations also involves major changes in policies toward foreign investment in China and toward Chinese relationships with the West. In place of Mao's intransigent isolation from the outside world, Deng initiated a new openness in relations with Western nations: Foreign capital, technology, and loans are actively sought to aid in the task of development; a modern tourist industry has been formed to attract visitors from around the world; fashionable consumer goods are imported, adding variety and novelty to everyday life; and business, academic, and cultural exchanges have been arranged to foster contact with other countries. As Deng explained: "China has now adopted a policy of opening its doors to the world in a spirit of international cooperation."

In the wake of slackened central control over the economy—a key feature of the Four Modernizations—demands also arose for a "Fifth Modernization": greater democracy. These demands came to focus upon Democracy Wall in Beijing, where people were free to post for public notice whatever political messages they wished, including criticisms of the party, government policies, and unpopular officials. At first Deng tolerated this unique expression of free speech, which emerged in late 1978, especially while it was directed against his political opponents. But he soon recognized the danger it posed to his own authoritarian rule, and he denounced it as "anarchy." Democracy Wall was extinguished as a forum for political dissent On January 16, 1980, Deng called for the right to put up wall posters to be stripped from the Chinese Constitution. He commented later: "We may have made a mistake in allowing it to last for so long." Private economic initiative was not intended to stimulate freedom to engage in political activity.

In cracking down on political dissenters, Deng not only placated hard-liners in the party, particularly the army, but also used the occasion to place his own loyal followers in positions of power and to purge the party of extreme Maoist elements. Seventy-five years of age in 1980, Deng has always been keenly aware of the difficult problem of political succession and the uncertainty it raises for his strategy of modernization. Deng's goal has been to make a lasting mark on China; as such he is concerned about who and what would follow him. He has wanted to ensure that hard-line Maoism will not rule China again.

The main fruit of Deng's striking departure from Maoist practice—"market socialism" at home and cooperative relations abroad—has been a reinvigoration of the economy. Economic stagnation during the last years of Mao's rule has given way to expansion, growing productivity in both agriculture and industry, and rising living standards. Between 1978 and 1992, Chinese real gross national product (GNP) grew at an annual rate of 9 percent, enough to double the size of its economy every eight years.

Deng's desire to open up China's economy to foreign investment was exemplified in the 1984 "Chinese Investment Guide," 608 pages long and put out by the Chinese government. China, which had for years given little or no encouragement or information to foreigners wishing to do business with it, now let investors know exactly what it wanted. By 1992, China had $40 billion of foreign exchange reserves and was attracting as much as $20 billion of direct foreign investment commitments each year.

In 1979 Deng created four "Special Economic Zones" to attract foreign capital, and in 1984 he opened fourteen coastal cities to foreign investment, essentially creating freer trade and investment areas in those cities. Workers were not assigned by the state but hired on a contract basis. There was more individual incentive to be productive, and productive workers were allowed to retain the fruits of their labors. Within seven years, the Special Economic Zones had per capita gross national products twice that of China as a whole, despite substantial growth throughout the country.

In addition to opening its economy to the outside world, China under Deng expanded its internal economy immensely. Rigid state ownership and control were relaxed; private enterprise was allowed; decollectivization was encouraged. In his 1984 "Little Yellow Book," Deng said that his goal for China was "socialism with a Chinese face," and also that year he commented in a speech that "some capitalism...cannot hurt us."

Coincident with China's economic expansion has come greater social freedom. While individuals can still not vote in China, nor do they have meaningful civil liberties, the harsh edge of Chinese communism has been softened to allow greater diversity in living situations, dress, and the like. The time is gone when everyone—from the highest party officer to the lowest peasant—is expected to wear Mao suits (the Mao suits, in reality, were as much a sign of inequality as equality; the materials and tailoring of the suits intended for high party officers were of much better quality than those for the ordinary person). In 1985 China held its first beauty contest, and rock music and punk haircuts, as well as individual and Western dress, soon proliferated on the cultural scene.

In its foreign relations, China moved even further along the course that had been signaled during Mao's final years. Premier Zhao Ziyang commented to then-Vice President George Bush in 1985: "Gone are the days when China decides its relations with other countries on the basis of social systems." Chinese international politics were dictated by national interest. It was the West that offered China capital and markets; it was the West to which China turned in its geopolitical orientation. Relations with America have been particularly warm, as the United States has provided China with access to technology and has been allowed to conduct naval operations in its waters. U.S.–Chinese international cooperation reached a high point in a series of Chinese votes at the United Nations Security Council meetings during 1990 and 1991 that allowed the Desert Storm operation to move forward against Iraq.

In January 1987, upwards of 50,000 students demonstrated in Shanghai's People's Square calling for "democracy, human rights, and freedom." These demonstrations initiated the chain of events that led to the Tiananmen Square massacre of 1989. Just as with the Democracy Wall episode, Deng himself may actually have supported some of the initial demonstrations to be in a position where he could make personnel changes in the government. Regardless, Hu Yaobang—General Secretary of the Chinese Communist party and as such Deng's designated successor—resigned and was replaced by Zhao Ziyang. Zhao, in addition to having served as national premier, served as party secretary in Sichuan province, which had implemented free market reforms. Zhao was considered more reliable in political matters than Hu, who at times talked of democratic initiatives and greater political freedom.

Hu died on April 15, 1989. His funeral in the Great Hall of the People was attended by tens of thousands of jeering students in Tiananmen Square, waving banners for democracy and shouting such slogans as "Down with Dictatorship!"—Hu being associated in the students' minds with calls for greater freedom. The protests spread to other cities, and soon as many as 100,000 protesters were in Tiananmen Square, after marching through Beijing.

Deng took a hard line. "We must crack down on these students, whatever the cost," he said, indicating the willingness to use violence. For several weeks tens of thousands of protesters would gather daily in Tiananmen Square, with up to half a million supporters in the streets. Zhao took a more conciliatory approach than Deng. "Reasonable demands from students should be met through democratic and legal means," he held.

Mikhail Gorbachev and Deng were to have a summit meeting together in May 1989, the first such Sino–Soviet meeting in thirty years. At this point, order temporarily broke down in Beijing. Gorbachev—at the height of his international acclaim—was greeted by banners bearing such slogans as "Welcome Gorbachev, the True Reformer" and "The Soviet Union has Gorbachev, but who does China have?" Now hundreds of thousands of protesters descended on Tiananmen Square, and over a million Beijing residents took to the streets. All international news media were on hand for the summit, so this spontaneous uprising against Deng's regime was broadcast live all over the world. Protests were also held in thirty four other Chinese cities.

The summit turned into a shambles—meetings were cancelled, shuffled, or postponed as all of Beijing seemed to pulsate with opposition to the regime. At one point, Gorbachev had to enter the Great Hall of the People through the back door, so massive were the demonstrations in front of it. The government was humiliated.

Deng moved to restore order. As soon as the summit was over, he warned protesters in no uncertain terms that he would use force to preserve the regime. Turning to the army, he massed forces on Tiananmen Square to intimidate individuals from protesting. Live television coverage was literally unplugged. Martial law was imposed. Students and other protesters built a final "Goddess of Democracy" statue (very similar to the Statue of Liberty), but the end was at hand. On June 4, 1989, Deng gave the order to remove protesters from the square. Military forces using tear gas, tracer bullets, and armored personnel carriers stormed human barricades, opening fire and killing hundreds and injuring thousands. Protestors were suppressed in other cities as well. The stability of the regime was assured, but its international reputation declined.

Following the Tiananmen Square massacre, China became something of a pariah internationally—at least officially. The United States Congress, for example, attempted to limit trade with it, but these efforts were vetoed by former President Bush. Over time, limitations that other countries attempted to place on trade with China have been lifted.

The internal response to Tiananmen Square was greater control. Deng increasingly mentioned Mao for a time, after neglecting references to him for a decade. Zhao Ziyang was removed as Communist General Secretary and replaced by Jiang Zemin, an economic reformer but political conservative. He had cracked down on demonstrators in Shanghai.

There initially was some concern following Tiananmen that China might falter from its economic course, but these concerns have proven groundless. Deng has continued to move forward with his vision of a China in which free enterprise plays a continually greater role in the economy, in which the country's political apparatus remains under rigid control, and where greater diversity is allowed in exercising consumer and personal lifestyle choices. This trend was confirmed most recently at the October 1992 Communist Party Congress, where Deng's initiatives were praised and economic reformers were placed in positions of power.

The transition China has undergone during the Deng era has been immense; in its own way it is almost as significant as that during the tenure of Mao, whose era of supremacy over China was not quite twice as long as Deng's. Chinese gross national product more than tripled during the Deng era. The nation no longer resembles that of fifteen years ago. Where once was bland, uniform poverty, now there is economic diversity, shops brimming with goods, motorized bicycles, radios, and even televisions. The economic expansion of China during recent years has been the most substantial increase in prosperity for as great a proportion of the world's people as has occurred since the post–World War II era.

China's torrid rate of growth was reflected in an annualized 14 percent rate of GNP increase during the first eight months of 1992, with 20 percent more industrial output. China is already the world's 19th largest trading nation; international trade during 1992 was $120 billion, up from $30 billion in 1980. To give some idea of what these numbers mean, in 1978 China produced 3 million television sets. By 1987, a mere nine years later, this figure had risen to 116 million. If China joins Japan, Korea, and other Asian Pacific nations as economically explosive, then the balance of world economic power could move in that direction. Indeed, because of China's huge population, it could become the largest economy in the world, although its standard of living per capita would still be exceeded by many other countries.

Deng's legacy, thus, despite his political record and the uncertain future of China, must be as one of the great liberalizers (though not liberals) of the twentieth century. He redirected and sustained China along a course that may forever change it and the rest of the world through at the very least China's growing influence on the rest of the globe.

The difficulty Deng experienced in attempting to stifle political freedom while allowing relatively more economic freedom typifies the dilemma that communist parties everywhere faced at the beginning of the 1980s. They could either change their economies and remain competitive with the rest of the world, or they could resist change and their economies would continue to stagnate. To allow economic change engenders political change, however, because freedom of choice in one area of a person's life leads to a desire and the ability to pursue freedom in other areas of life. To what extent Deng's successors are able to continue along the same course of economic freedom and political control that he trod remains to be seen.

There comes the inevitable question of trying to compare Mao and Deng. During both of their long tenures over China, each wrought great changes. Mao brought China together and isolated it from the rest of the world, at the same time removing foreign influences from China. Deng liberated the productive forces of hundreds of millions of Chinese, and by doing so he greatly raised its standard of living and set China on a very different course than it was heading on during the early 1970s and before.

Communism continues to exist in China to the extent that the nation remains a one-party state, coercive in its means of political control, and with a continuing substantial state component in the economy. But this component diminishes each year, both because the state economy is further liberalized and because as the private sector of the economy grows, the state sector diminishes in relative size as well as importance. It is indeed ironic that Deng twice had to sack party leaders because in promoting economic reform they also became supporters of political change. This indicates the enduring tie between economics and politics, and that if China is to continue along its path of free market economics, it must also ultimately change politically.

China became a socially much more stratified and diverse nation during the Deng era. Millionaires and stock markets were not consistent with Mao's vision of China's future, but they are a part of Deng's perspective. Mao will become increasingly irrelevant in China, just as his prominence has declined markedly during recent years. In the event that a reformer of a new generation comes along who unleashes political change, then it is very possible that Mao's statues will go the way of Lenin's.

THE FUTURE OF COMMUNISM AND OF FORMERLY COMMUNIST NATIONS

Communism's future is bleak. It has been utterly repudiated in the nation that was its first exponent and primary nurturer, the Soviet Union; and communist economic policies have been virtually repudiated in the other major nation that embraced communism, China. The further collapse of communism around the world leaves only a few states that still proclaim and practice Marxism-Leninism.

Marx failed to foresee the problems of large-scale bureaucracy inherent in the large-scale, collectivized economic organization of a society. In the *Communist Manifesto* he predicted that after the communist revolution, "political power" would disappear—or, as Engels put it, "the state would wither away." Even Lenin wrote in *The State and Revolution*, before he came to power, that in a communist society there would be no need for a "special machine," since "all would take a turn in management."

Experience has shown that large-scale enterprises lead to large-scale organizations, which in turn lead to large-scale bureaucracies, in the face of which the individual is impotent. Large-scale bureaucracy is more likely to develop in collectivized than in private-enterprise economies, since the pervasive force of bureaucratization is mitigated in the competition of private-enterprise economies. Command economies, on the other hand, by enforcing their planning decisions through the power of the state, are far more dictatorial than free -market economies.

It is ironic that it is in the area of economic productivity that communist societies have most failed. Communism was intended to unleash people's productive energies by ending the exploitation of labor by capital. That communism has failed may be because its underlying assumption about the perfectibility of humanity is erroneous: It may be that it is not possible for individuals as a community to practice the altruism that true communism would require. Moreover, communist ideas about people's inherent, biological equality may be mistaken. In this case, a system of capitalism, at least in economic production—based on competition and assuming differential rewards founded on differential contributions and talents—tempered by some socialist ideas and practices in the area of human welfare, may be both the economically most productive and socially most humane system of human organization attainable. The name of this system is, of course, the welfare state.

Moreover, as the nineteenth century moves ever further away from our own age, Marx can provide little guidance in resolving an issue that confronts humankind today more starkly than ever before: nationalism. In Marx's view, national sentiment is but part of the ideological superstructure of capitalism. However, he felt that capitalism itself contributes to the disappearance of nationalism. "National differences and antagonisms between people," he wrote in the *Communist Manifesto*, "are vanishing gradually from day to day, owing to the development of the bourgeoisie, to freedom of commerce, to the world market, to uniformity in the mode of production and in the conditions of life corresponding thereto." This optimistic and cheerful forecast fully reflects the typical outlook of nineteenth-century thinkers—Marxian, non-Marxian, anti-Marxian—who looked at the world through the narrow lens of economic theory. In that narrowly economic perspective, the whole world was destined to become one market; commerce would flow freely among nations and continents; and nationalism would disappear as an obsolescent prejudice of the preindustrial age. One world market would mean one world community living in peace and harmony and enjoying progressively rising living standards.

Although trade among nations has expanded enormously since Marx's time, such commercial expansion has not resulted in a corresponding decline of nationalism. Nationalist sentiments rivet many—perhaps most—countries in the world today. It is a remarkable fact indeed that today nationalism is strongest in former communist states. Indeed, nationalism is what in large part both internally and externally caused the demise of the Soviet Union.

Although Marx stated in the *Communist Manifesto* that "the working-men have no country," subsequent events have nullified this assertion. Before World War I a number of European Marxist and socialist parties publicly committed themselves not to support their capitalist governments in case of war. But when war broke out in 1914, these declarations were quickly forgotten, and workers in France, Germany, and other belligerent countries supported their governments as loyally and patriotically as did the capitalist bourgeoisie. This same pattern has been repeated again and again since that time. Once again, it simply may be that communism's underlying premise about human malleability are erroneous.

The future of communism and former communist nations is most uncertain. Communism's forward progression in the world is at a dead stop, and it appears to be only a matter of time before its withdrawal is complete. Communism will continue to affect the world for decades, however, just as fascism did after its defeat in World War II. Areas in which communism will have continuing influence include former communist nations themselves, the relations these nations have with other nations, and the world political system itself through the creation of a score of new countries that the downfall of communism has engendered.

The short interval between communism's collapse and the present has already demonstrated that the fate of former communist states will be turbulent. Yugoslavia, the Soviet Union, and even Czechoslovakia have dissolved as a result of their changes of government. The direction that formerly communist nations will take—both internally and externally—remains to be seen, and must be watched with the greatest interest.

FOR FURTHER READING

ASCHERSON, NEAL, *The Polish August*. New York: The Viking Press, 1982.

BERGSON, ABRAM, *Productivity and the Social System: The USSR and the West*. Cambridge, Mass.: Harvard University Press, 1978.

BIALER, SEWERYN, *Stalin's Successors: Leadership, Stability, and Change in the Soviet Union*. Cambridge: Cambridge University Press, 1980.

BROGAN, PATRICK, *The Captive Nations: Eastern Europe, 1945–1990.* New York: Avon Books, 1990.

BROWN, A.M., and JACK GRAY, eds., *Political Culture and Political Change in Communist States.* London: Macmillan, Inc., 1977.

BRZEZINSKI, ZBIGNIEW, *The Grand Failure: The Birth and Death of Communism in the Twentieth Century.* New York: Collier Books, 1990.

BUTTERFIELD, FOX, *China, Alive in the Bitter Sea.* New York: Bantam Books, Inc., 1982.

COLLINS, JOHN M., *U.S–Soviet Military Balance.* New York: McGraw-Hill Book Company, 1981.

DJILAS, MILOVAN, *The New Class: An Analysis of the Communist System.* New York: Praeger Publishers, Inc., 1957.

———, *The Unperfect Society: Beyond the New Class.* New York: Harcourt Brace Jovanovich, Inc., 1969.

GORBACHEV, MIKHAIL, *Perestroika: New Thinking for Our Country and the World.* London: Collins Publishers, 1987.

GWERTZMAN, BERNARD, and MICHAEL KAUFMAN, eds., *The Collapse of Communism.* New York: Random House, Inc., 1991.

HAMMON, PAUL, T., ed., *The Anatomy of Communist Takeovers.* New Haven: Yale University Press, 1975.

JOHNSON, PAUL, Modern Times: *The World from the Twenties to the Nineties.* New York: Harper Perennial, 1991.

KENNAN, GEORGE, F., *The Nuclear Delusion: Soviet–American Relations in the Nuclear Age.* New York: Pantheon Books, Inc., 1982.

LAFEBER, WALTER, *America, Russia and the Cold War, 1945–1980.* New York: John Wiley & Sons, Inc., 1980.

McCLELLAN, DAVID, *Karl Marx: Selected Writings.* London: Oxford University Press, 1977.

PANKHURST, JERRY G., and MICHAEL SACKS, eds., *Contemporary Soviet Society.* New York: Praeger Publishers, Inc., 1980.

PARKIN, FRANK, *Class Inequality and Political Order: Social Stratification in Capitalism and Communist Societies.* New York: Praeger Publishers, Inc., 1971.

RUSH, MYRON, *How Communist States Change Their Rulers.* Ithaca, N.Y.: Cornell University Press, 1974.

SCAMMEL, MICHAEL, ed., *Russia's Other Writers: Selections from Samizdat Literature.* New York: Praeger Publishers, Inc., 1971.

SCHRAM, STUART R., *The Political Thought of Mao Tse-Tung* (rev. ed.). New York: Praeger Publishers, Inc., 1969.

SMITH, HEDRICK, *The Russians.* New York: Quadrangle, 1976.

SOLZHENITSYN, ALEXANDER I., *The Gulag Archipelago.* New York: Harper & Row Publishers, Inc., 1973.

ULAM, ADAM, *Dangerous Relations: The Soviet Union in World Politics.* New York: Oxford University Press, 1983.

WECHSLER, LAWRENCE *Solidarity: Poland in the Season of Its Passion.* New York: Simon & Schuster, Inc., 1982.

ZAGORIA, DONALD, ed., *The Soviet Union and Asia.* New Haven: Yale University Press, 1982.

Index